PRESTON'S COLOURFUL PAST

KEITH JOHNSON

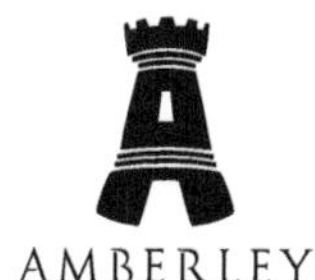

AMBERLEY

First published 2026

Amberley Publishing
The Hill, Stroud
Gloucestershire, GL5 4EP

www.amberley-books.com

British Library Cataloguing in Publication Data.

A catalogue record for this book is available from the British Library.

ISBN 978 1 3981 2193 5 (print)
ISBN 978 1 3981 2194 2 (ebook)

Origination by Amberley Publishing.
Printed in the UK.

Appointed GPSR EU Representative: Easy Access System Europe Oü, 16879218
Address: Mustamäe tee 50, 10621, Tallinn, Estonia
Contact Details: gpsr.requests@easproject.com, +358 40 500 3575

Contents

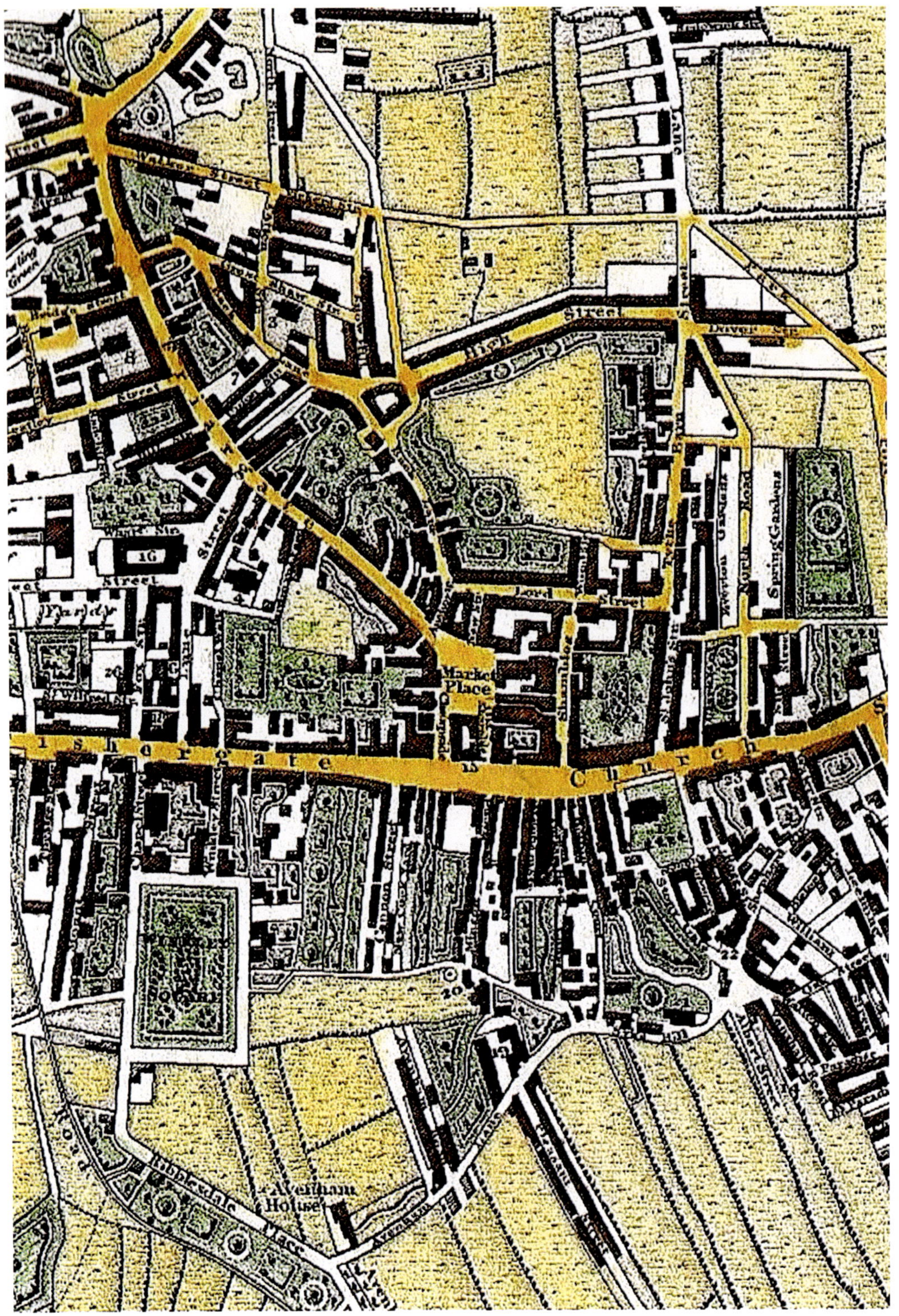

Map of Preston by Edward Baines, 1824.

Introduction

Preston, like many towns and cities, has a colourful past, and it is thanks to the artists and photographers of the past that we are able to get a glimpse of the people and places in which they dwelt. Visit the art gallery within the Harris Museum and Library and you will find, amongst the paintings on display, a rich tapestry of life in bygone Preston. Be they oil or watercolour paintings, the artists, including Preston's own Devis family of painters, have created images that reflect their era. Lords and ladies, notable political and military figures and everyday folk have had their image created by strokes of a brush.

Especially fortunate for Preston was the work of Edwin Beattie, who not only sketched the Preston scene in Victorian times and beyond, but also produced many watercolours of the streets, buildings and alleyways that existed then. In later years the likes of James Brindle, Patti Mayor, Ted Robinson and members of the Preston Arts Society would capture the likeness of local scenes and people in a colourful way.

Postcards have also been a great source of colourful images since Edwardian days. 'Wish You Were Here' greetings have been sent near and far from Preston with images of our pleasant parks, tourist attractions and carefree days.

In 1906, the *Lancashire Daily Post* began to print the occasional photograph amongst their illustrative etchings and sketches in the daily newspaper. Cumberland wrestlers, local footballers, cricketers and political personalities were all caught on camera.

One *Lancashire Daily Post* photographer of the period, Arthur Nield, would go on to contribute countless black-and-white photographs of sporting events, processions and parades for the next forty years until his retirement in 1945. For my generation, the *Lancashire Evening Post* chief photographer was Roy Payne, who joined the *Post* in 1950 and spent four decades focussing his camera lens on people and places locally.

By necessity, the photographs he took for three decades were printed in black and white. That would change in his later years, however, when the production of newspapers with colour images became normality. The revolution in newspaper printing began in March 1986 when Eddie Shah launched his tabloid *Today* newspaper in the UK, using the latest full-colour offset printing technology to provide a publication sprinkled with colourful photographs and graphics throughout, including advertisements. It caused ripples in Fleet Street at the heart of the newspaper industry and forced the UK newspaper proprietors to follow suit and introduce the latest electronic technology and full-colour printing as they invested in the most modern printing presses.

The Goss Printing Press Company in Preston was one of those who benefited from the newspaper industry's equipment upgrade, an example being the purpose-built Broughton Printers site on the outskirts of Preston. Those Headliner presses, costing over £9 million, were designed to print in colour at 70,000 copies per hour. It would become a place where the presses ran around the clock, with not only the *Lancashire Evening Post* but many regional and national titles, including the *Daily Express* and the *Daily Star*, rolling off the production lines.

Thanks to advances in the colourisation of images, we are now able to reproduce those old black-and-white images to reflect the colourful scene that the camera lens captured. We have all leafed through the old family album and seen the fading monochrome images of earlier generations and wished we could see them in glorious colour. Fortunately, modern technology enables us to end speculation and discover that your cherished auntie wore a blue dress with pink flowers upon it and your uncle was resplendent in a navy blue double-breasted suit as they joined a family gathering.

We are now able to view the images that pioneering photographer Robert Pateson took around the town in the 1860s in a new light. We are able to appreciate the colours that he saw with his own eyes as he focussed his camera lens in Avenham, Winckley Square, Broadgate and beyond.

Likewise, those images captured with a click of a camera by photographers from the 1920s onwards can now be enhanced to produce a cavalcade of colour. All the pomp, pageantry and processions of old parades teaming with colourful banners, colourful participants and colourful crowds. Royal visits, military parades and Preston Guilds were all occasions to hang out the bunting and wave the multicoloured flags. The mill girls from Horrockses took part in many a procession, parading in the vibrant fashionable frocks produced by them in their Preston factory and worn throughout the land. To this day we are still blessed with an annual Caribbean Carnival, first held in 1972, an extraordinary event that brings colour to the streets of Preston in the most imaginative way.

We have embraced the introduction of colour in our everyday lives with the clothes we wear. In cinemas, the days of glorious technicolour were welcomed with delight, as was the introduction of colour television, and the cars upon our roads are no longer predominately black as Henry Ford would have wished.

Amberley have been at the forefront of introducing colour photographs into local history books, which traditionally had only greying images to illustrate the text. Hopefully, the script that accompanies the photographs within these pages will prove that Preston has indeed had a colourful historical past, with a colourful chronology and colourful characters in abundance.

'Colourful' is oft described as vivid and vibrant, and I hope that the contents of this book appear so in your eyes. It has not been viewed through rose-tinted glasses, but depicts life as it really was, clear eyed. It is a journey taken looking through the kaleidoscope of colour and it transported me, and now maybe you too, from one end of the Preston rainbow to the other.

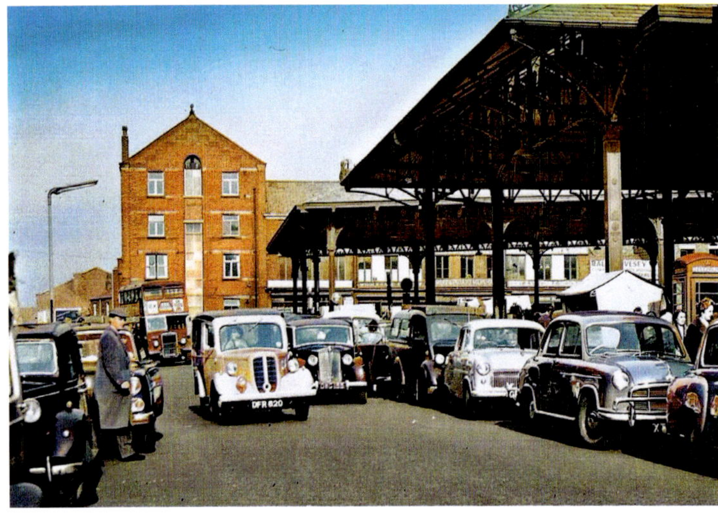

Market Street, 1958
Colourful cars and a Ribble red bus.

Town Centre Life in Our City

The colourful images that follow from the late Victorian days onwards give us a glimpse of Preston town centre in the decades that followed and before city status was granted in 2002 by Queen Elizabeth II. The city streets that we are familiar with today were well established at the dawn of the twentieth century. Take a glimpse along the ancient thoroughfares of Friargate, Fishergate and Church Street, once known as Churchgate, which all lead to the historic Market Place, and wander along the likes of Lancaster Road, Lune Street, Market Street and Orchard Street. Hopefully this will be a nostalgic journey as you reflect on the ever-changing scene and recall those things lost in time.

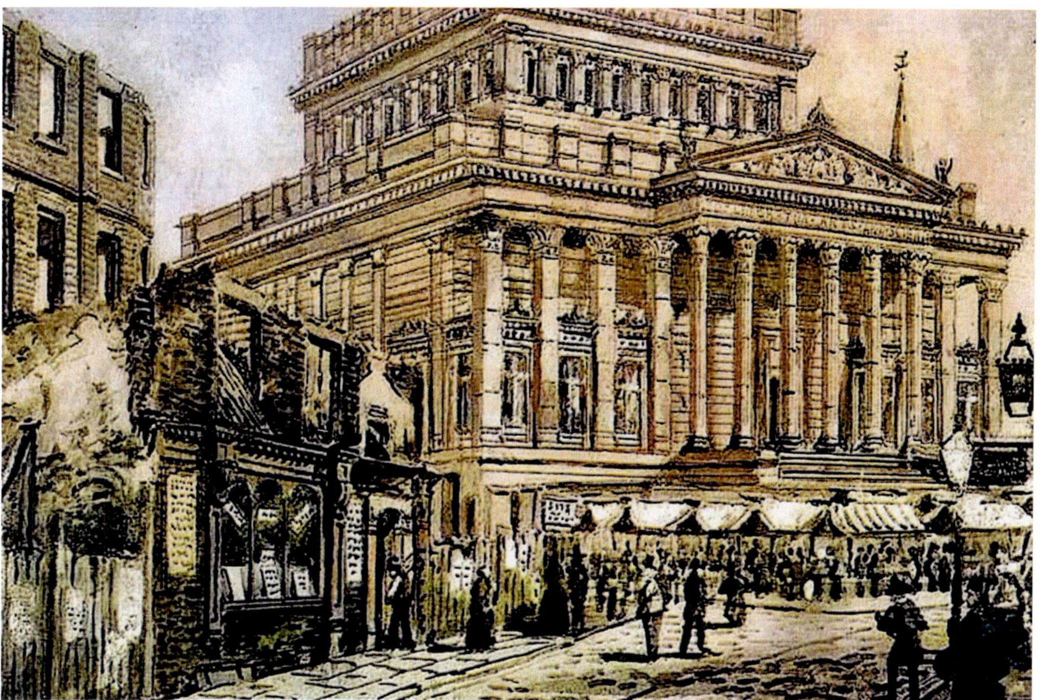

Friargate Looking Towards the Market Place, 1895

Edwin Beattie produced the original watercolour with the newly opened Harris Museum & Library centre stage. The properties to the left were being knocked down to widen the entrance to Friargate. The remains of the late seventeenth-century George Inn are clearly shown, its concert hall sign a reminder of days gone by. It was replaced by the George Hotel, a three-storey structure that is shown behind being constructed to the left of the painting, which opened in 1898. Market-day activity can be seen in front of the Harris; beneath the canopy-covered stalls traders sold everything from textiles to crockery.

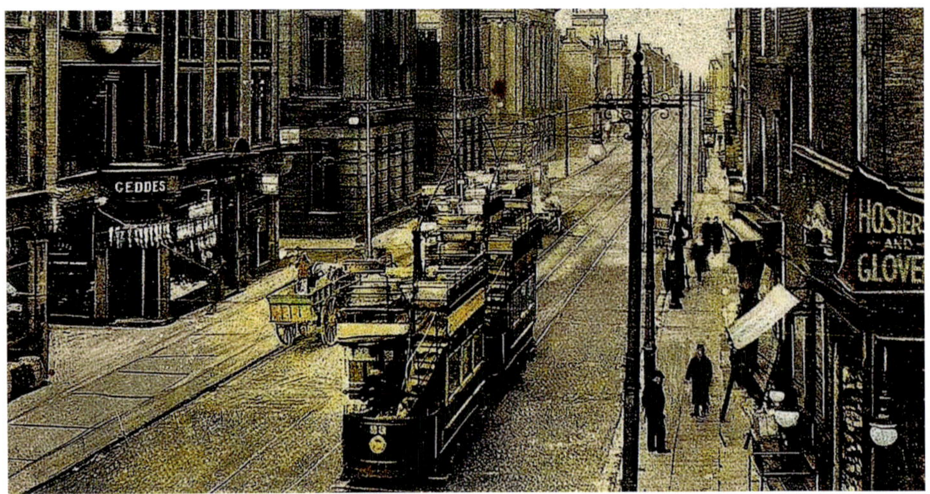

Lancaster Road from Church Street, 1905

To the left the Miller Arcade (1899), the Harris Museum (1893) and the Preston Sessions House (1904) had transformed Lancaster Road, constructed in a short period in 1827. Any visitors to Preston in the Edwardian era had the opportunity to travel on the upper deck of an electric-powered tram and tour the town – it might have been a bumpy ride but was certainly enjoyable. In the Miller Arcade, at the Geddes store you could pick up the best, freshest poultry in town all year round, according to their adverts, and when the time was right a brace of young pheasants for 4s.

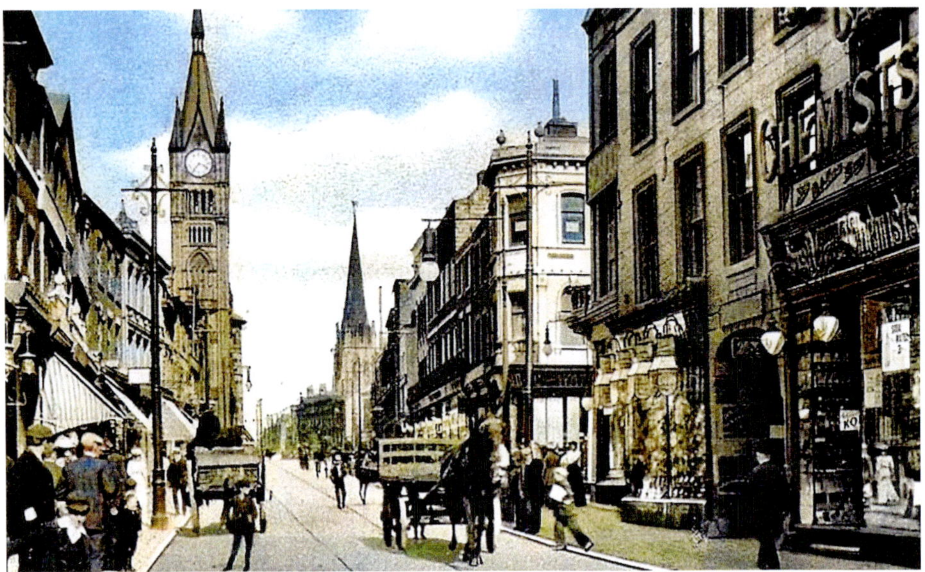

Fishergate Looking Towards the Parish Church, 1909

This late Edwardian tinted postcard reflects the days when horses and carts shared the highway with electric-powered tram cars, introduced in 1904. In the distance to the left stands the ill-fated Gothic Guild Hall tower, destroyed by fire in 1947. To the right is the earlier location of 'Boots the Cash Chemists', situated next to the arched entrance to Woodcocks Court, where printers, engravers, plumbers, wholesalers and porter bottlers earned their living.

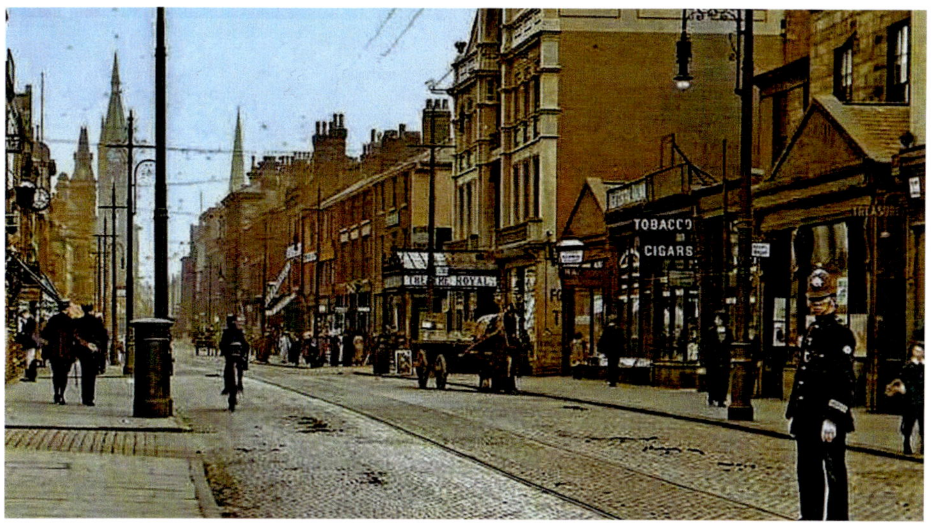

Fishergate from Charnley Street, 1911

A police constable seems to have an eye on photographer Alfred Shaw as he gave us a glimpse of the properties on the southern side of Fishergate. The Theatre Royal dominated the scene, having been rebuilt in 1898 on the site of the original 1802 theatre. For Christmas 1911 the comic play *Preserving Mr Panmure* was the star attraction. Also to the right, and to this day above Primark, can be seen the upper storeys of what was William Cartwright's mansion, the engineer of the old tramway that linked the Preston-Kendal canal with the Leeds-Liverpool canal at Walton Summit.

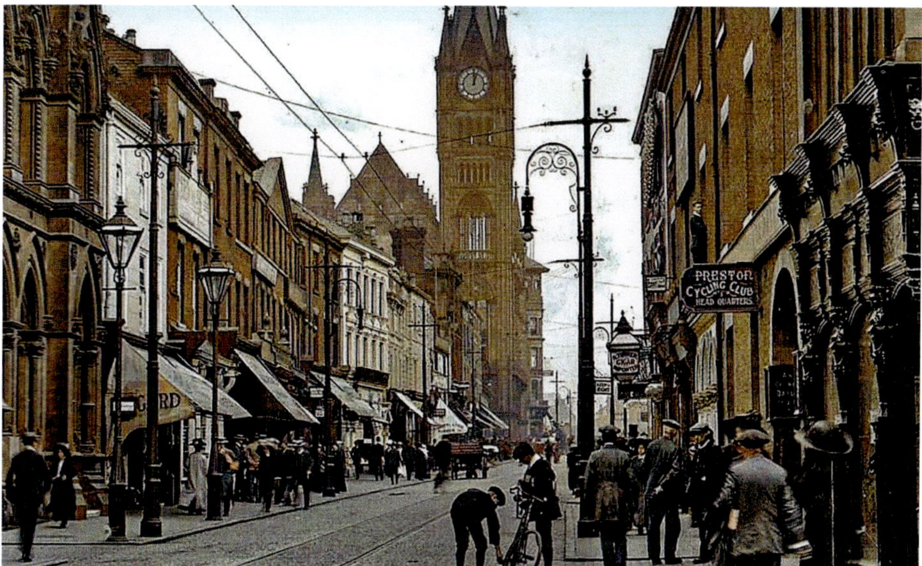

Fishergate Looking Towards the Town Hall, 1911

To the left is the Gothic façade of the Preston Gas Company building, which stood where the Fishergate entrance to St George's Shopping Centre is now. To the right is the Shelley Arms and a passageway that led to Preston Cycling Club's HQ. The club was formed in 1877. Sandy Sellers was an early champion cyclist, winning races on his penny-farthing in record-breaking times. A pair of youngsters can be seen by the roadside checking out their bicycle.

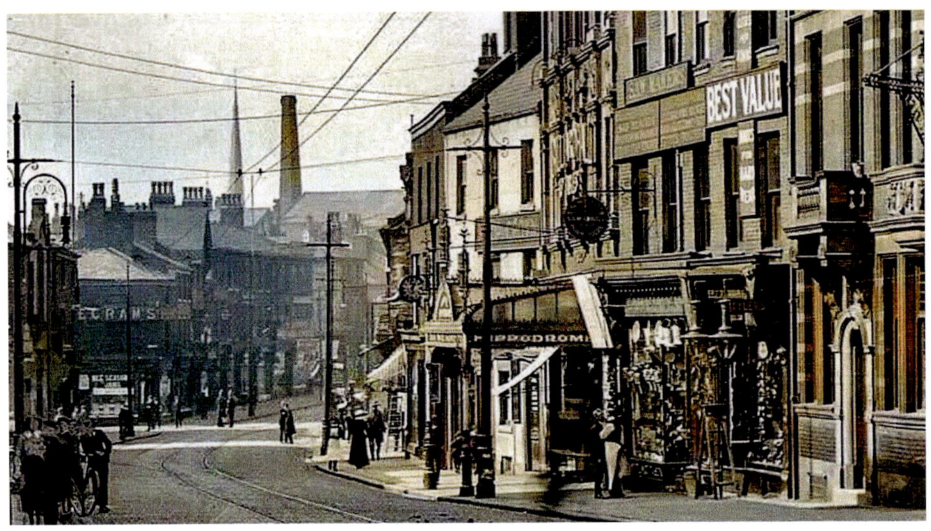

Friargate from Orchard Street, 1912

To the right is the Black Horse Hotel of 1795, which was upgraded a century later with its red-brick façade. Between the Black Horse and the Royal Hippodrome were Tyler's boot and shoe stockists and Slingers the ironmongers. The Royal Hippodrome opened in January 1905 and in January 1912 a popular *Babes in the Wood* pantomime was performed. The theatre closed in 1957 and after demolition the C&A store, which later became Wilko, was constructed. In the distance to the right, on Lune street corner, is the grocery store of James Pegrams & Co.

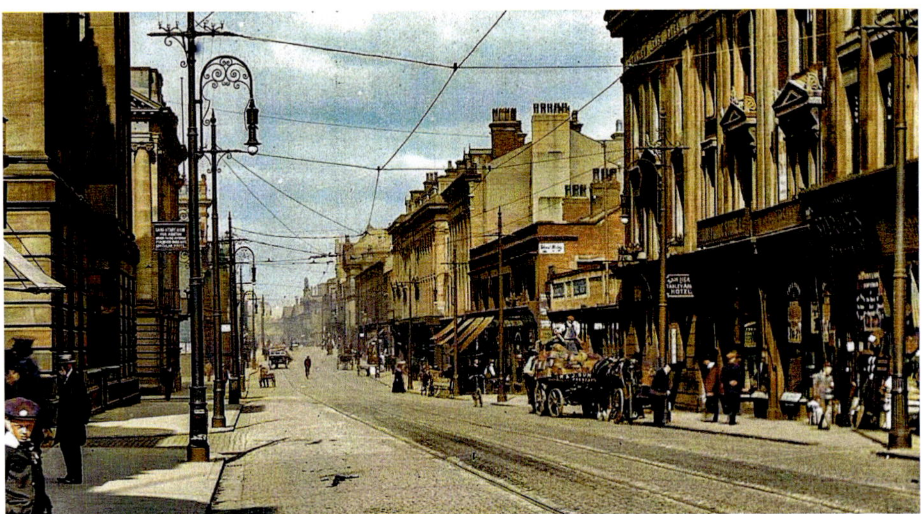

Lancaster Road Looking North from Church Street, 1912

In 1849, buildings at the Church Street end of Lancaster Road were knocked down as the road was opened up for development. Consequently, the Stanley Buildings immediately to the right date from 1854. At the far end, the Stanley Arms was the first to be occupied. Nearer to Church Street was a new post office, replacing the one in the Old Shambles (1720). Other traders along the Stanley Buildings included the County Drug Store, Hubberstey the grocer, Preston Camera Club, Pearl Life Insurance and James Starkie & Sons of the Iron and Wire Mills, off Church Street. A heavily laden horse-drawn cart and a hand cart are parked outside the Stanley Arms.

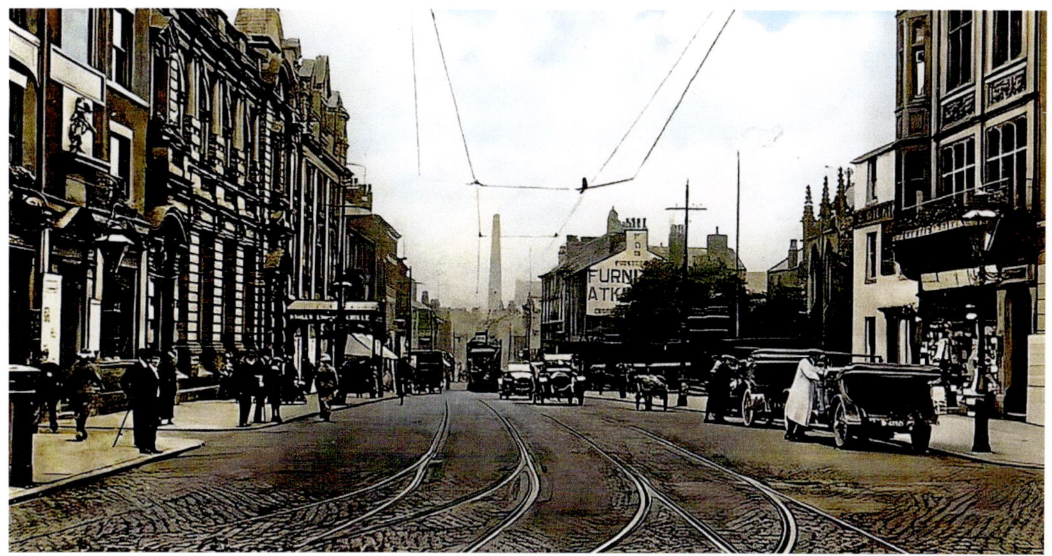

Church Street Looking Eastward, 1921

Those were the days when chauffeur-driven automobiles were often parked outside the Bull & Royal, and the Eagle & Child public house stood at the top of Stoneygate. Motor cars were becoming a common sight on the main thoroughfares, and the visible tracks of the electric trams were a reminder of the most popular mode of public transport. Generally, a couple of old pennies would get you to the outskirts of town and a circular route ticket to Fulwood and back was four old pennies' worth of travel.

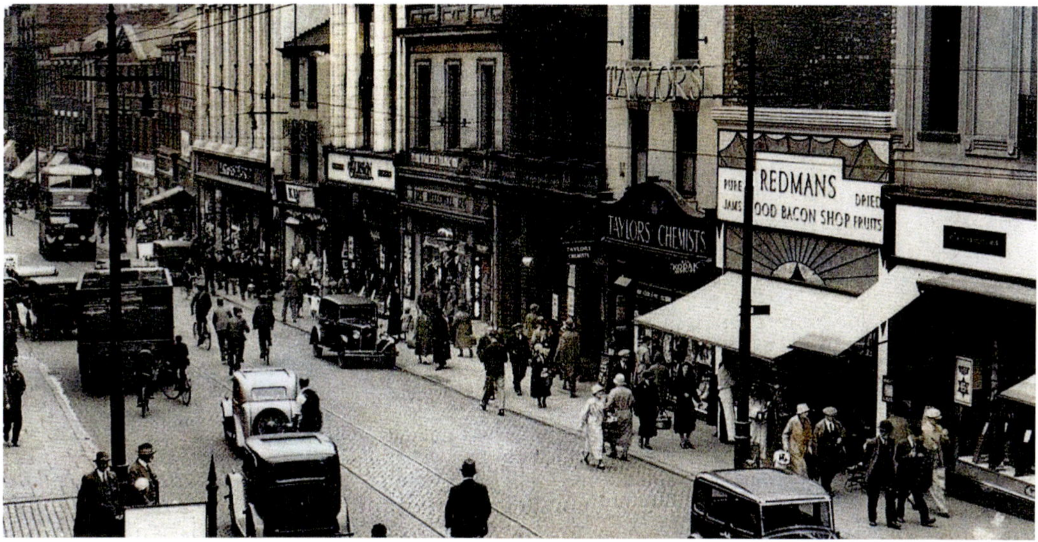

Fishergate, North Side, from Cheapside, 1933

The Preston Gas Company building towers over the landscape in the distance. Burton's the tailors occupy the premises on the corner of Cheapside, and Hellewells have premises further along – days when suits and raincoats were all the fashion. Redman's the grocers, who also had an outlet in Miller Arcade, had built a good reputation in Lancashire with their slabs of butter, bacon off the roll and slices of ham drawing customers. The popularity of bicycles is evident; numerous cyclists pedal along, weaving their way past the buses, trucks and saloon cars.

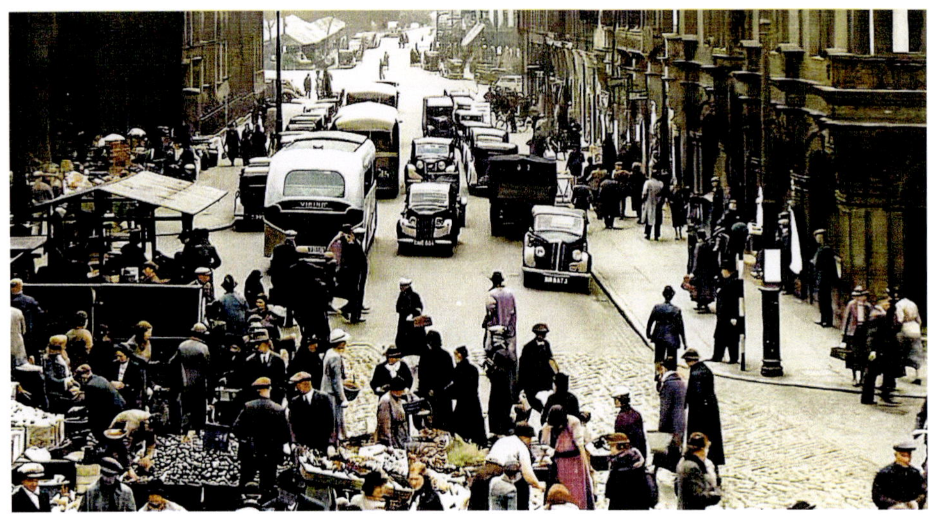

Market Street from Orchard Street, September 1934

It's market day and there is an overflow from the covered market as fresh fruit and vegetables are on offer. Further along is the fish market with its own canopy and numerous fishmongers display their fresh produce – fish from Fleetwood and shrimps from Southport for sale. In the distance on the Market Place the stallholders had just received news that plug-in electric lighting would be provided to illuminate the covered stalls during the winter months. On the corner to the right is the Farmers Arms, which by the 1970s was the Jolly Farmer.

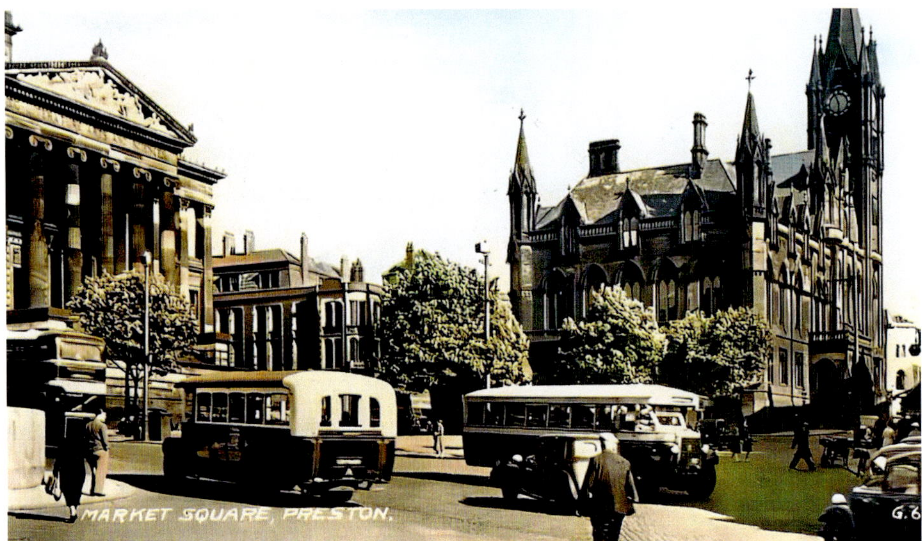

Preston Market Place, April 1938

During the summer visitors to the Harris Museum and Art Gallery, shown to the left, had the opportunity to see an exhibition of famous paintings illustrating Christianity in art, arranged by curator Sidney Paviere. With bus terminals dotted around the town centre, many stopped by the Market Place. Here two single-decker Leyland Lion buses with English Electric-built bodies can be seen coming and going. During the weeks ahead the Market Place would see PNE returning with the FA Cup and a royal visit from King George VI and Queen Elizabeth.

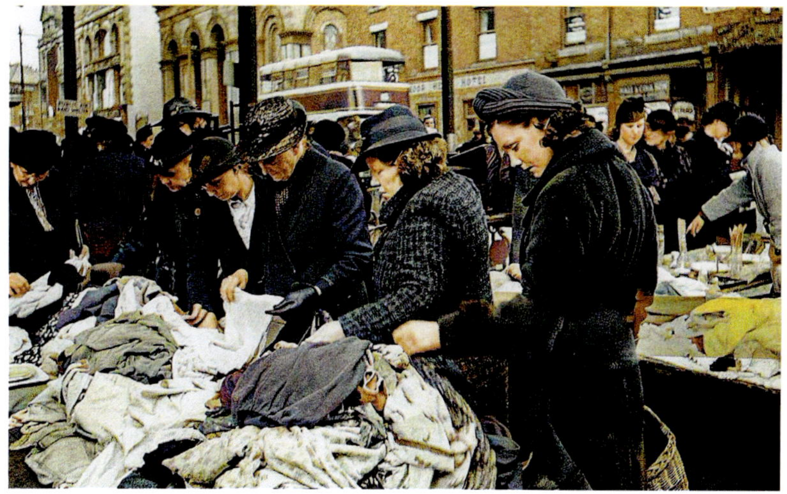

Covered Market Facing Lancaster Road, October 1941

The smartly clothed ladies rummage through the second-hand clothing on the market stall following the introduction of wartime clothing rationing in June 1941. All new clothing required coupons; a dress needed eleven, a shirt eight and a pair of shoes seven out of an adult's sixty-six coupons per year. A Preston Corporation bus can be seen passing the Black A Moor Head hotel (the Lancaster Gate today). Beyond is the Grecian façade of the Lancaster Road Congregational Church, opened in 1863. By 1972 the closed church and adjacent school buildings in the Bishopgate area had been swept away as the towering Preston Office Centre was built.

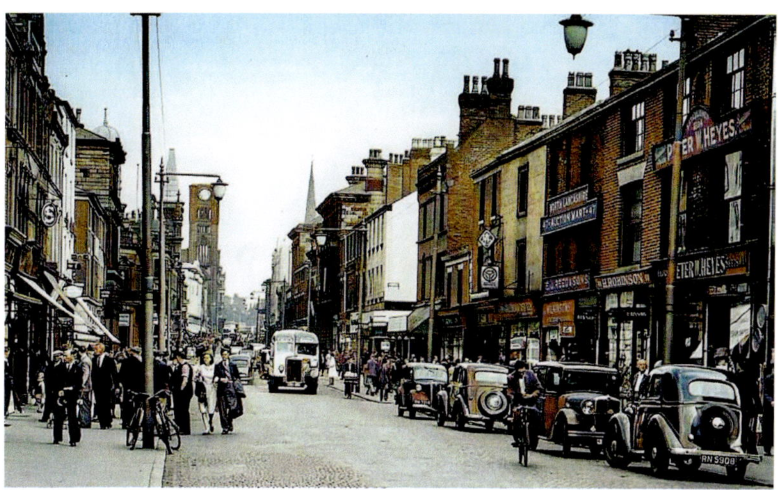

Fishergate from Fox Street, 1948

In the distance is a reminder of the destructive Guild Hall fire of March 1947 that left the clock tower burnt out. To the right, at No. 48, were the premises of Peter W. Hayes, the 'Seedsman', established in 1894 with floral delights galore. Next door in the upper salesrooms at No. 47 are estate agent EJ Reeds, selling family homes in Penwortham, Ashton and Fulwood for under £2,000, and at the North Lancashire Auction Mart you could bid for furniture or bric-a-brac. On the ground floor is Wilkinson's, electrical suppliers, who were offering to repair your wireless for 7s 6d plus parts. To the right above Bruccianis café (1932) is a large letter 'S', signifying that the Singer Sewing Machine Co. operated from there.

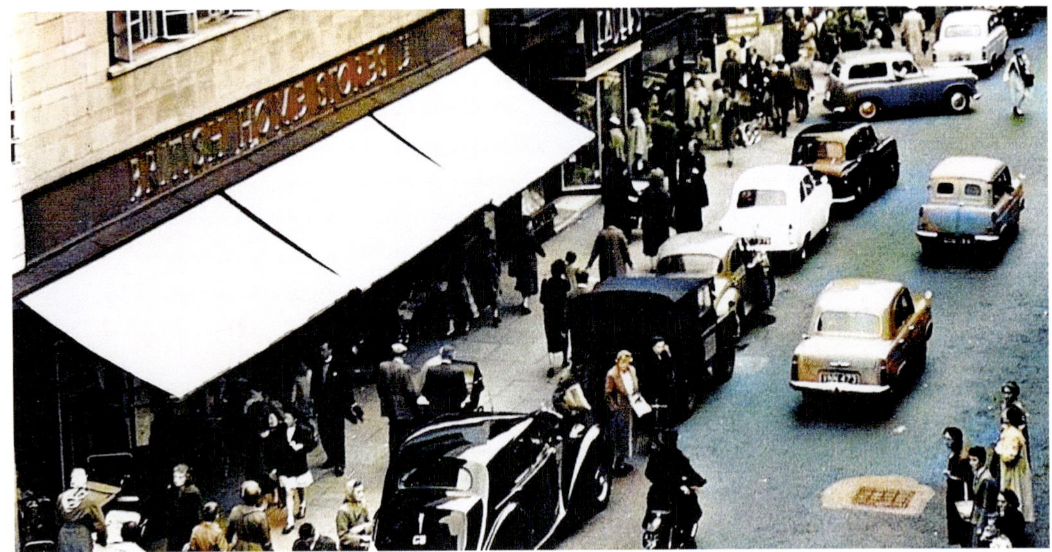

Fishergate, January 1957

The traditional January sales had increased footfall in the town. Owen Owen and BHS were leading the fashion trends with frocks and socks and pots and pans. Within three years the Owen Owen store of 1937 would be restructured beyond recognition. Their neighbours, BHS, had acquired the premises of drapers Frederick Matthews in February 1935 to add to their nationwide chain. Owen Owen, taken over by the Lewis Group, departed Fishergate by 1992 and BHS ceased trading in 2016.

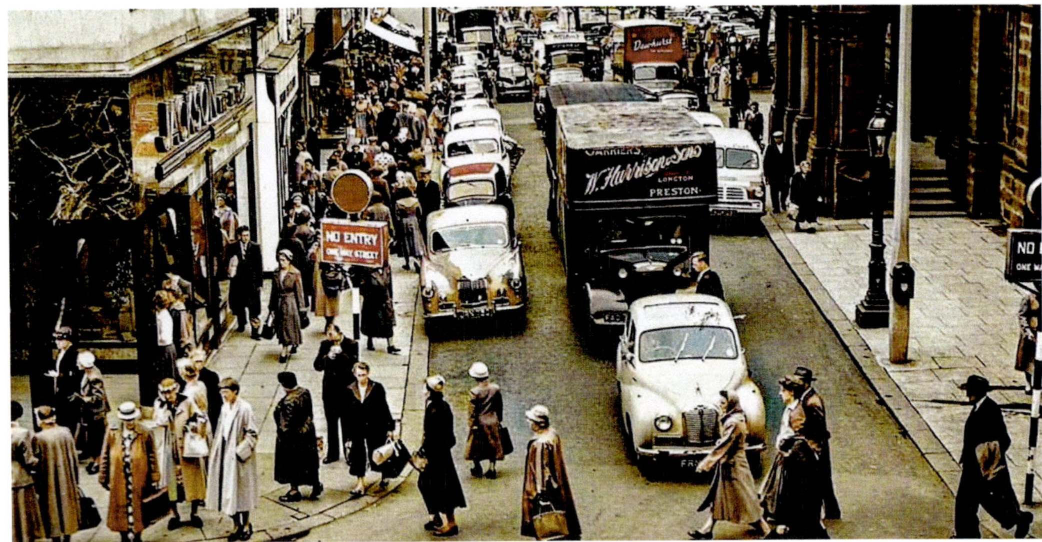

Cheapside from Fishergate, March 1957

Jackson the tailor was offering to help you step ahead with men's two-piece suits made to measure for between £8 and £10, just in time for Easter. Decades of cheap and cheerful shopping had taken place along Cheapside, including retailers who had become familiar names on the high street such as shoe supplier Stead & Simpson, the Maypole Dairy Company and Hepworth the tailors. Even double parking didn't appear to be a problem back then, with vehicles parked up outside the blackened remains of the fire-ravaged Town Hall building to the right.

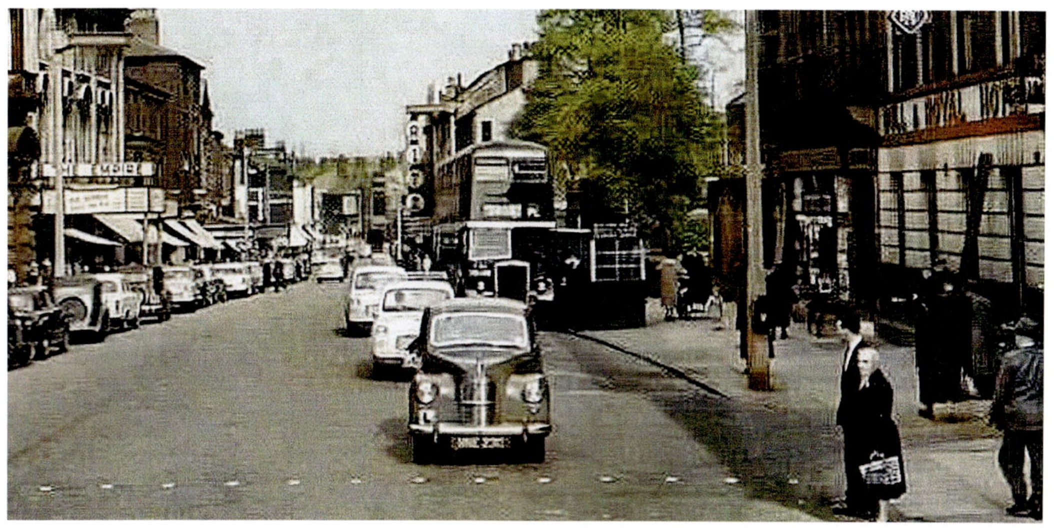

Church Street from Lancaster Road, April 1957

The Eagle & Child public house is no longer at the top of Stoneygate, having been demolished by 1933. The trams and tram lines have long since disappeared, and a Preston Corporation bus can be seen about to depart for Plungington. Back then Church Street was a very popular shopping area, and there was plenty of choice at the cinemas too. To the left, at the Empire, they were screening the *King And I* starring Yul Brynner; further along, at the Palladium, Errol Flynn in *Istanbul* was on offer; and across the street at the Ritz they were showing Debbie Reynolds in *Bundle of Joy*.

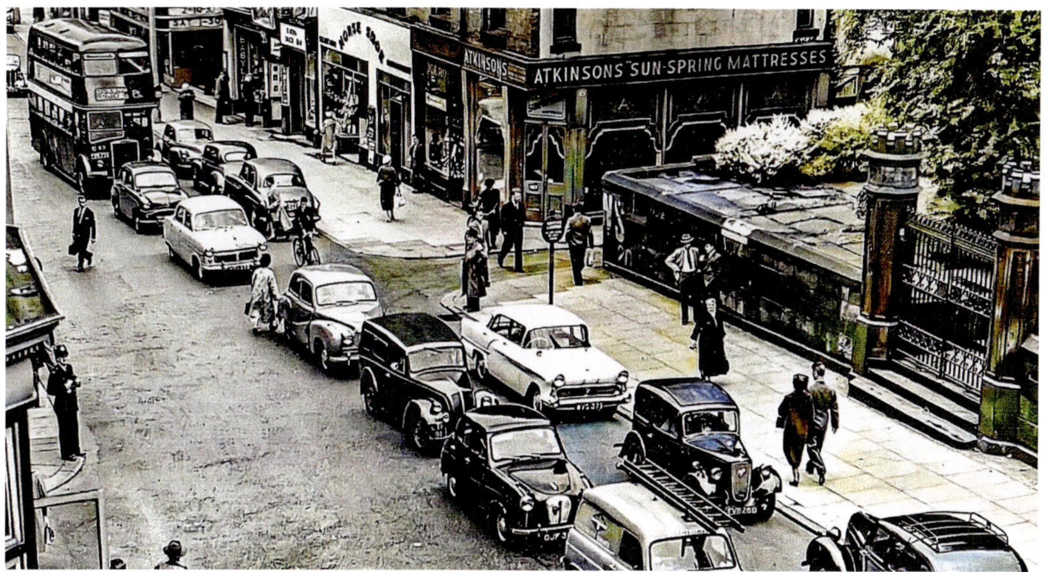

Church Street Looking Towards St John's Place, July 1957

Its Monday morning and traffic builds up along Church Street, despite petrol rationing, with a line of vehicles parked alongside the kerb. At the Ritz cinema they are advertising a double bill with *True as a Turtle* the main feature film. Atkinson's, the long-established bed suppliers, are on the corner of St John's Place. In the graveyard of the parish church (today's Preston Minster) the grave slabs, removed in 1977, are on view.

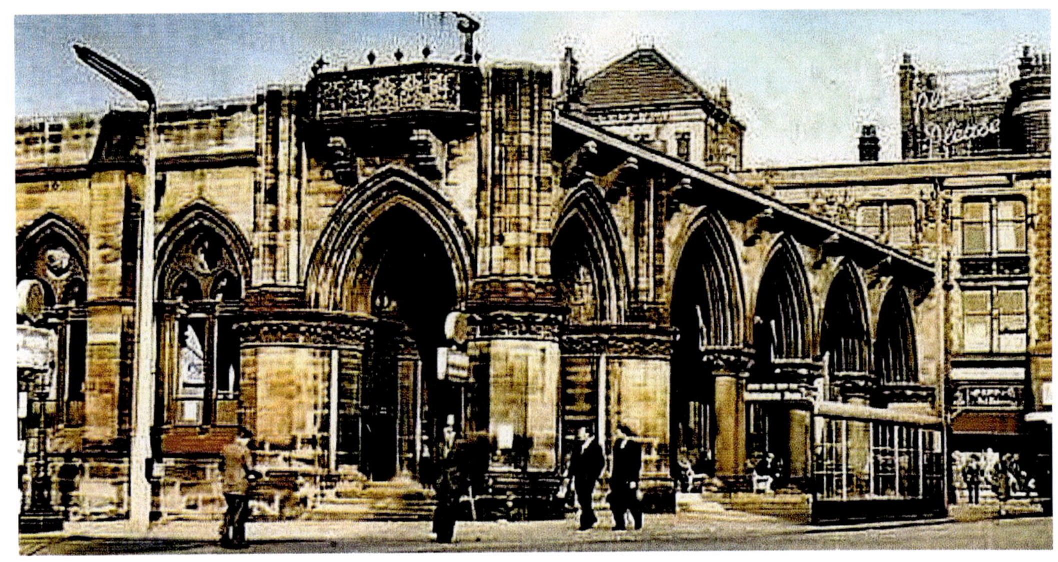

Victorian Town Hall from Fishergate, 1957

A decade after the destructive fire of March 1947, the Town Hall awaits its fate. In the alcoves of the building there were still benches to rest awhile or to wait for the next bus to Farringdon Park from the glass-fronted bus shelter. To the right above the Miller Arcade is a 'Players Please' sign advertising the popular cigarettes available at the tobacco kiosk within. Opened in 1899, the Miller Arcade was acquired by the Arndale Property Trust in 1946 and was known as Arndale House until 1972.

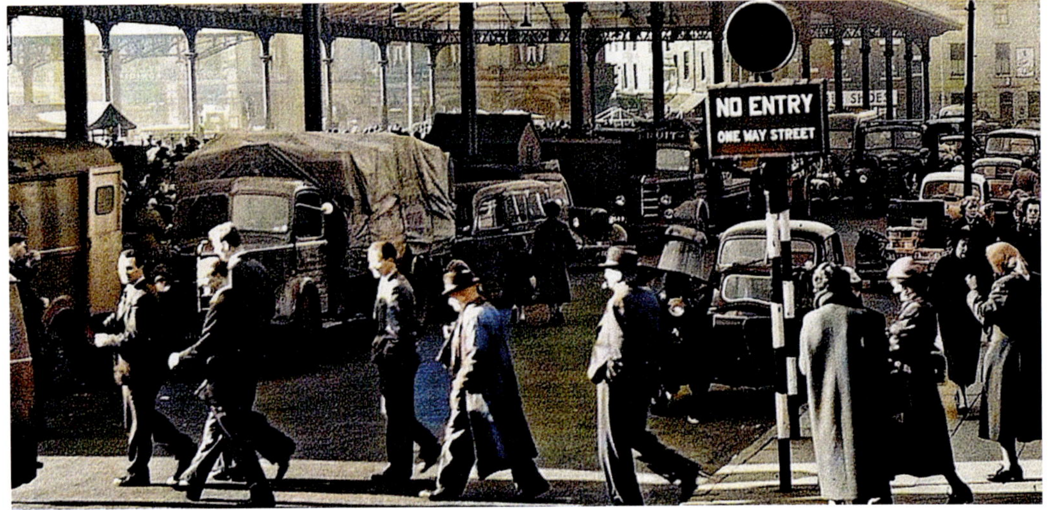

Liverpool Street, October 1958

The street running from Lancaster Road down to Starchhouse Square had the Covered Market along one side and wholesalers along the other. The townsfolk crossing the one-way street cast long shadows in the autumn sunshine. A busy market day lies ahead for the traders unloading their goods. The familiar fruit, vegetable and fish stalls operated beneath market canopies alongside the cosmetic, clothing, carpet and curtain stalls until the Indoor Market was erected on Liverpool Street facing the Covered Market. Liverpool Street is now home to the Arc cinema, which opened in February 2024, and the Animate leisure complex.

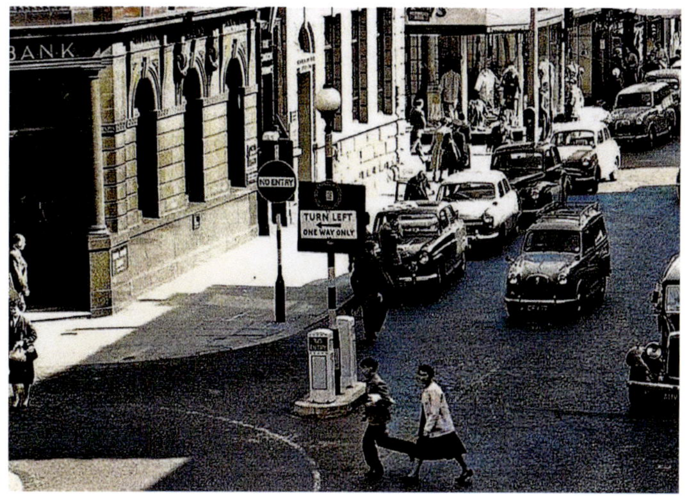

Fishergate from Lune Street, November 1959

The introduction of a one-way traffic system from Lune Street to Church Street along Fishergate led to much criticism in the *LEP*. Gridlocked traffic was commonplace at rush hour throughout town. In this image a row of vehicles are parked along the side of the road; there were calls to ban town centre street parking. On the corner was William Deacon's Bank Ltd, who had just opened their first drive-in branch on the corner of Lytham Road and Garstang Road, now the Little Wonders children's nursery. William Deacon's was part of the Royal Bank of Scotland which became part of NatWest, who have occupied the site since September 2023, having moved from No. 35 Fishergate (their city centre branch) in 1991.

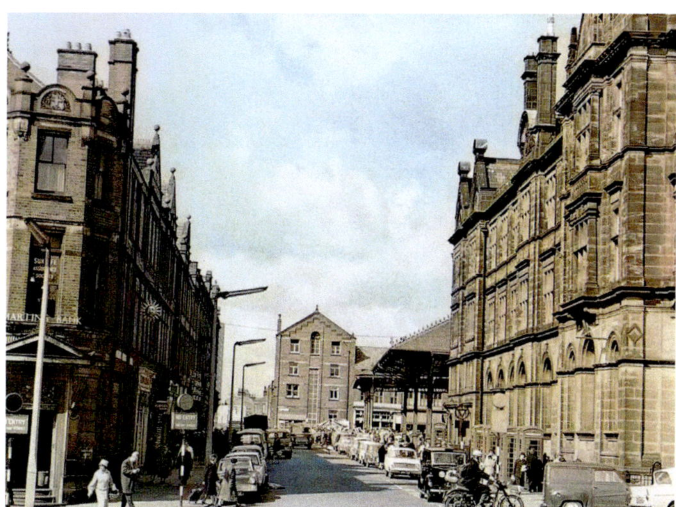

Market Street from Friargate, 1960

To the left is the George Hotel and adjacent shops on Market Street built *c.* 1896. The hotel replaced the original George Inn when Friargate was widened. Its days as a licensed premises were short-lived, however, as by the mid-1920s it was a branch of Martins Bank, then later a branch of Barclays before it became a Ladbrokes betting shop. To the right is the old General Post Office with its row of iconic red telephone boxes dating from *c.* 1936. According to the sign, no entry is permitted from Friargate as cars park freely on either side of the main road.

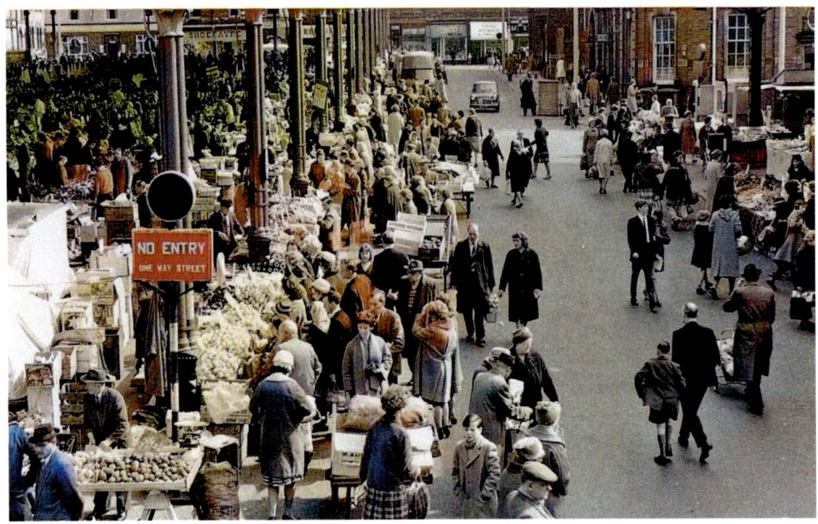

Market Days, Earl Street, 1960

The hustle and bustle of the open-air market saw the Covered Market to the left awash with traders and customers, while the fish market to the right had its own unique aroma with fresh fish on display. At the top of Earl Street is Lancaster Road with the former Preston Central Police Station, within Amounderness House, to the right. It was occupied by the Preston Borough Police before they merged with the Lancashire County Constabulary in April 1969. They moved to Lawson Street in 1973, then to Lancaster Road North in 2009.

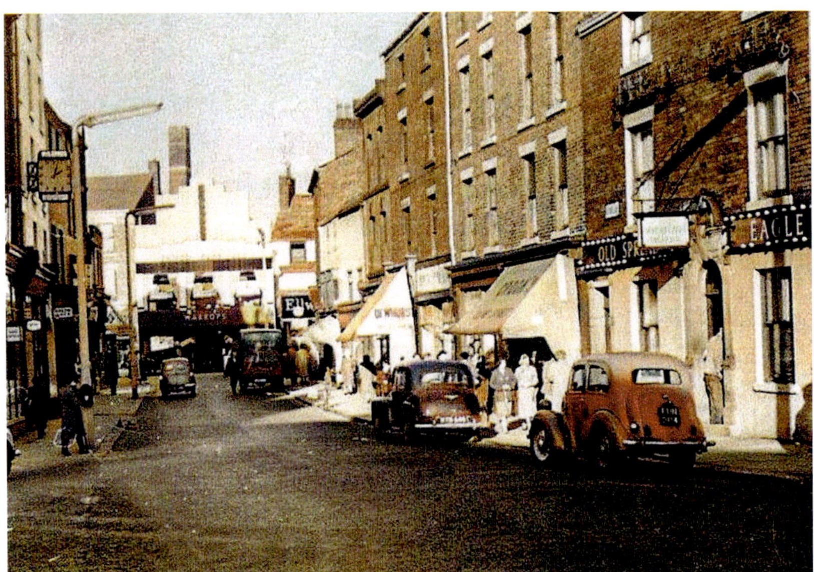

Lune Street Looking Towards Friargate, 1960

The Old Spread Eagle (1807) is pictured to the right across from the Corporation Arms. Both inns and the properties leading down to Friargate were about to be swept away as the Ringway development proceeded. Many a visitor enjoyed a drink here before going to the dances at the Public Hall. In the distance on Friargate are the Harrops furniture store and Ellwood's fabric shop, set for demolition in 1967.

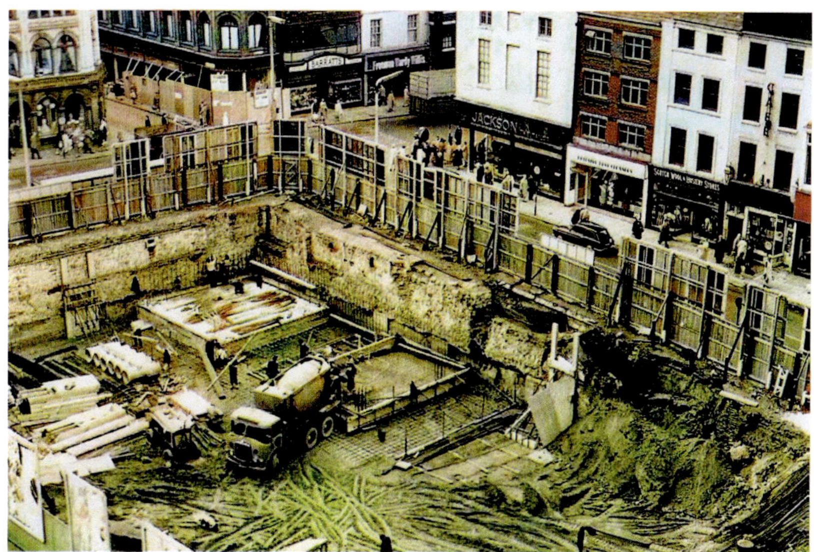

Market Square, October 1962

The square became a rectangle after the burnt-out Gothic Town Hall was demolished. Work is clearly underway on its replacement here as Crystal House foundations are being laid. Behind the hoardings is a cement mixer pouring out concrete as townsfolk walked past. Patrons of the EH Booth's café on the first floor of their store, shown top left, on the corner of Glovers Court, nowadays a Waterstones bookshop, had a bird's-eye view of the development.

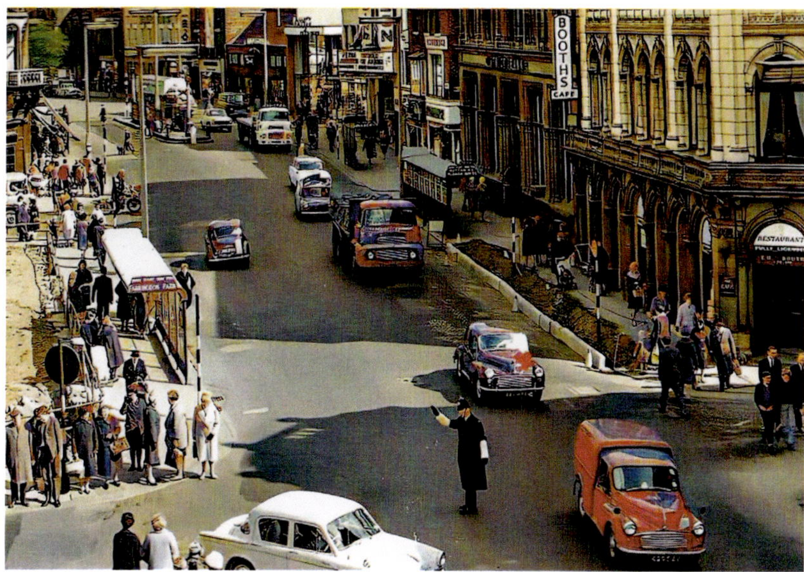

Fishergate Looking Towards Church Street, April 1963

A police constable directs traffic at the junction with Cheapside as pedestrians wait to cross the road. To the left the Town Hall has gone and to the right pavement repairs are taking place outside Booth's. The first-floor café was a welcome place for shoppers to take a break. In the distance, traffic negotiates its way past the centrally placed island of the underground toilets, and the former Gaumont cinema has been transformed into the Odeon.

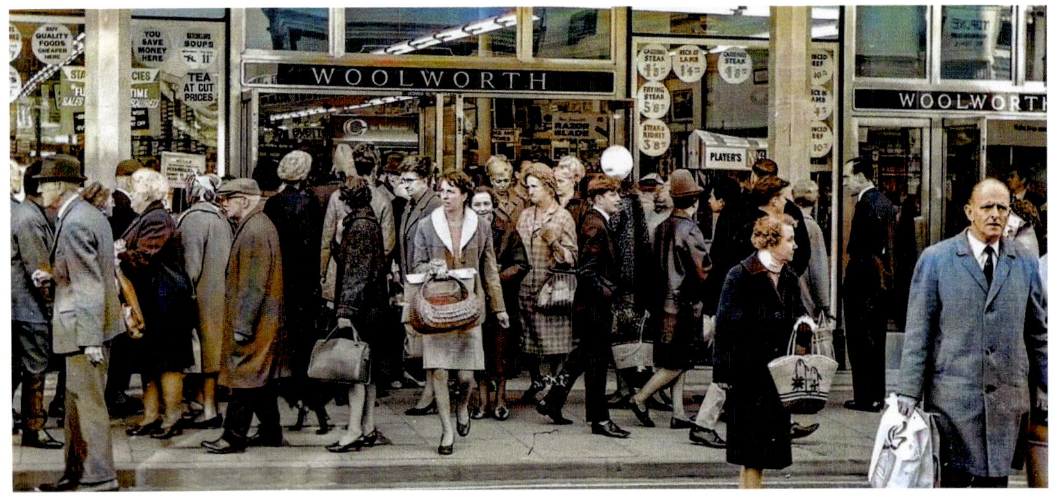

FW Woolworth & Co., Nos 30–31 Fishergate, December 1963

This popular store opened originally at No. 9 Fishergate, at the top of Glovers Court, in February 1910. It was only the second Woolworths in the UK at the time. In 1934, they moved to a newly built store with an art deco frontage at Nos 30–31 Fishergate. This image shows a busy Saturday of Christmas shopping, typical throughout the 1960s. In the 1950s, Woolworths introduced their own clothing brand, Winfield, named after their founder, Frank Winfield Woolworth. Besides the toys, toffees and trinkets, the store was stocked with plenty of groceries including choice cuts of steak and lamb.

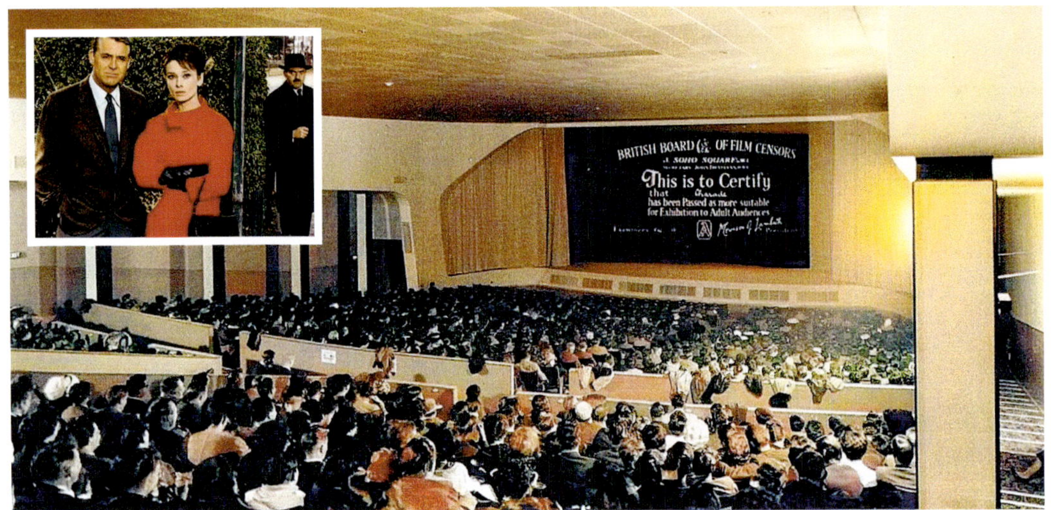

Odeon Cinema, Church Street, February 1964

It's time to dim the lights as the newly released *Charades* starring Audrey Hepburn and Cary Grant (inset) is about to begin, watched by a full house. At the time the Odeon was one of five cinemas in the immediate town centre. The Palladium closed in 1968, the Empire in 1974, the ABC in 1982 and the Ritz in 1986. A threat to the last of the town centre cinemas emerged in 1990 when the UCI cinema (today the Odeon) opened on Preston Riversway; a year later the Warner Village cinema in Walton-le-Dale, which became Vue in 2004, also opened. The Odeon had introduced the Odeon 2 screen in January 1970, but despite the best of efforts the cinema closed in September 1992.

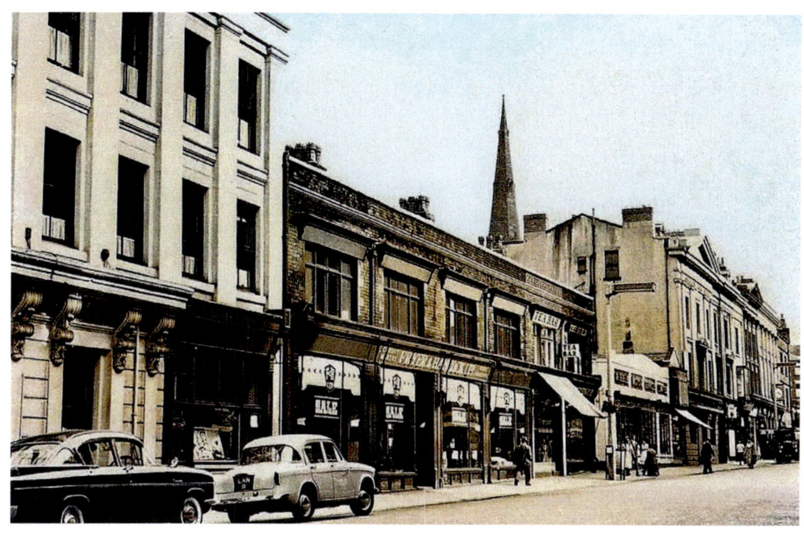

Lancaster Road, East Side, from Harris Street, 1964

The premises in the foreground up to the Stanley Arms were earmarked for demolition, with plans for the new Guild Hall in the pipeline. Fryer & Hancock, cabinetmakers and house furnishers, were holding a sale. Established in late Edwardian days, they also had a showroom in Lord Street and a works in Gt Shaw Street. At the other side of Wards End, beyond the original Tea Bar, was the passageway leading to the Ribble bus station, and beyond that was the Ribble travel information centre.

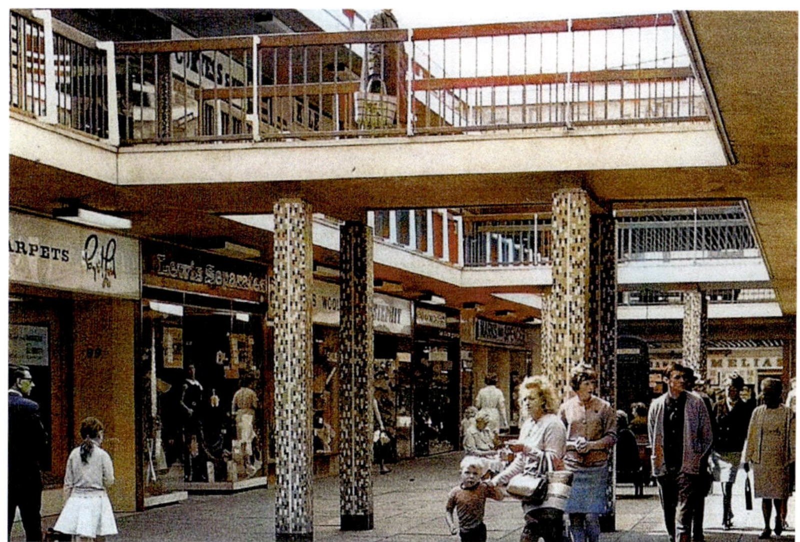

St George's Shopping Centre, 1969

The shopping centre opened in November 1964 with forty of the planned 120 outlets. It cost £5.5 million and was owned by the Murrayfield Real Estate Company. Among the traders seen here are Cyril Lord the carpet retailer; Lewis Separates; a Martin Dawes TV outlet; the grocers Melias, previously on Friargate; Curtess Shoes, who later had a corner shop on Orchard Street, currently a Greggs branch; and a Marks & Spencer store, whose upper storey leads onto Fishergate to this day.

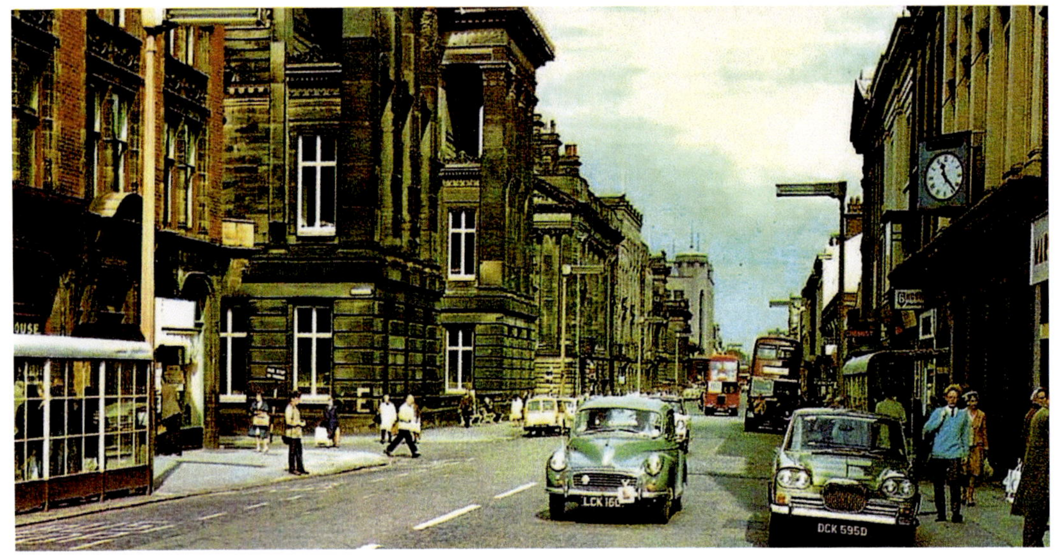

Lancaster Road from Church Street, *c.* 1969

At this time bright and colourful clothing was in vogue, which is evident amongst the shoppers, many of whom would have commuted to town on the nearby buses. Buses had grown in popularity over the years, leaving trams a distant memory from the 1930s. Car ownership was also increasing at this time and a Morris Minor car displaying 'L' plates, perhaps driven by an eager new learner, heads towards Church Street.

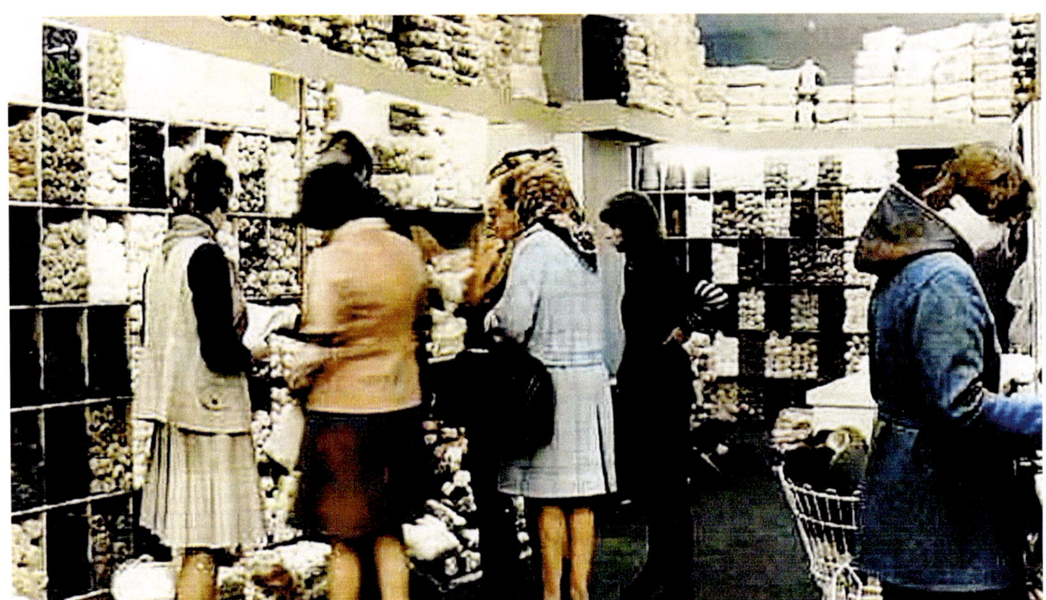

Jaspers Wool Shop, Cheapside, 1979

A large variety of colourful wools are on display, with shop assistants on hand as a lady browses through the catalogues to choose a knitting pattern. Back in 1979 when this picture was taken, knitting was a common hobby for many people, with a number of specialist wool suppliers dotted all over town. Pictured here is the interior of Jaspers on Cheapside, a family-run business that started life in Perthshire.

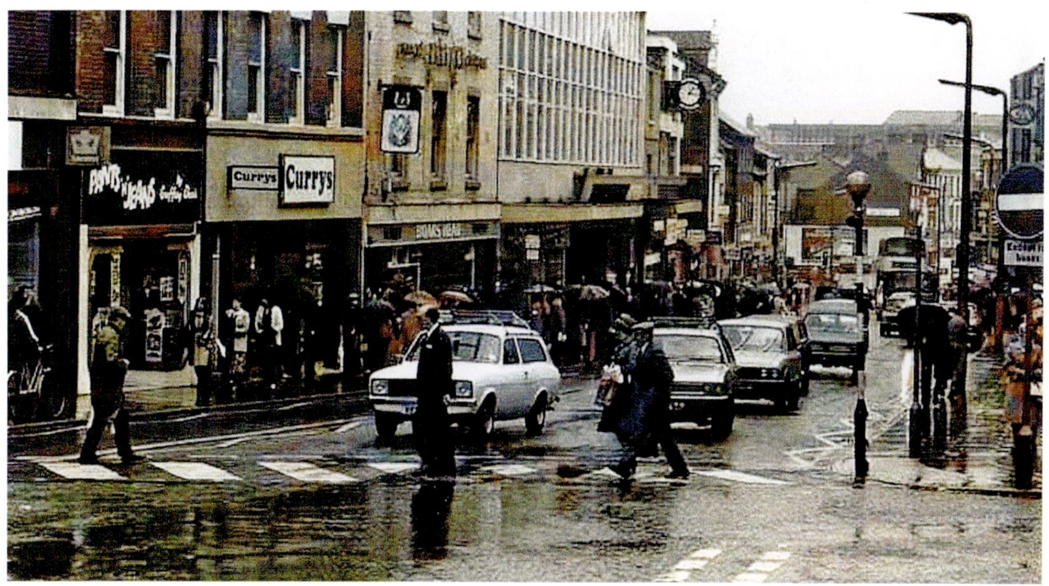

Friargate from Market Street, 1980

The shoppers are still out despite the rainy day, with umbrellas ready to shelter them when the showers arrive. The zebra crossing was clearly popular, as cars and buses wait for the pedestrians to pass. Next to the Boars Head public house, which closed in 1983 and was converted to a retail store, was a popular branch of Currys, the place for electronic gadgets.

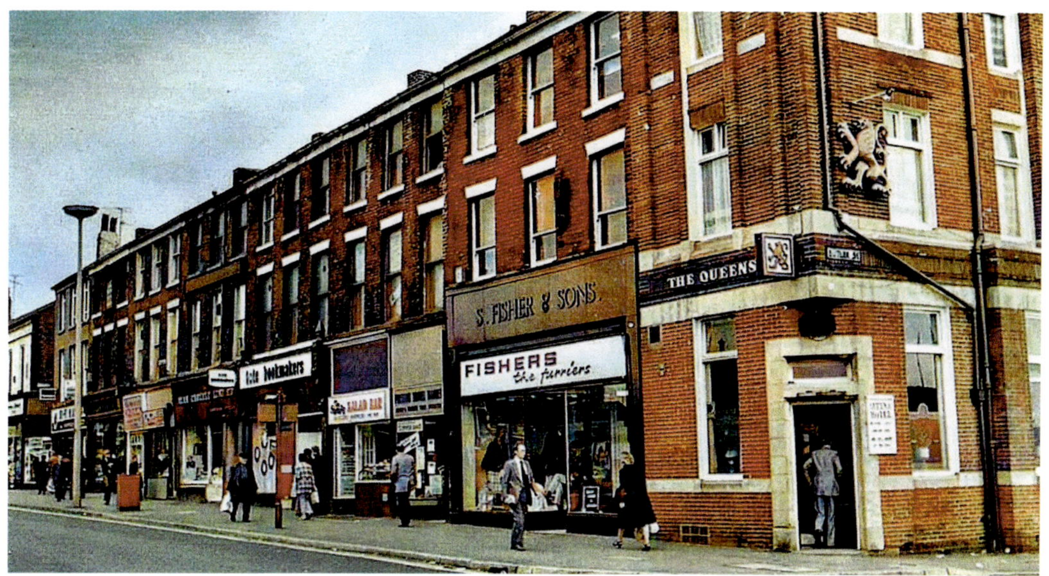

Queen's Buildings Fishergate, 1980

The Queen's Hotel, serving Lion Ales on the corner of Butler Street and dating back to the 1850s, would soon disappear, along with the shop premises occupying the Queen's Buildings facing Fishergate, their demolition necessary for the development of the Fishergate Centre. Well-established traders such as Fishers the furriers, the Shanty salad bar, the Tote bookmakers and Carlyle the opticians were all destined for pastures new.

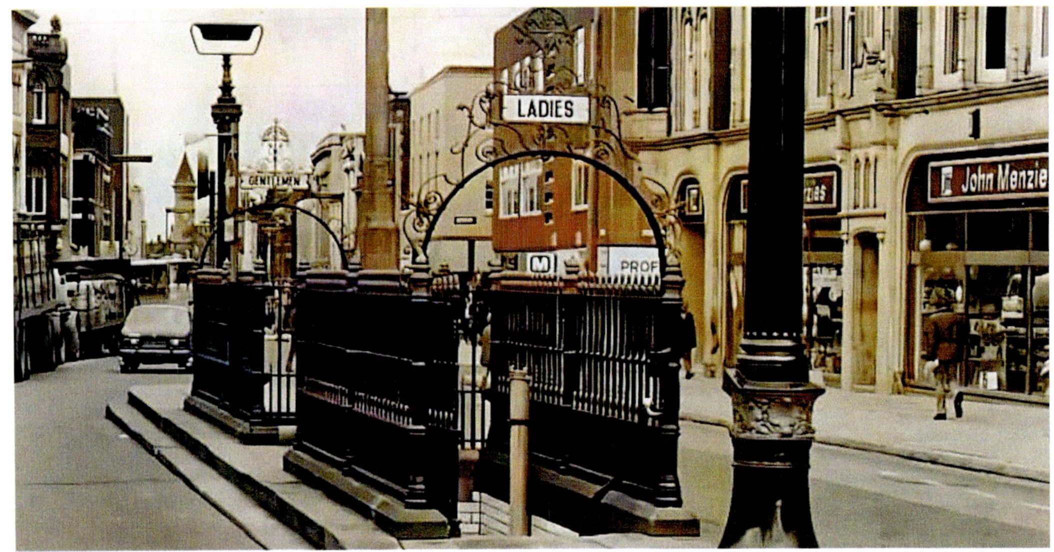

Underground Loos, Church Street, 1981

If you needed to spend a penny you could visit the underground public lavatories situated at the top of Church Street. They were built in four months in 1902 and opened days before the Preston Guild of that year, costing £2,000. Their central location was designed so that the new electric tramway could have a double line – one on each side. Fortunately, the ornate ironwork of the toilet block entrances has been preserved and can be seen at the front of Miller Arcade where the popular John Menzies store was thriving.

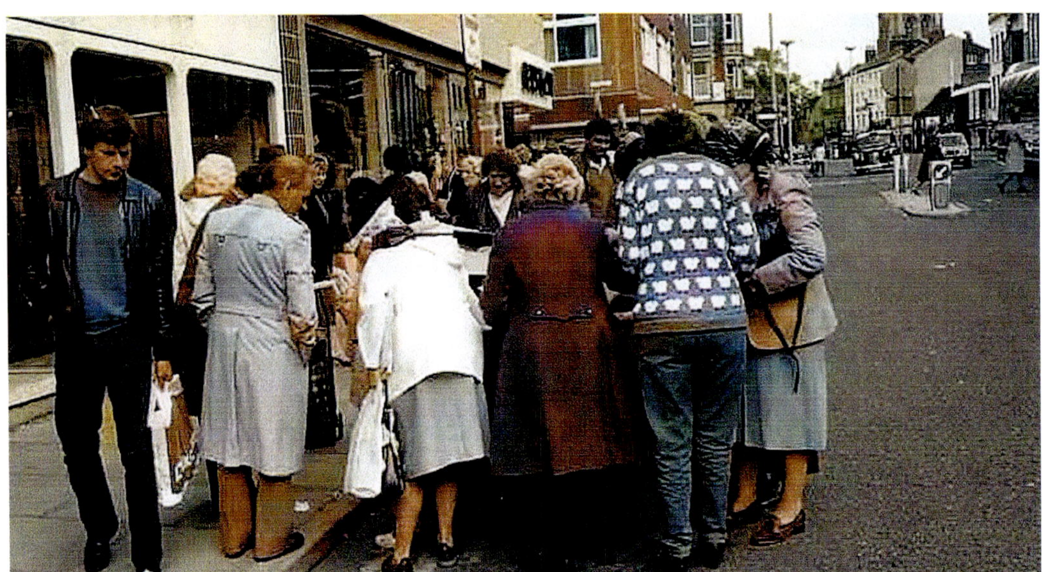

Occasions Store, Fishergate, February 1982

The January sales were over, but the closure of the Occasions store next to Burton's provided some irresistible free bargains for shoppers. A skip had been filled with discarded stock from greeting cards to calendars, trinkets to toys, balloons to baubles and stationery to sketch pads. Burton's the tailors had recently moved from Cheapside to replace Jackson's on the corner, nowadays home to an Ann Summers store.

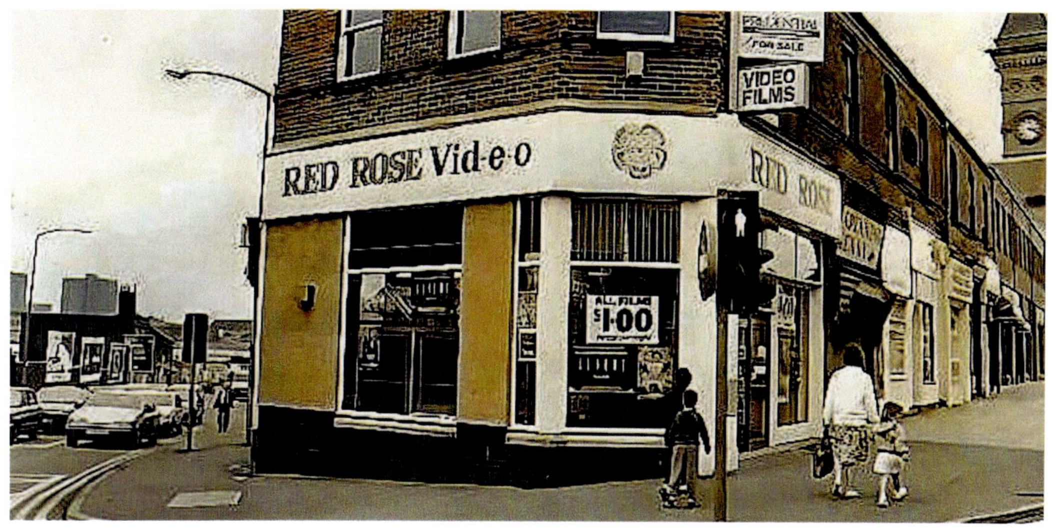

Corporation Street, Fishergate Corner, 1984

On the corner of the Victoria & Albert Buildings is a reminder of the days when video stores were all the rage. For your Saturday night entertainment, you could hire a VHS video for £1. Back then the row of shops on Fishergate, from the corner towards town, included the Spinning Jenny, a haberdashery store; Preston Computers; Villas & Vacations, a travel agent; the Mulberry Bush, a fancy goods outlet; a barber; and a tailor. The corner premises today is Chinese takeaway outlet Chun Cha, until recently home to the Kingswood estate agents.

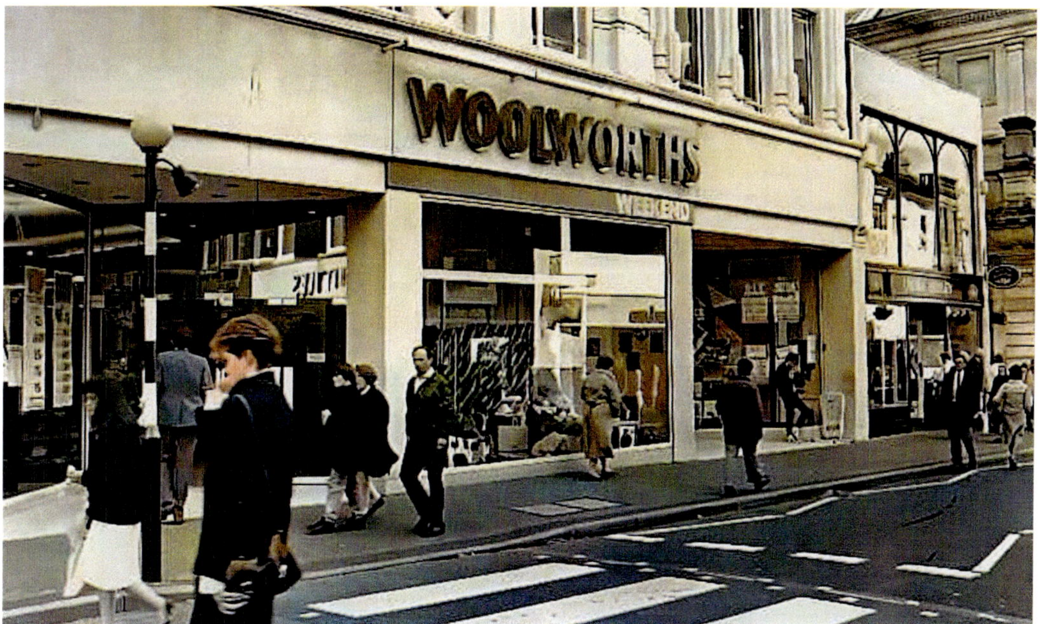

Woolworths, Fishergate, 1987

After decades of popularity, Woolworths waved goodbye to Preston in late December 2008. Today a Next store operates from the location. To the right is a Laura Ashley outlet which had taken over the former Barclays bank premises. When Laura Ashley departed in 2020 it became a Trespass clothing store.

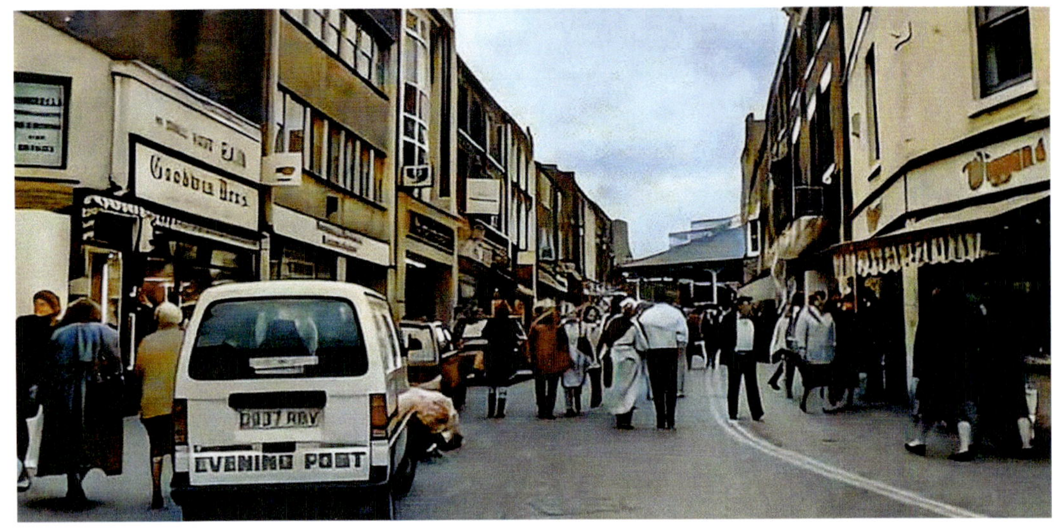

Orchard Street from Friargate, 1987

It is a busy shopping day as a *Lancashire Evening Post* van ignores the yellow lines and makes a quick stop to deliver the latest edition of the paper. The Goodwin Bros umbrella shop to the left carries the warning 'We Shall Have Rain'. To the right is Wiggins, bakers and confectioners, tempting customers with their pies and pasties. The street was constructed in 1836 to enable access to the Orchard in the days before the Covered Market was completed (1875). It is a street with ever-changing traders, but back in the 1980s it was noted for its bakers, butchers and cheese merchants.

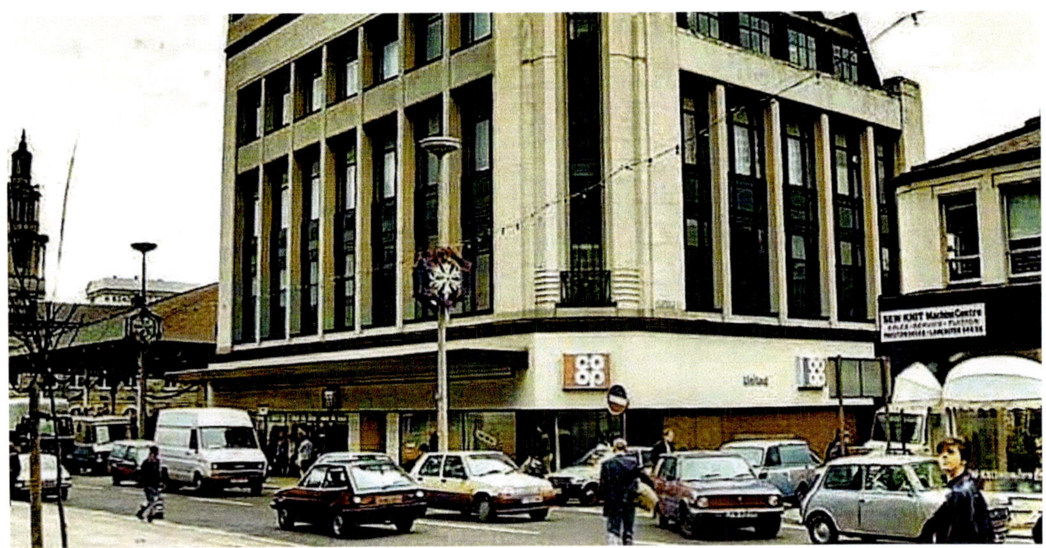

Co-op Department Store, Lancaster House, Lancaster Road, December 1988

Opened in May 1939 and built in the art deco style by local builders John Turner & Sons, the Co-op department store was described as a furnishings emporium. It was extended along Liverpool Street in 1972 when the Indoor Market Hall was built. It is pictured prior to its closure in 1988, having been bought by Preston Corporation with plans to eventually merge it into the Market Hall. The ground floor was occupied by a popular Chinese restaurant called Great Times from 1991 until closure in 2015. Parts of the upper areas are occupied by city council staff from time to time.

On the Streets Where We Have Lived

The streets that we have lived in have changed dramatically down the decades. Thanks to pioneering photographers such as Robert Pateson and Alfred Shaw we have images of Preston streets from Victorian and Edwardian days. Pateson, who had a studio on Fishergate, opposite Fox Street, took photographs of the Avenham and Winckley Square areas, where homes were inhabited by the gentry and genteel folk at the time. Whilst Alfred Shaw, from Blackburn, captured terraced rows and corner shops in areas where the millworkers spent their daily lives.

During the post-war period, Preston, like many towns in Lancashire, embarked on a slum-clearance programme. It meant the sweeping away of endless rows of terraced houses on cobbled streets, such as Higford Street, off New Hall Lane, where I was brought up. Homes that had flagged floors, coal fires and outside toilets. Where a tin bath was brought out when it was bathtime and the private landlord came on pay day for the few shillings rent that was due. Though the bulldozers have demolished them, cherished memories linger on.

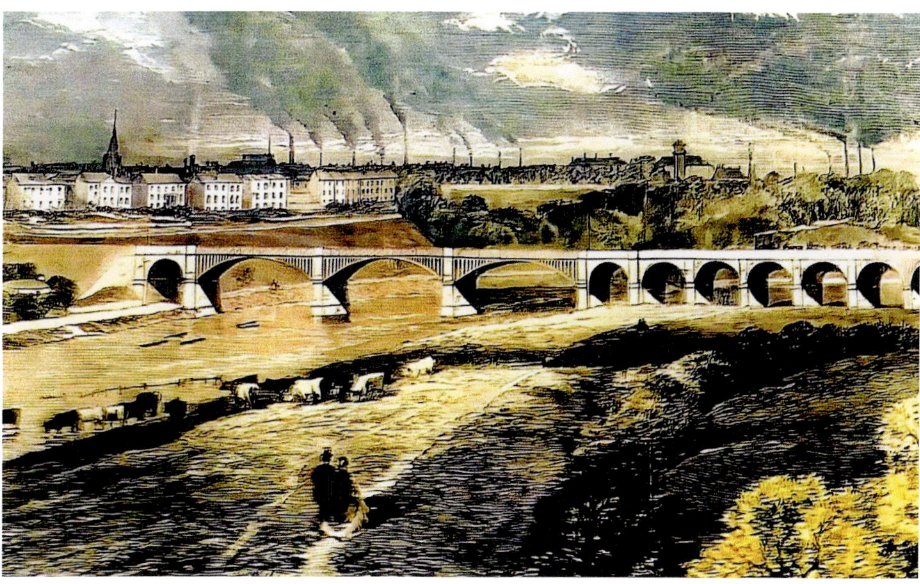

Preston from Penwortham, 1855

Spanning the River Ribble is the East Lancashire Railway Bridge (1846), with its three main arches over the water and a footpath running alongside the railway tracks. Fine houses can be seen in the Avenham area and beyond. Cattle can be seen grazing on the shoreline. In April that year, John McGowan of the Ribble Fishery Establishment on Fishergate informed the public he had commenced fishing locally and would be providing daily fresh salmon, sparlings, turbot, trout, crabs and lobsters.

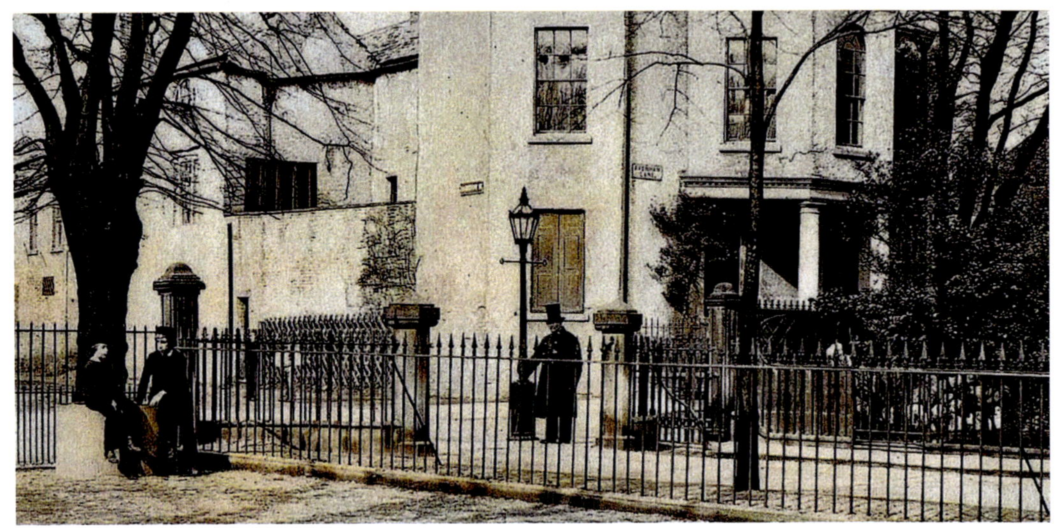

Avenham House, Avenham Lane, Corner of Bairstow Street, 1860

When Robert Pateson took this photo Avenham House was the residence of Revd Alfred Beaven, headmaster of the Preston Grammar School. The house had been owned by Richard Newsham Sr, four times mayor of Preston. He died there, aged ninety, in June 1843. His son, Richard Newsham Jr, bequeathed the family art collection to the town when he died in 1883. Avenham House was demolished in 1901 when the top end of Bairstow Street was upgraded. To this day the gabled end of No. 31 Bairstow Street has the stone lettering 'Avenham House'.

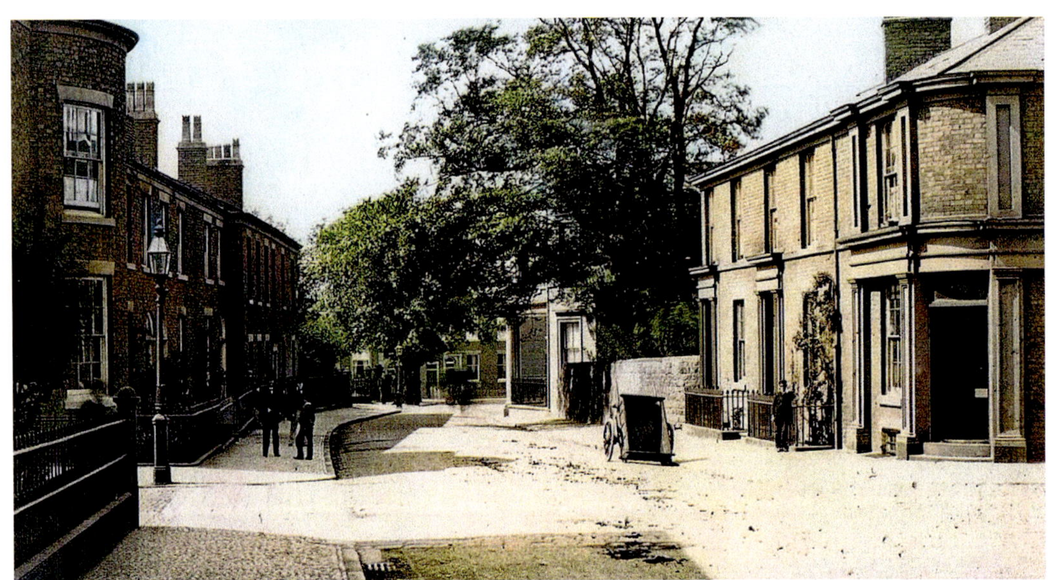

Avenham Lane Looking Towards Ribblesdale Place, 1862

This scene has changed little over time, except for a third storey being added to the building on the corner of Chaddock Street to the right, which dates from *c.* 1835. Centrally placed is the porticoed entrance to Avenham House at the head of Bairstow Street. To the left, beside the gas lamp, is the entrance to the fashionable-housed Latham Street. Notably, the cast-iron railings enclosing cellars of the houses on Avenham Lane remain to this day.

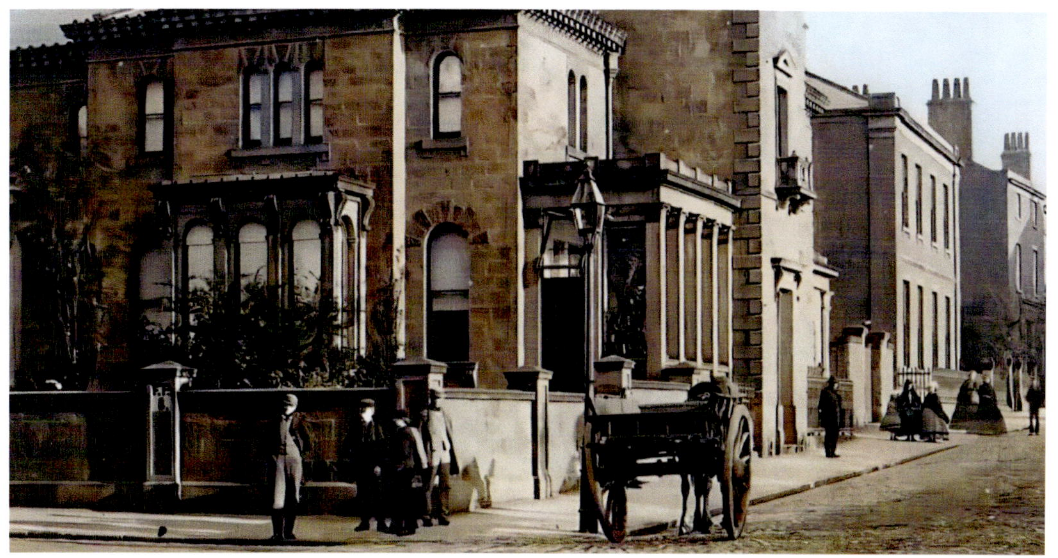

Cross Street, Winckley Square Corner, 1862

The Italian-style villa was built in 1850 by wealthy cotton master William Ainsworth. The mill he was connected with was that of his father, Thomas Ainsworth, in Cotton Court, off Church Street. That mill had strict rules for operatives, with a seventy-hour working week often imposed. Later occupiers were Mr Parker, a wealthy grocer; the surgeon Dr Hammond; and county court officials. It was knocked down in 1969 and replaced by a red-brick apartment block named Winckley House.

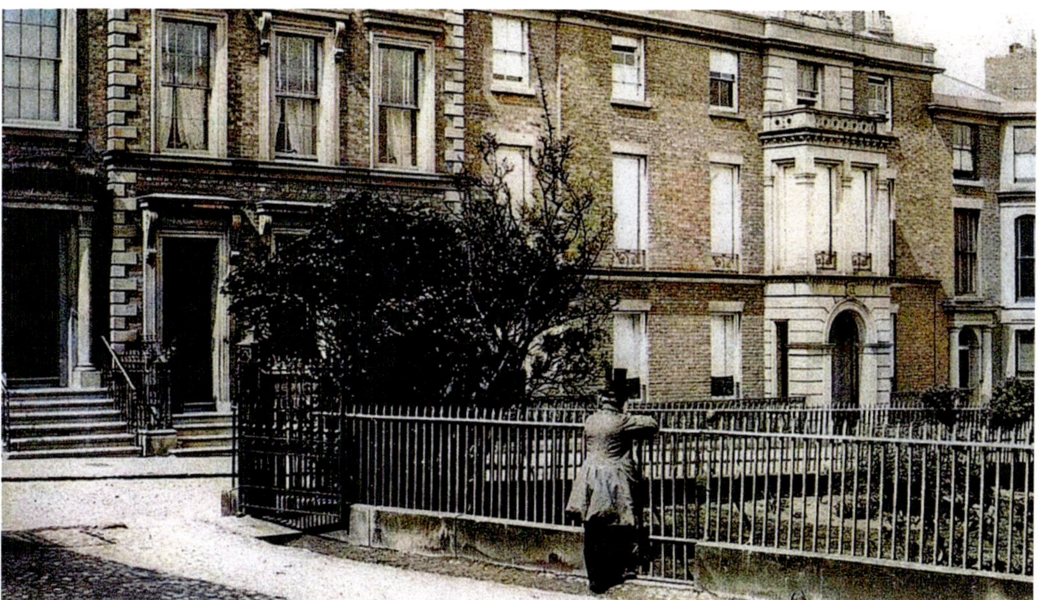

Winckley Square, South-West Corner, 1862

A Victorian gentleman leans on the railings as he looks towards the three-storey mansion of No. 23 Winckley Square, the home of barrister Thomas Batty Addison, chairman of the Preston Quarter Sessions and Recorder of Preston. Thomas and his brother John had the house built a decade earlier, living together until John's death in 1859. Thomas continued to live there until his death in 1874.

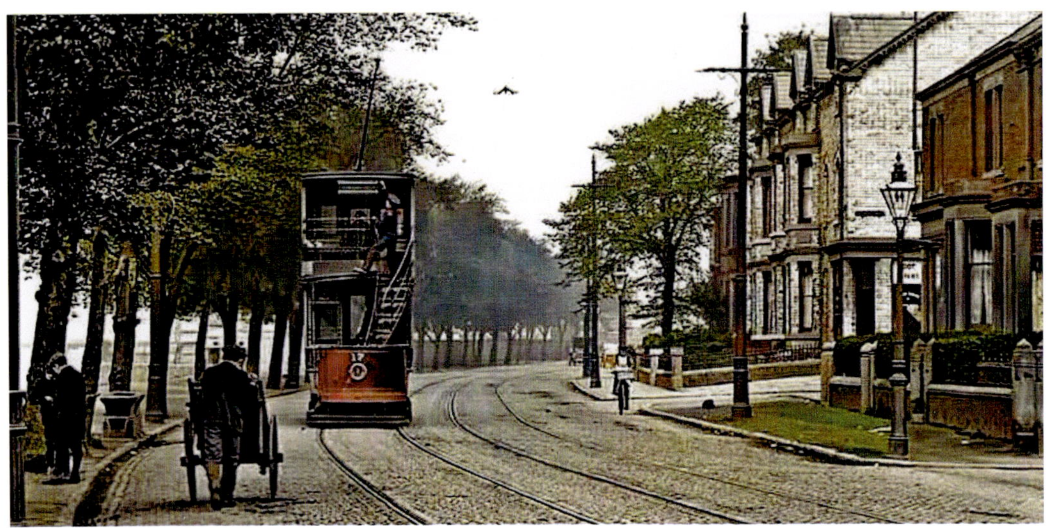

Broadgate, 1911

When Alfred Shaw visited Broadgate, he captured this tranquil scene with a handcart and an electric-powered tram trundling along the cobbled road. The tram conductor can be seen changing the destination board to Strand Road. In 1860, trees had been planted along Broadgate, and they were flourishing here. Recently, substantial flood-defence walls have been built, but back in 1904, 1910 and 1927, when the River Ribble burst its banks, the houses were flooded and ground floors and cellars left under water.

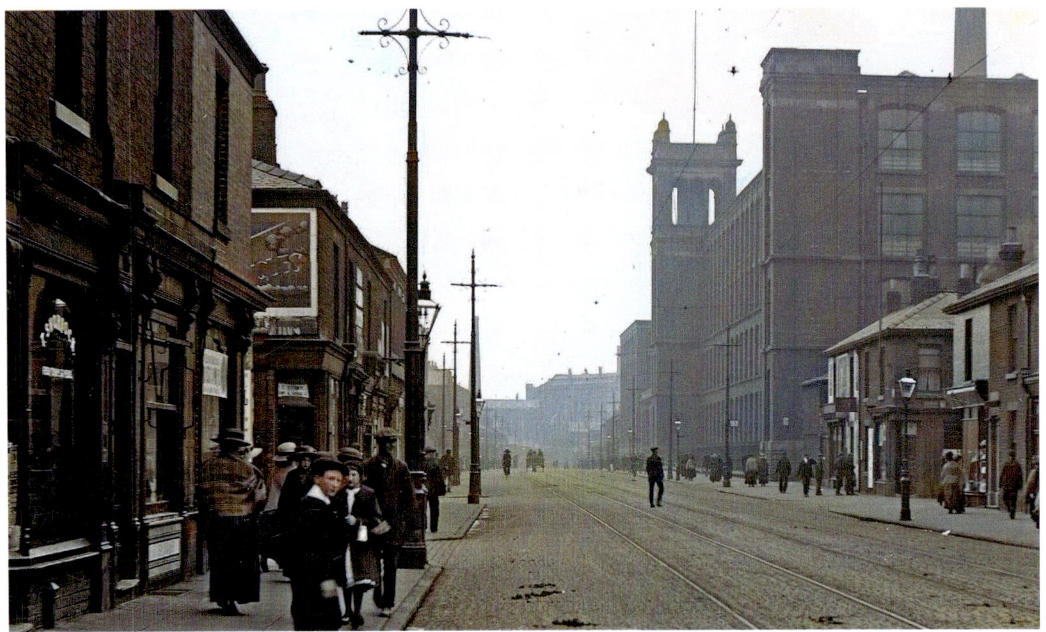

New Hall Lane Looking Towards Stanley Street, 1913

The streets off New Hall Lane were densely populated, mainly with millworkers. The flagship Centenary Mill to the right was erected in 1891. When this photo was taken Horrocks, Crewdson & Co. employed over 6,000 workers on New Hall Lane and in their Stanley Street Yard Works.

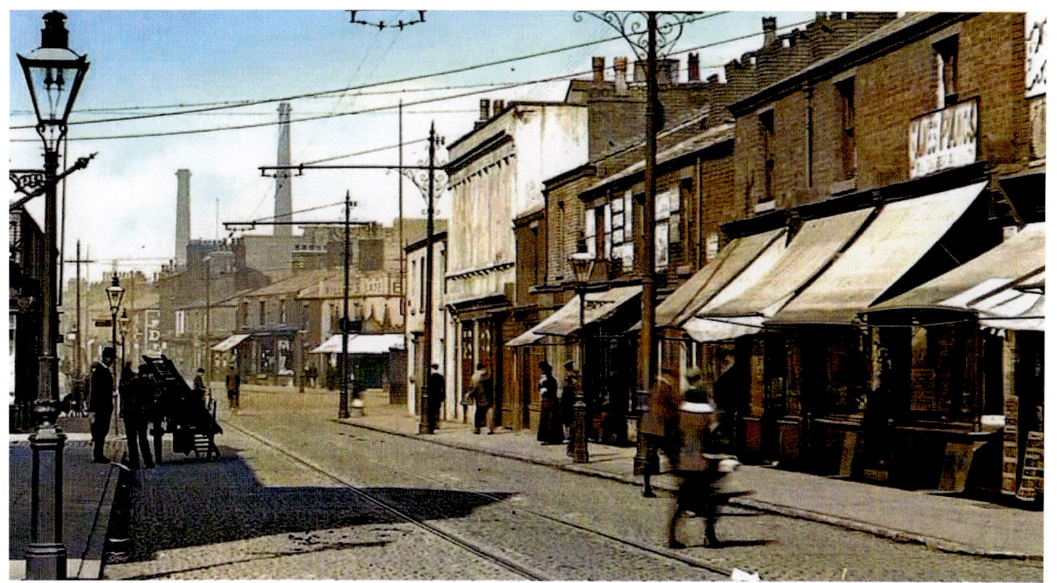

North Road from High Street Corner, 1913

This road was constructed in 1830 as stagecoach traffic increased and it became part of the extensive electric-powered tramway system. It was a busy neighbourhood shopping street. In the distance, as North Road stretches onwards, the tall chimneys of the mills on Hanover Street and Park Lane tower above the rooftops.

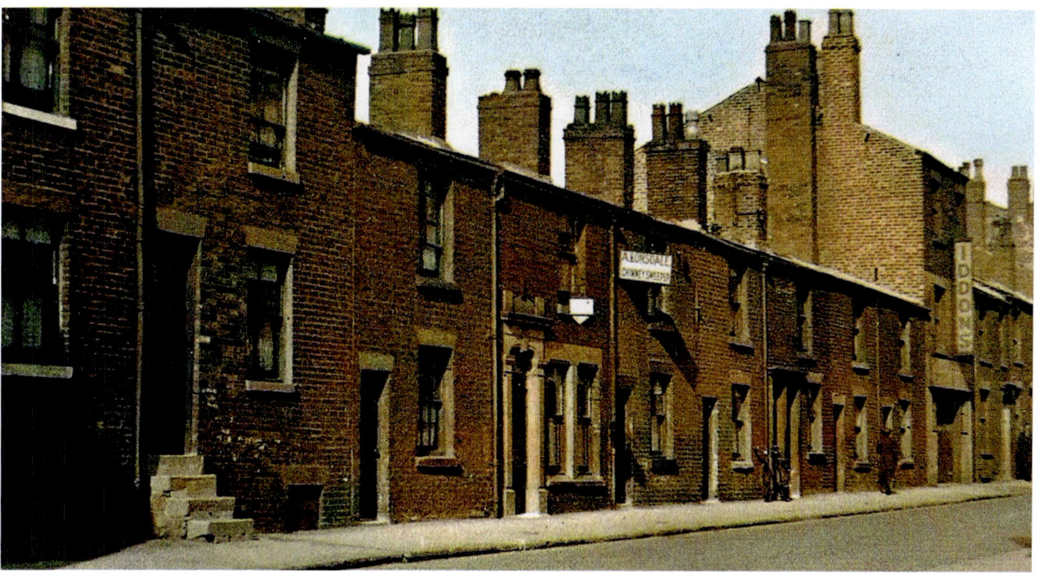

High Street from Lancaster Road, 1932

This street stretched down from Tithebarn Street to Starch House Square. A publication in 1861 described it as being about 220 yards long and containing a row of poor houses with small back yards. Behind them a huge sewer discharged itself on the surface, creating a filthy bog. Fifty years later the street had an air of respectability, with tradespeople of all description residing there. All were swept away with the coming of the Ringway, apart from a couple of business premises at the North Road end.

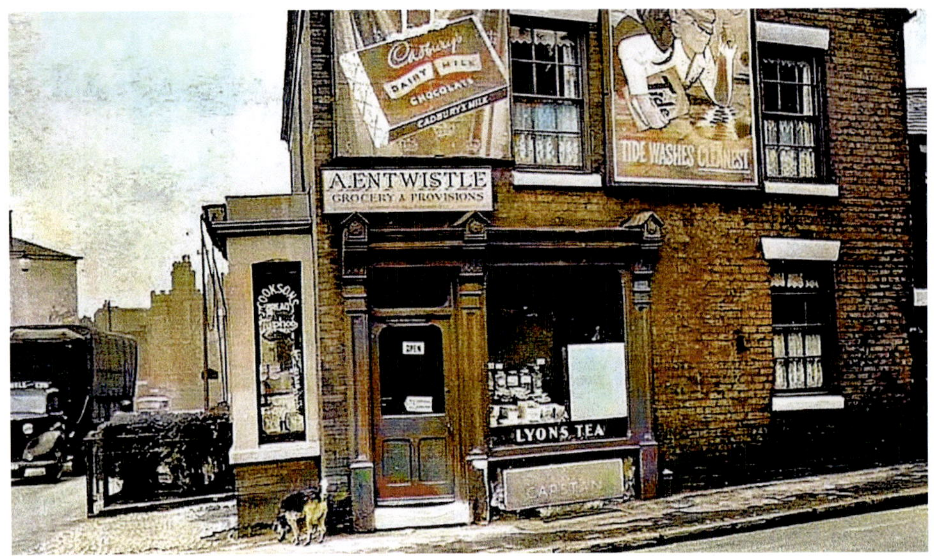

Newton Street, Corner of Deepdale Road, 1952

The grocery store of Albert Entwistle was a typical local community store, serving the terraced homes in the neighbourhood. Typhoo & Lyons Tea, Cadbury's Dairy Milk, Capstan cigarettes and Tide washing powder, all familiar brands, are advertised on billboards and in shop windows. To the left, as the canvas-covered lorry passes up Deepdale Road, the County Arms can be seen on the corner of Ribbleton Lane, along with the outline of HM Prison Preston.

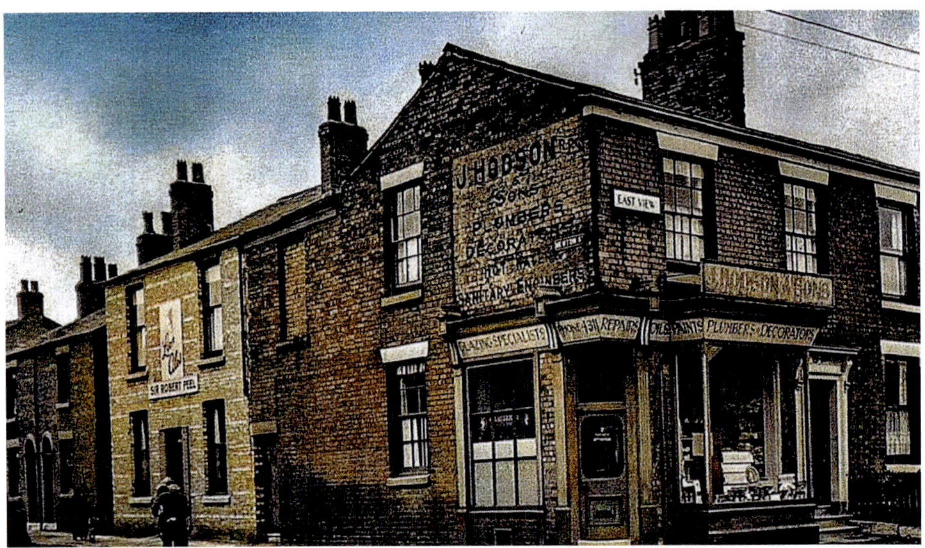

Newton Street, Corner of East View, 1952

Facing onto East View was the corner premises of J. Hodson & Sons, plumbers and decorators. Adjoining it was the Sir Robert Peel Inn (1850), displaying a Lion Ales sign. In the 1980s, with the street redeveloped and lined with maisonettes, the licence of the inn was taken over by the corner premises. In June 1982, after extensive modernisation, this opened as the Hollywood Bar, a popular pub of the era with drag artists and disco music. It later became the Finney Sport's Bar, which closed in 2010.

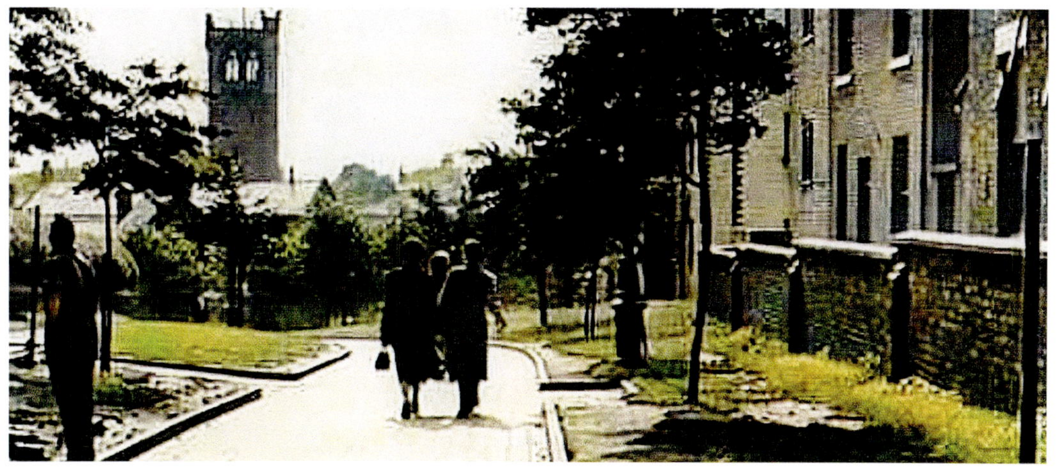

Stoneygate, August 1953

The popular footpath from Church Street down to Shepherd Street was in the news after a *LEP* reader expressed his dismay following the Parks Department's attempts to beautify the grass verges either side of the footpath. He wrote that the flower beds had been trampled, lovely blooms ravaged and young sapling trees damaged beyond repair. The Parks Superintendent, Mr A. V. Pearson, agreed with the correspondent, stating that Stoneygate was the worst spot for young hooligans causing damage. In 1937, under a Corporation clearance scheme, many of the terraced homes and thatched cottages in St John's Place, Library Street and Rose Street had been swept away, along with the dilapidated Cock Pit.

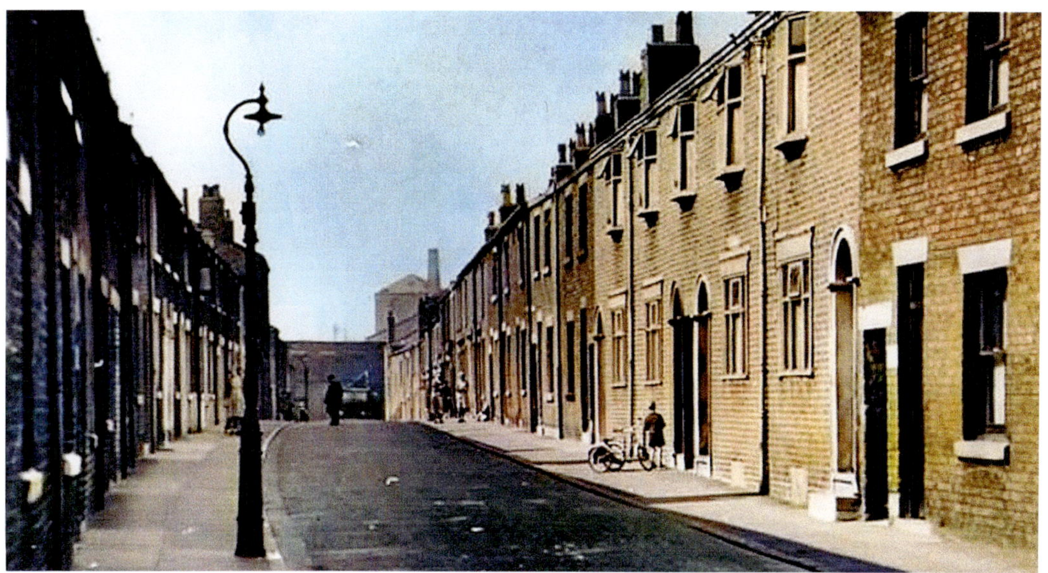

Pleasant Street, off Avenham Lane, November 1955

Preston Corporation announced that all the houses on Pleasant Street and neighbouring Brunswick Street were earmarked for demolition, with plans for high-rise apartment blocks to be built in that area. The Town Council had allocated £1,722 for almost forty properties and a stable to be purchased. The local Ratepayers Association were not happy, citing the case of a widow who bought her house in 1953 for £450 and was to receive compensation of just £30.

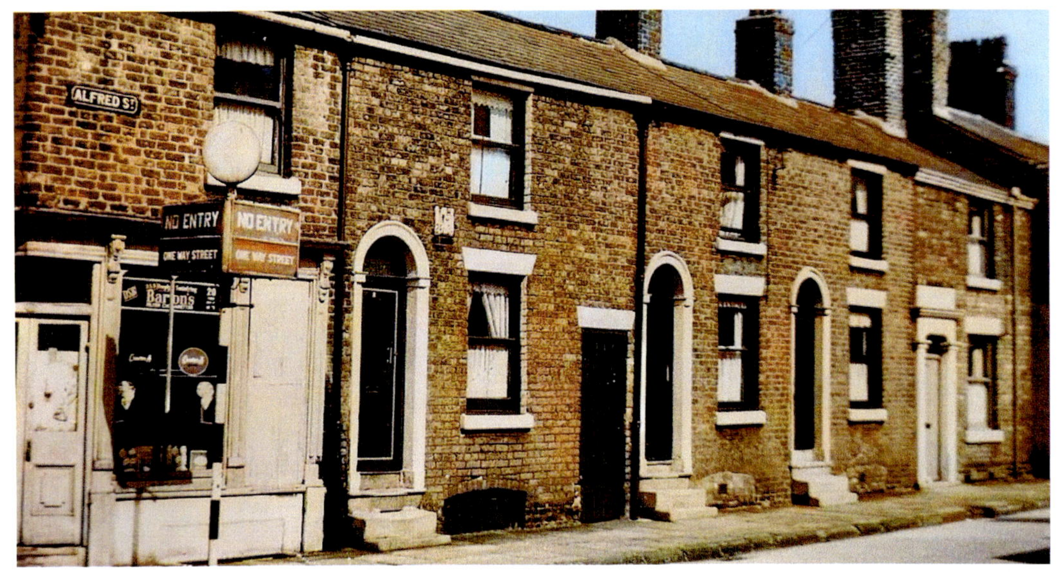

Above: Alfred Street, off North Road, 1955; *Below*: Alfred Street Junction with North Road, 1955

Built *c.* 1830, Alfred Street stretched from North Road to Park Road at its junction with Pole Street. It consisted of terraced rows of houses with a cellar where handloom weaving took place. After the decline of handloom weaving, almost a century later the street's residents included a fishmonger, flagger, gardener, sawyer, tailor, grocer, printer, lamp lighter, reed maker, engineer and a couple of police constables. The grocers shop on the corner of North Road was run by Miss Sarah Jane Gradwell, who died suddenly after falling downstairs in late December 1925, aged fifty-five. Thirty years later, the shop was still thriving. In 1955, the residents of Alfred Street received notice that their homes were due for demolition as part of the ongoing slum-clearance programme. In April 1960, when building work was underway, an old brick-lined well over 200 years old was discovered in the backyard of what was No. 39 Alfred Street.

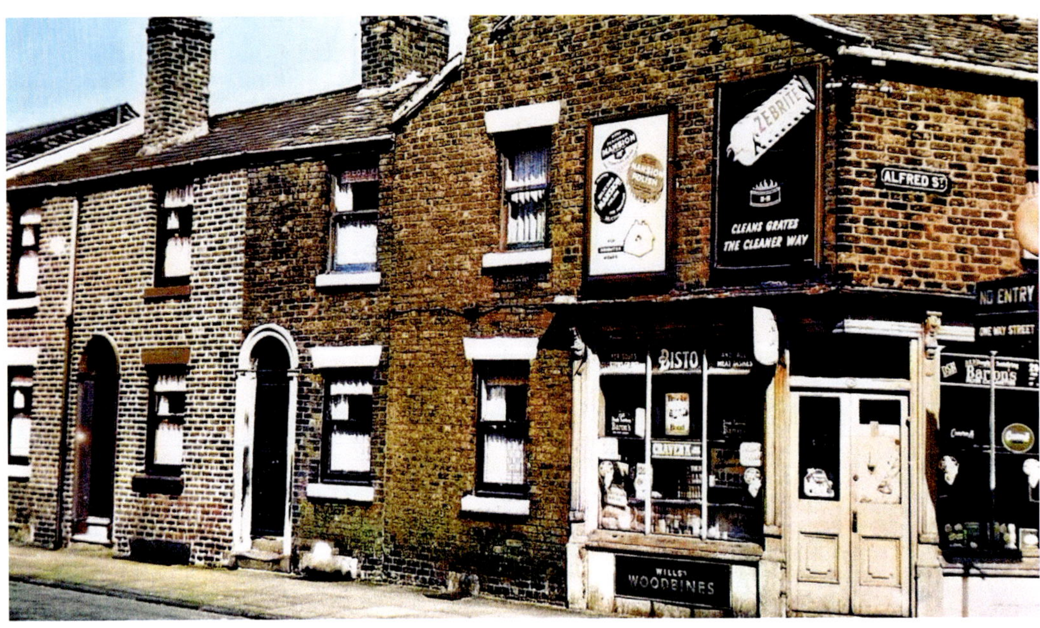

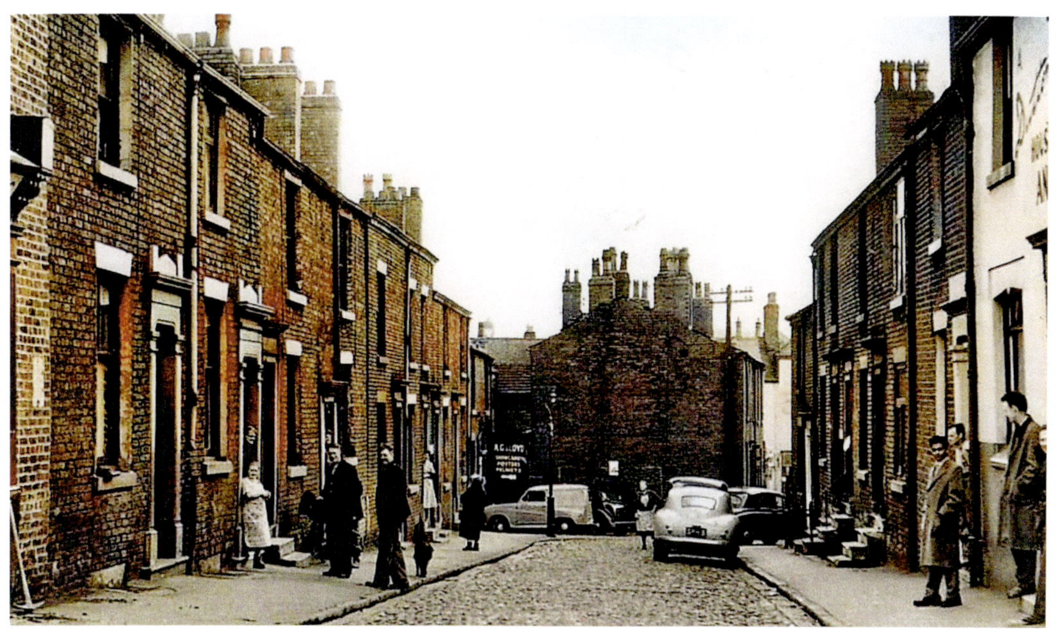

Above: Nile Street, 1956; *Below:* Church Street, North Side, 1956

This typical cobbled terraced street situated off Church Street was destined for demolition. The Anchor Inn, to the right of the image, stood on the corner of Lords Walk from *c.* 1840. In the 1950s three dressmakers, a shoemaker, a joiner and an upholsterer were among the residents of Nile Street. The shop of Cookson's bakers and confectioners was on the corner of Church Street. Started by Edward Cookson, it had grown into a flourishing enterprise. The bakery was taken over by Allied Bakeries in 1954, although they still traded under the Cookson banner, offering their 'healthy brown bread wrapped and sliced' from the Church Street shop. The Cookson's Exhibition bakery, based at Lytham, closed in 2001.

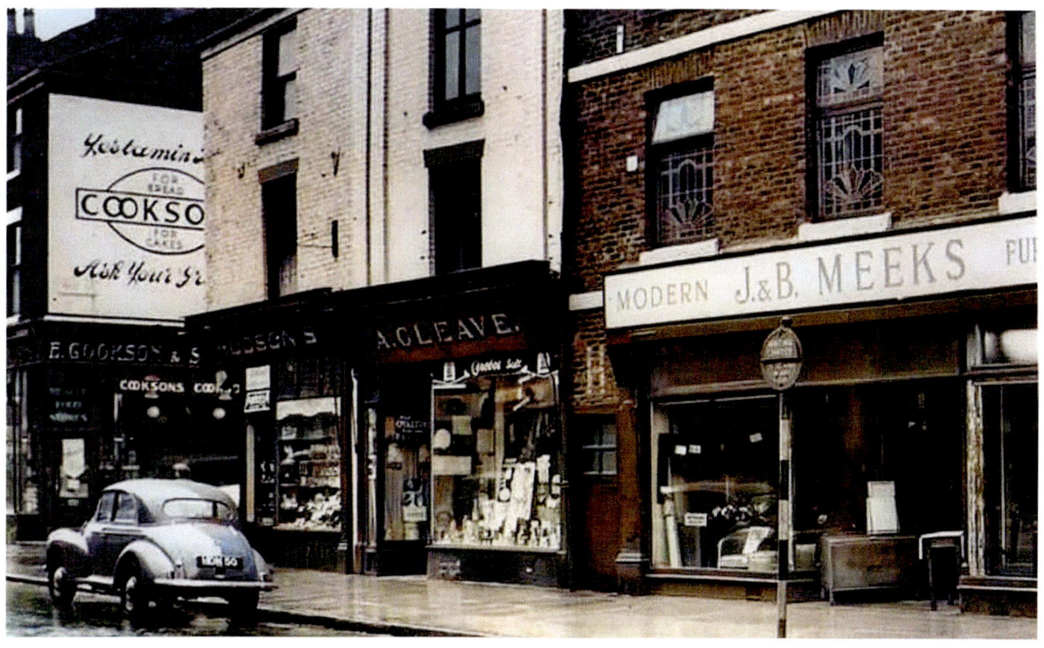

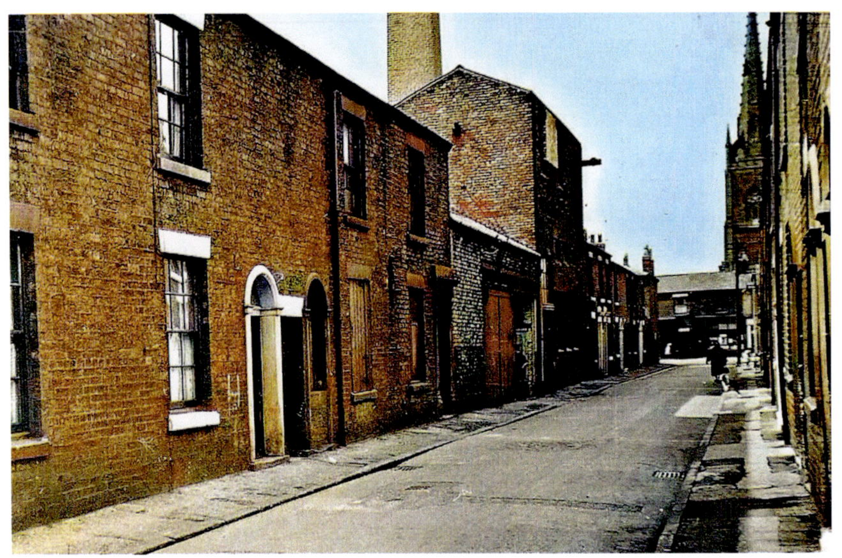

Milton Street Looking Towards Adelphi Street, April 1959

The tall building with the chimney to its rear was the Adelphi Works of brass founders WL Holland. To the right, in the distance, is the spire of St Peter's Church. A public inquiry was held in April, with residents of Mill Hill, Milton Street, Pollard Street and Cunliffe Street voicing their opposition to a Compulsory Purchase Order eventually issued in November to permit demolition of the century-old dwellings where maisonettes would be built.

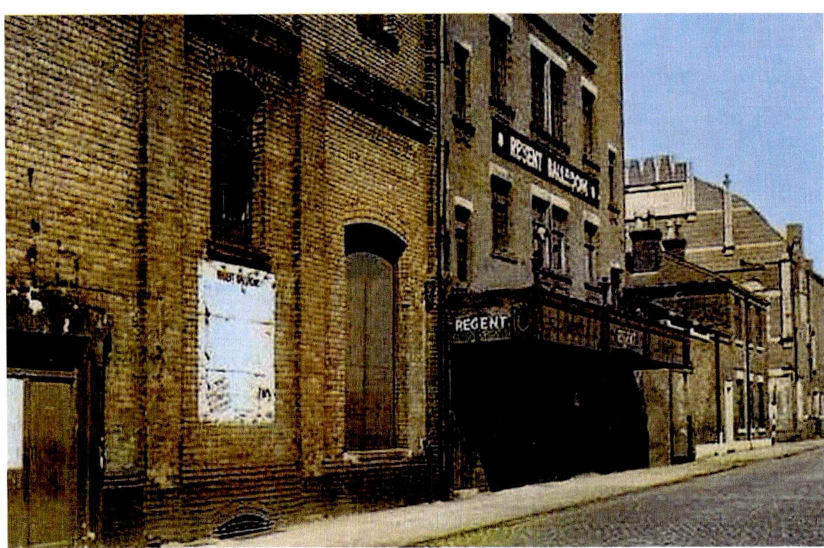

Tithebarn Street, West Side, October 1959

To the left is the Prince's Theatre, on Crooked Lane corner, which had opened in 1882 as the Gaiety. Alongside is the Regent Ballroom and in the distance is the King's Palace Theatre (1913–55), all of which helped to establish Tithebarn Street as a place for entertainment. Prince's closed in late October 1959 and was demolished in 1964. The Regent dated back to 1929 and was built by cinema entrepreneur Will Onda, who embraced the dance band era. In the 1950s Eddie Regan and His Orchestra were the resident band, and for *3s* you could dance the night away.

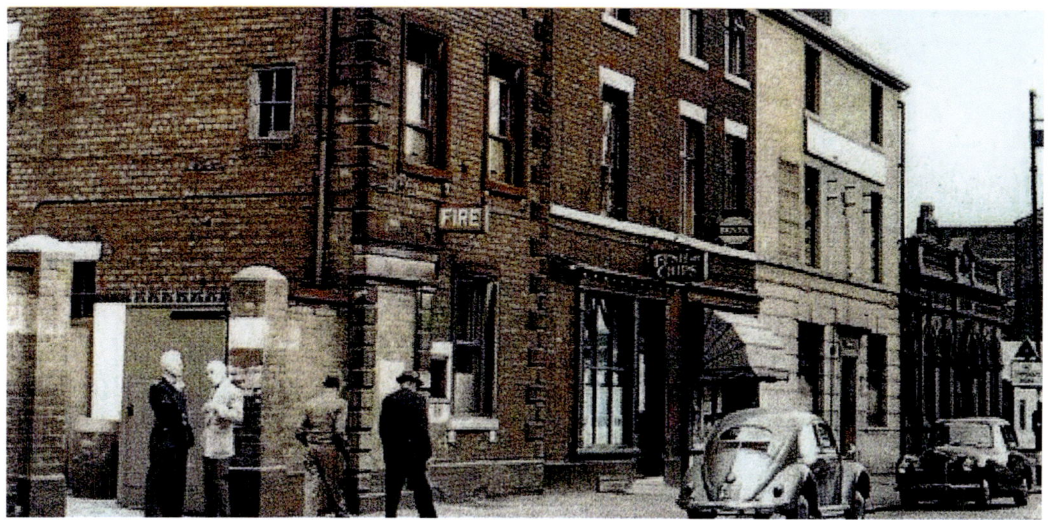

Tithebarn Street, East Side, October 1959

A fire officer stands at the yard gates of Preston Fire Station, possibly discussing the events of the previous night when the Preston Fire Brigade dealt with five fires in three hours: a rubbish fire at India Mill, derelict properties in Lawson Street and Selbourne Street, a chimney blaze in Nimes Street and a small blaze at Foster's vehicle works on Fylde Road. Alongside the fire station were a fish and chip shop, Johnson's pie shop, the Market Hotel and the single-storey Weights and Measures offices of Preston Corporation.

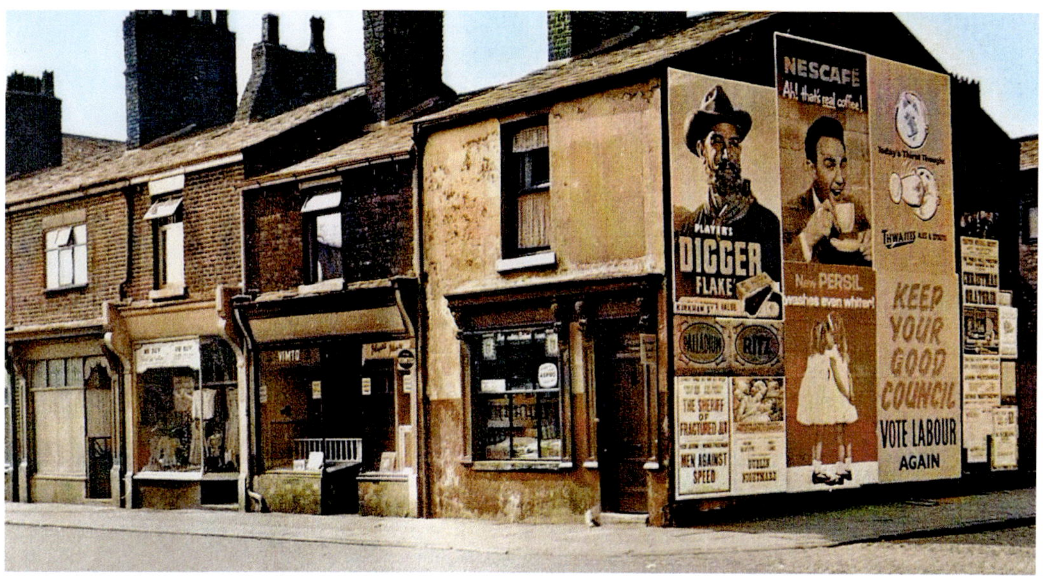

Fylde Road Junction of Kirkham Street, December 1959

Both Kirkham Street and the neighbouring Moss Street had several cellared dwellings built for handloom weavers c. 1825. In 1934, sixteen houses and eleven cellar dwellings were amongst the properties earmarked for the slum-clearance scheme. They were demolished by 1939. The corner shop remained until the 1960s, with its walled advertisements of well-known brands and the films showing at the Ritz and Palladium on display.

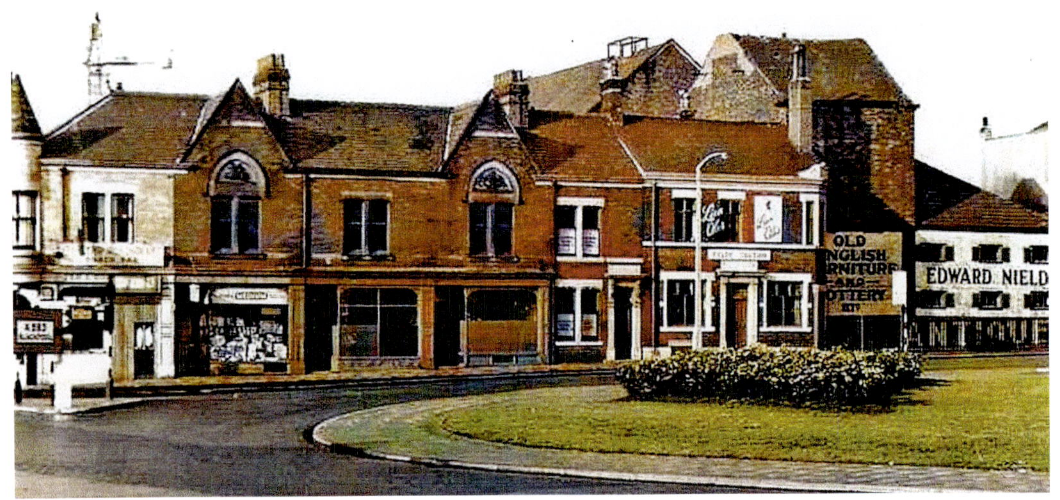

Corporation Street Junction with Fylde Road, 1960

This short stretch of road was originally known as Friday Street. Edward Nield's antiques premises to the extreme right were next to the Star cinema (1921). Neild often provided period furniture to film companies, including for an adaption of Dickens' *Old Curiosity Shop*, made at Elstree Studios in 1934. Next door was the Fylde Tavern (1840), displaying the Lion Ales sign. All were swept away in the Harris College developments of the 1960s.

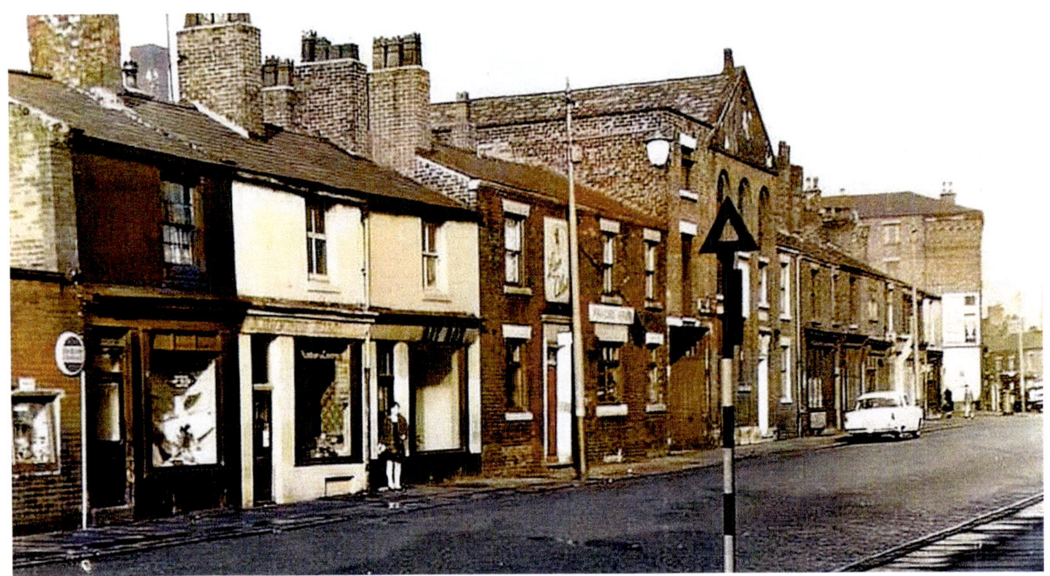

Fylde Road, Opposite St Peter's Church, 1960

This entire row of buildings up to Kirkham Street was demolished *c.* 1990 and replaced by colourful UCLAN Computing and Technology buildings. Three shops can be seen to the left of the Paviors Arms (1850) which displays the Lion Ales sign. The inn closed in 1982 and became a private dwelling. Next along was the tall former premises of corn dealer S. P. Redmayne, with further shop premises beyond occupied at times by stationers, fishmongers, cobblers and even an umbrella maker.

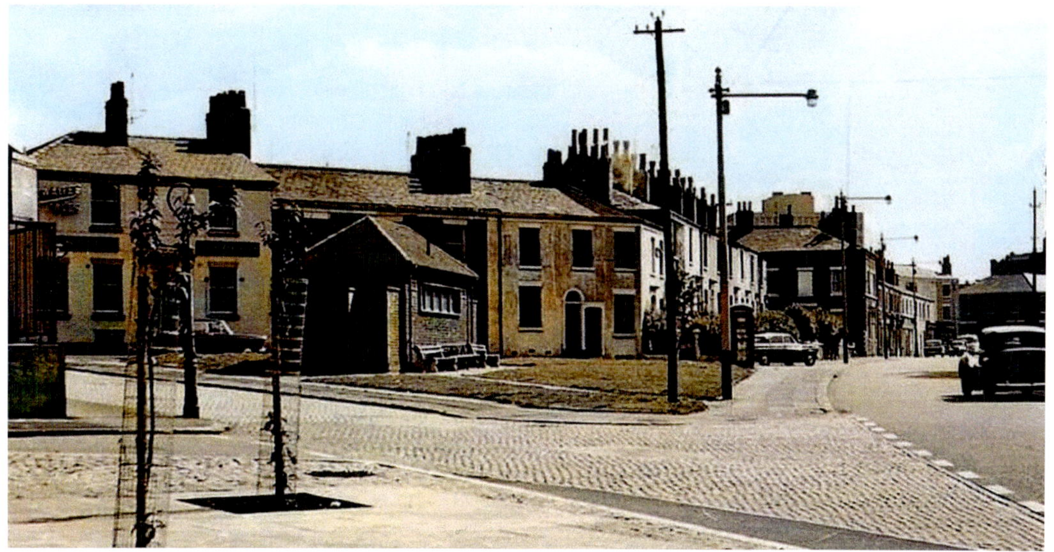

Fylde Road from Goss, 1960

This was the scene facing employees of the printing press manufacturers as they left the engineering offices. To the left, on the cobbled Victoria Street, was the Greenbank Tavern, a popular haunt for Goss workers, which closed in 1966. Further along, past the terraced row where joiners, fitters and a cabinetmaker lived, was the Moss Rose inn, which closed in 1958, at the corner of Atherton Street. By this time the brick-built toilet block had replaced the 'Iron Duke' urinal.

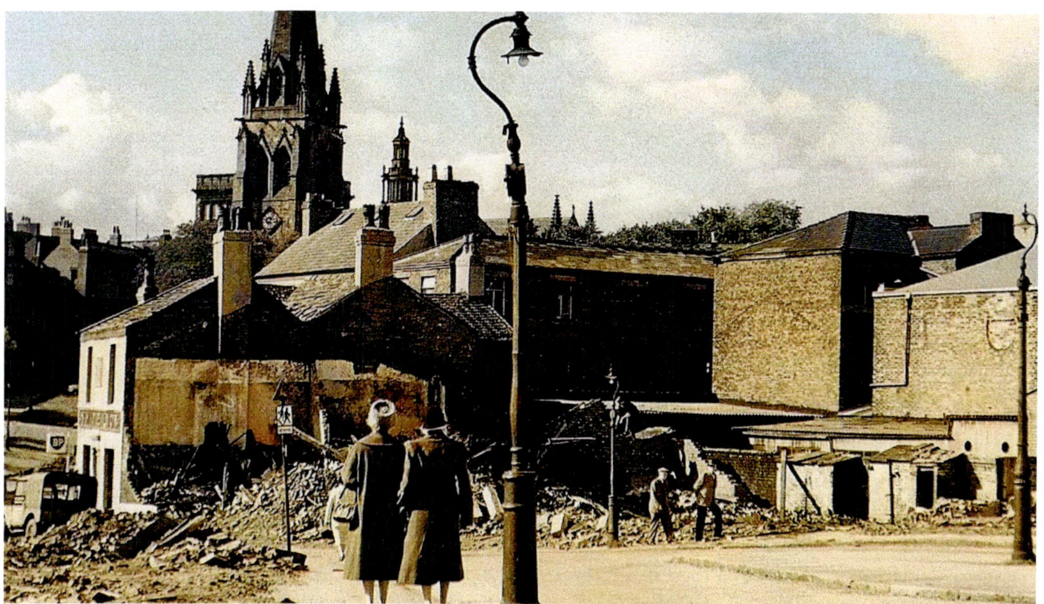

Avenham Redevelopment Underway, 1960

Two ladies make their way to Stoneygate, having to negotiate their way through the rubble as demolition takes place. The White Lion (1807) public house just ahead of them on Syke Hill was earmarked for demolition. In the distance, the spire of the parish church, the future Preston Minster, dominates the scene.

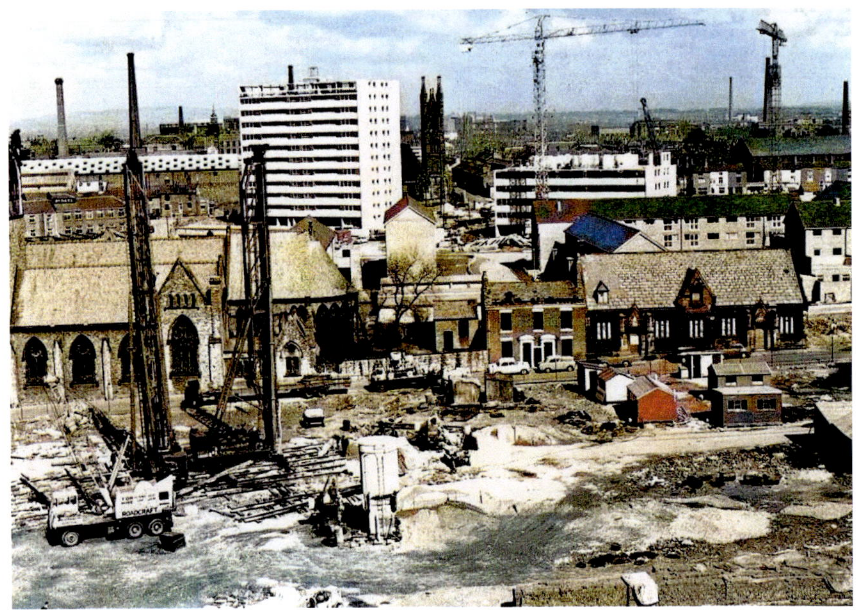

Avenham Redevelopment Progress, 1960

Work was well underway on the new apartment blocks of Lancaster House and York House, which would stand eleven storeys high and cost £130,000. Alas, their lifespan was short-lived, being demolished in 2005 and replaced by lower-level city-view apartments.

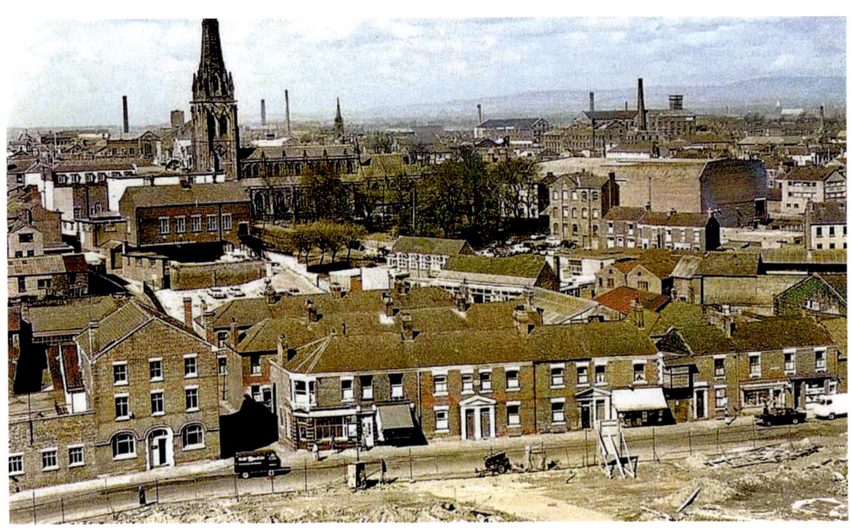

Avenham Lane Development Progress, 1963

In the foreground the foundations work is underway for the construction of the two tower blocks named Kendal and Penrith House – nowadays known as Sandown Court. When completed in June 1965 they both stood nineteen storeys and 53 metres tall. To the left, on the north side of the lane, is the former Drill Hall of the Loyal Regiment, occupied then by the Preston Mattress Company – a car park today. On the other side of Bolton's Court, the properties along Harrisons Terrace from Nos 101–09 still remain. They included a gents outfitters, confectioners and private dwellings back then.

Travelling Through Time

We often take for granted modern modes of transport that take us to the countryside or the seaside or to visit friends or relatives. However, it has taken considerable progress to reach our current transport situation. It all began in days of packhorses and carts, when toll roads and turnpikes greeted travellers and stagecoaches were driven into town alongside horse-drawn carriages. Sail boats, ferries and canal boats were all developed for the movement of goods and people before the coming of the railways. Eventually, horse-drawn trams gave way to electric-powered ones, and our roads became filled with motorised vehicles from omnibuses to saloon cars, then trucks to transport goods. The images that follow travel through time, chronicling the means of transport through the centuries.

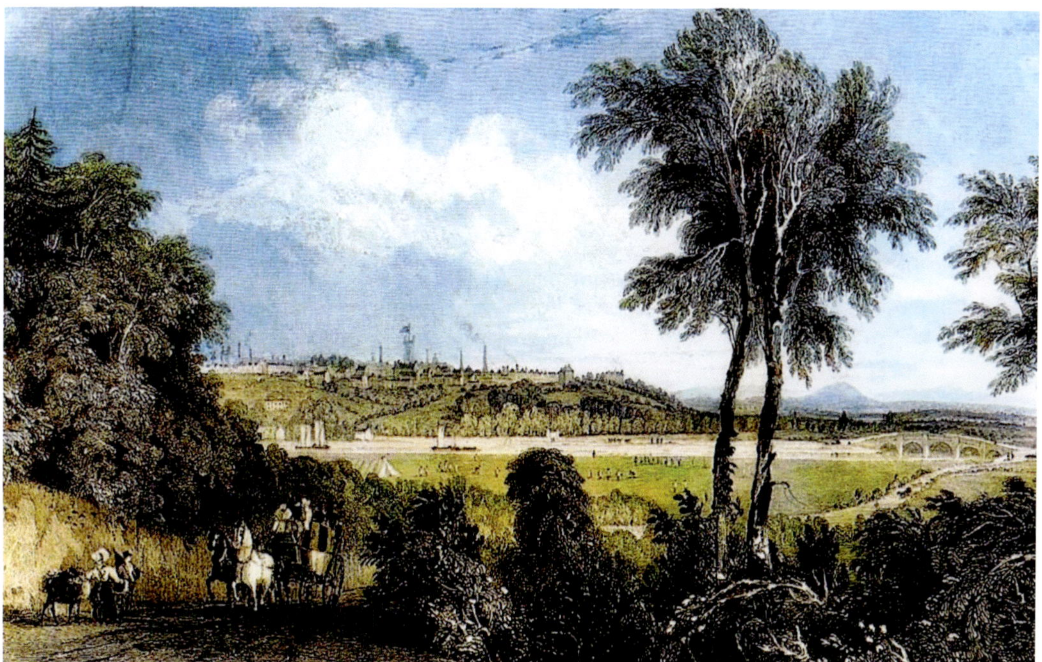

Preston from the South, 1833

The original etching by Thomas Allom shows the cotton town, with a growing population of 33,000, from across the River Ribble. There was clearly a need for transport by then. On the river, sailing boats are clearly visible and packhorses and a carriage drawn by two horses share the main road towards Penwortham, which is little better than a dirt track. To the right can be seen the stone Penwortham Bridge (1759), which replaced an earlier construction of 1755. To aid maintenance, toll charges were imposed.

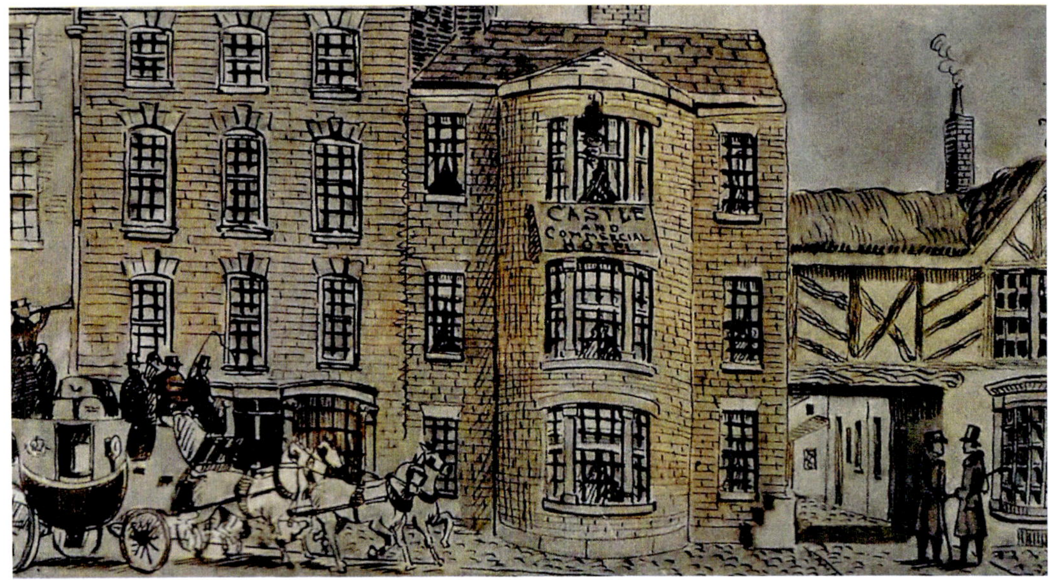

Stagecoach Arrives at the Castle and Commercial Hotel, Cheapside, 1820

Artist Edwin Beattie takes us back in time with this watercolour, to the days when stagecoaches were very much a favoured mode of transport. The Castle, along with the Spread Eagle on Lune Street, Legs of Man on Fishergate and Red Lion and Bull Inn on Church Street, all had livery stables with chaises and gigs for hire. Stagecoaches going to all places departed from the Bull Inn and Red Lion daily.

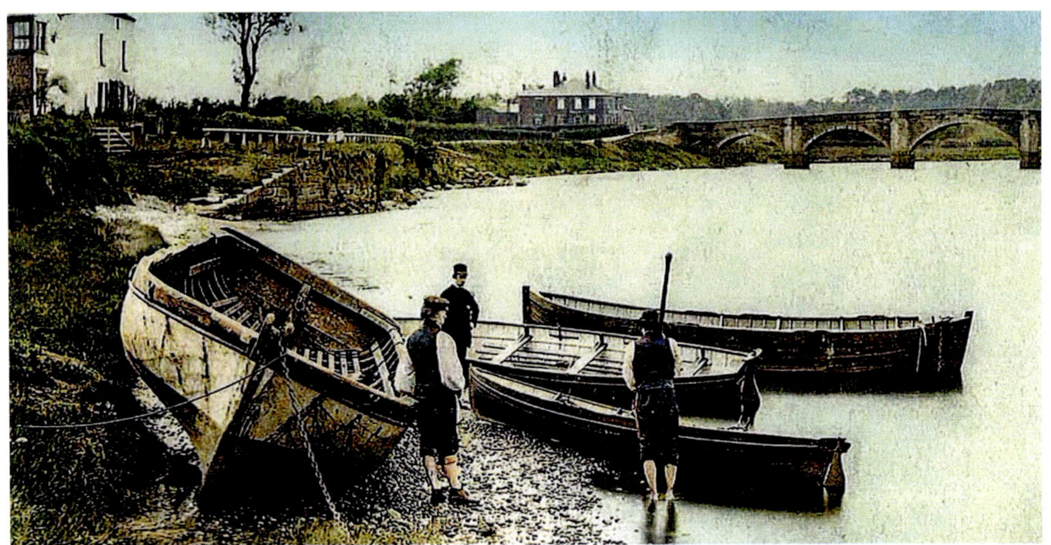

Penwortham Passenger Ferry, 1861

The ferry boats across the River Ribble to Penwortham operated from before the Penwortham Old Bridge, seen in the distance to the right, was constructed. Despite the bridge the ferry was still operational decades later. Shown to the left is the Ferry Boat Inn and centrally the Bridge Inn, nowadays the Tinkerbells nursery. This was a time when foot passengers were obliged to pay a toll of a halfpenny to cross the bridge and drivers of a coach and horse paid 1s per crossing, so keeping the ferry was a viable alternative for foot passengers. The Bridge Inn was licensed *c.* 1826 when the Ferry Boat Inn closed.

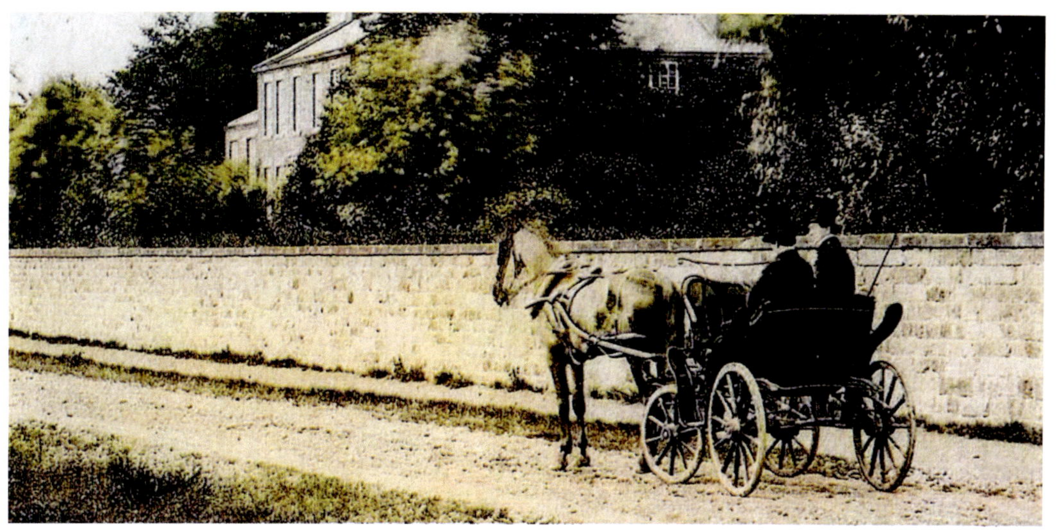

Doctors on Call, Riversway, 1862

Dr Noble and Dr Hall are on call and can be seen riding west towards Pedder Lane, past the Willows, along what is Riversway today. During the cotton famine of 1860–64, the doctors from the Preston Dispensary treated over 5,000 poverty-stricken patients each year. The Willows was built for George Galloway (1822–1912) and his son William Wilding Galloway (1854–1936), who, like his father, was connected with Horrockses. In his will, he gifted the Willows for it to be used as a convalescent home. After decades of providing healthcare, it is now a 'creative space' centre.

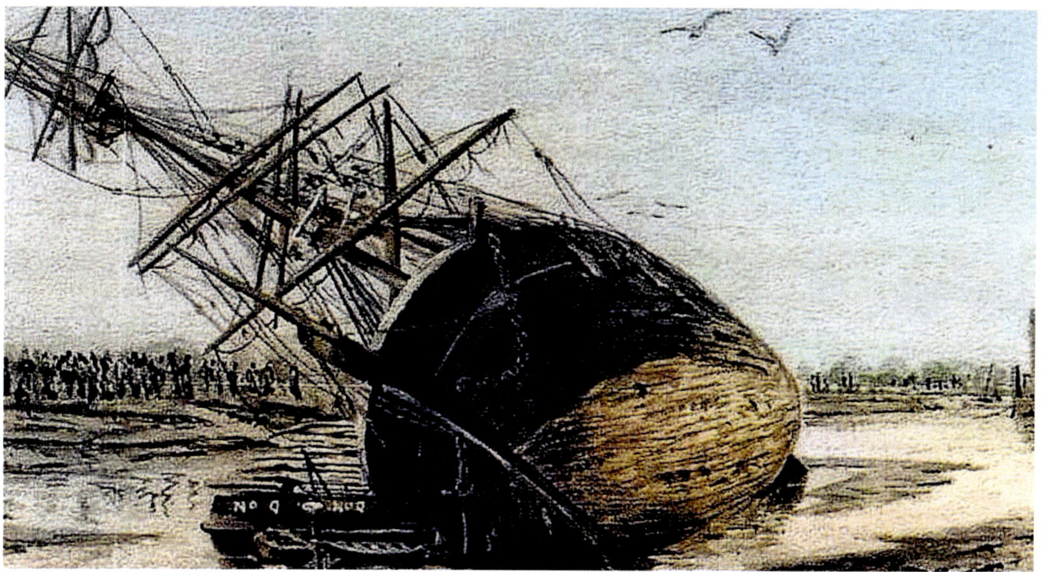

Barque *Oluf Nickelsen* in Trouble, June 1893

Edwin Beattie's watercolour shows a vessel in difficulty in the river estuary. A miscalculation by the captain meant that after being towed upriver from the sea to Chain Caul it was grounded and, by force of the current, heeled over. It was soon apparent it was very twisted and its masts out of line, with each tide making it more severely strained. Unfortunately, being old, it was facing the breaker's yard. It was the first vessel to come to such grief at Preston for a number of years.

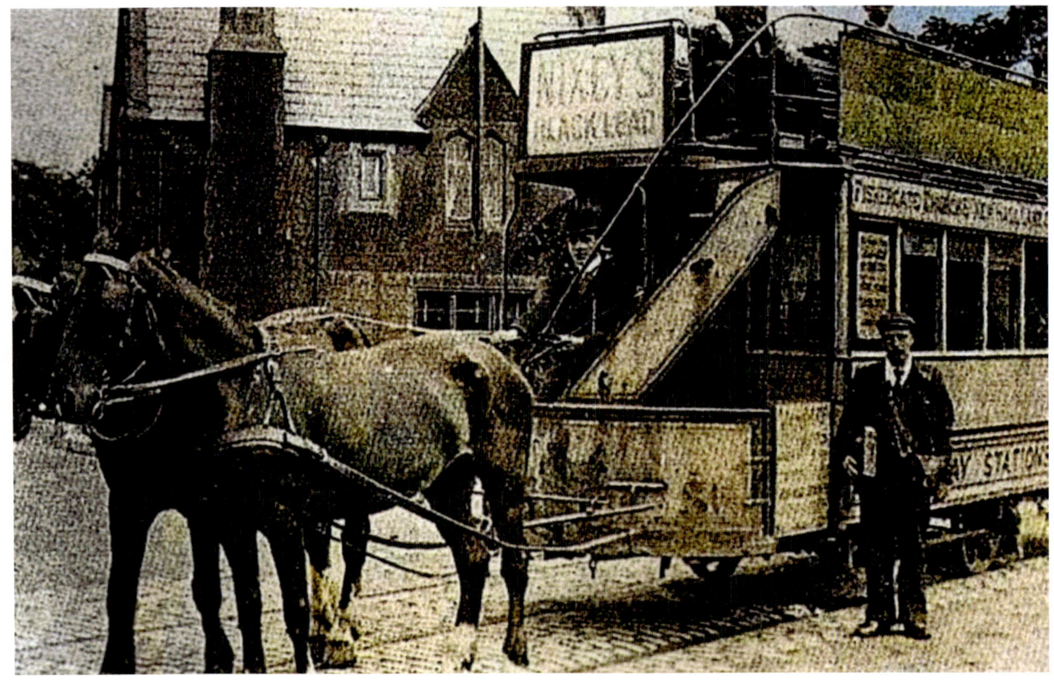

Horse-Drawn Tram, Preston Cemetery Gates, 1900

With the cemetery at Farringdon Park (1855) on the outskirts of town, it was difficult for locals to visit their dearly departed. It was only in April 1882, when the tramway from the bottom of Fishergate Hill to the Pleasure Gardens was extended, that a public service was provided there. In the years that followed a steady stream of tramcars halted at the cemetery gates, especially at weekends.

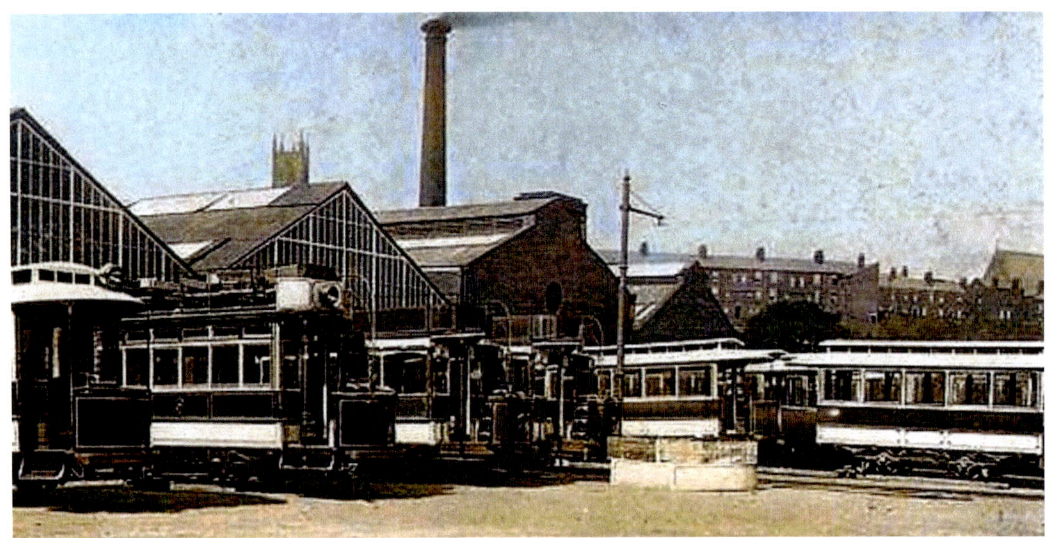

Dick, Kerr & Co. Ltd Yard Works, Strand Road, 1900

The scene outside the premises known originally as the Electric Carriage Works, as tramcars manufactured in Preston are prepared for transporting. The open-top double-deckers were built for Carlisle and Sheffield, whilst the single-deckers were earmarked for the USA.

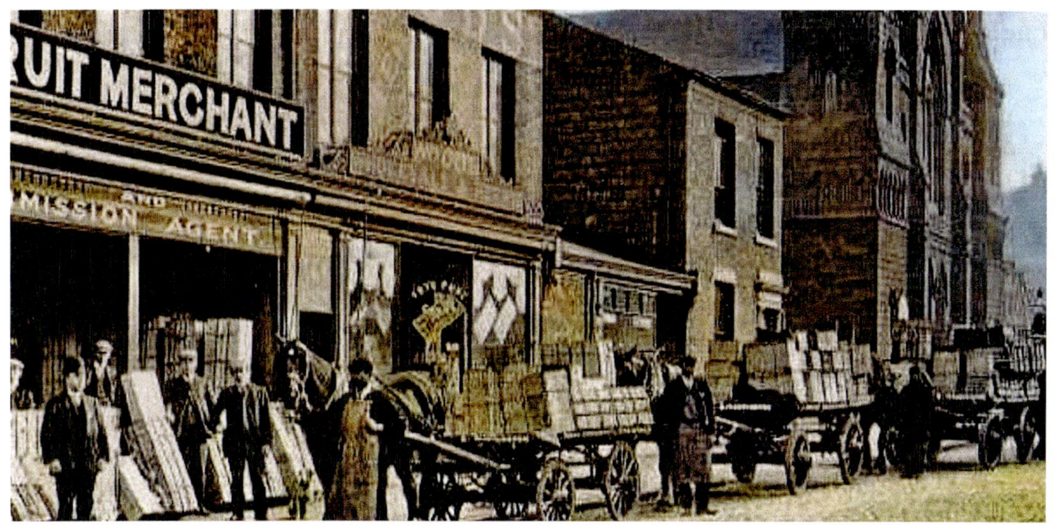

Liverpool Street Facing the Covered Market, 1910

The staff of the fruit merchant E. Waddington have loaded up their carts, fed and watered their horses and are about to go forth with their deliveries. This was a time when Liverpool Street flourished. To the right of the image is the Orchard Methodist Chapel of Gothic design, which was opened in May 1862 and closed in 1954. Like all these properties it was demolished to make way for the new Indoor Market Hall, which opened in 1972 and itself closed in 2018 to make way for the new Animate leisure and entertainment complex opened in February 2025.

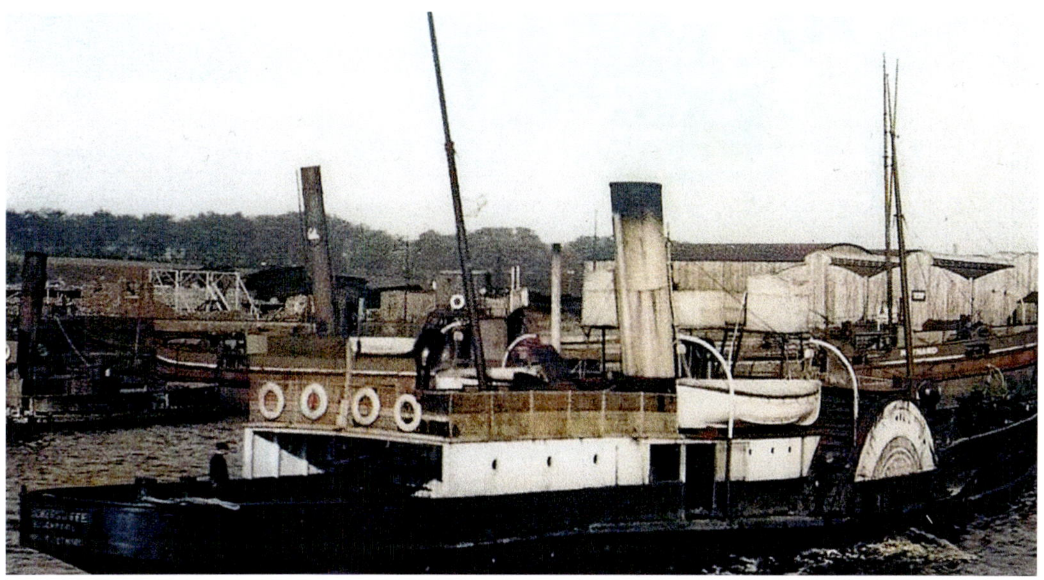

Paddle Steamer *Bickerstaffe*, Preston Docks, *c.* 1920

Bickerstaffe, built in 1879 by Laird Bros of Birkenhead, was one of a number of paddle steamers that operated in and out of the docks from its opening in June 1892. It was in the news in 1911 when a national rail strike coincided with the Preston holidays. Many stranded holidaymakers returned to town from Morecambe, Fleetwood and Blackpool aboard this vessel or the paddle steamer *Greyhound*. In 1929, after fifty years' service, *Bickerstaffe* was off to Garston and the ship breaker's yard.

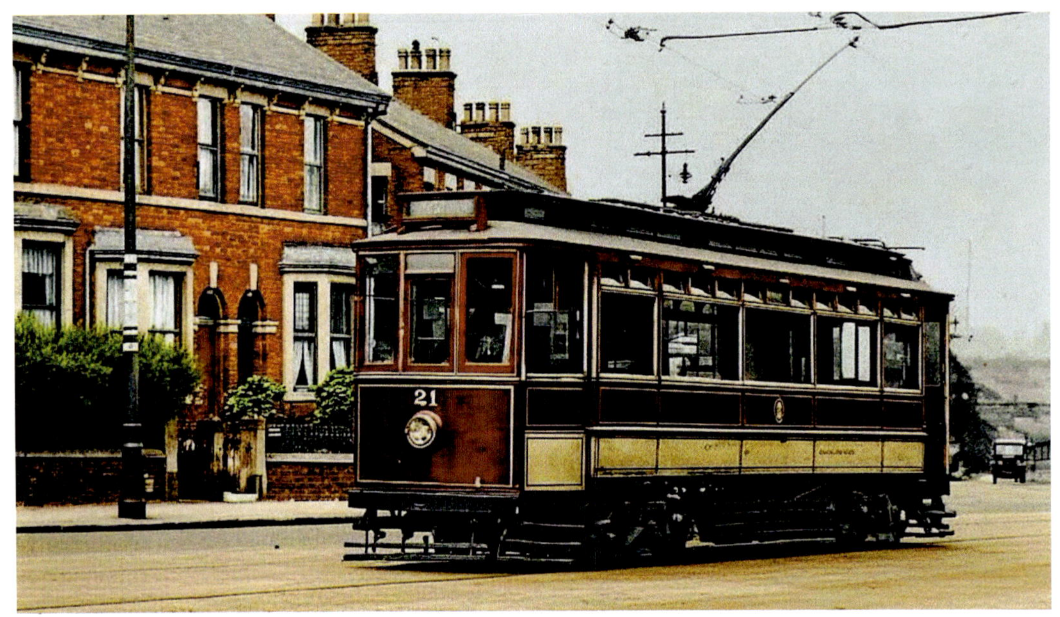

Tulketh Road, Egerton Road Junction, *c.* 1926

This single-decker tram was one of three built by Messrs Dick Kerr & Co. and supplied in 1912 for the Ashton route, being able to cope with height restrictions of the Fylde Road railway bridge (1840).

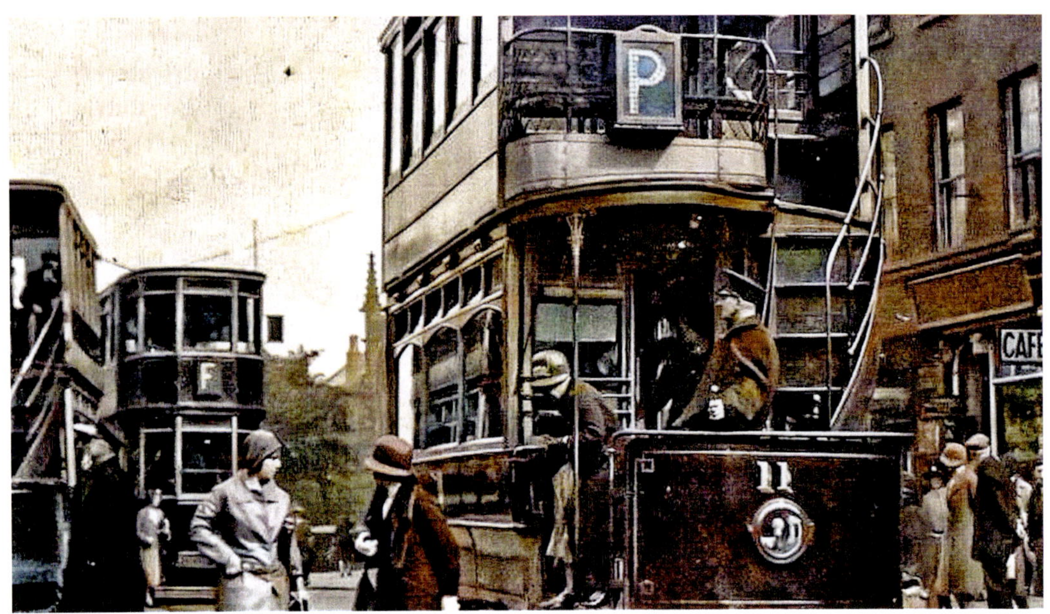

Church Street Beyond the Parish Church, 1931

A tram comes to a halt as a smartly dressed lady prepares to disembark. From the central tram terminal, opposite Miller Arcade, there was a steady stream of trams to Penwortham, Ashton, Deepdale, Fulwood, Ribbleton and Farringdon Park. At this time when the trams were competing with motor buses, the Preston Corporation Transport Department, who ran both forms of transport, reported an annual profit of £6,590.

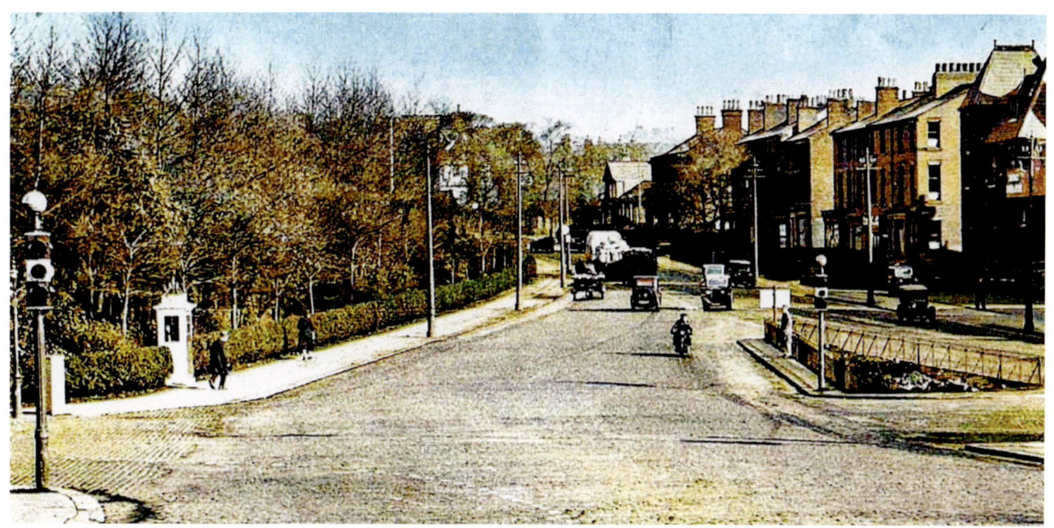

Fishergate Hill from Penwortham Bridge, November 1934

The junction with Strand Road was in the news with the installation of traffic lights on this route into town. Traffic lights were first introduced to Preston in 1932 on Blackpool Road, Garstang Road and Lancaster Road. After initial teething troubles, more were installed at both ends of Park Road and at this crossroads, taking into account traffic also from Broadgate. It wasn't long before fines of 10s were issued to those who failed to stop at the traffic lights. Cyclists appeared to be the main offenders, and they expressed the view that the police were making an example of them.

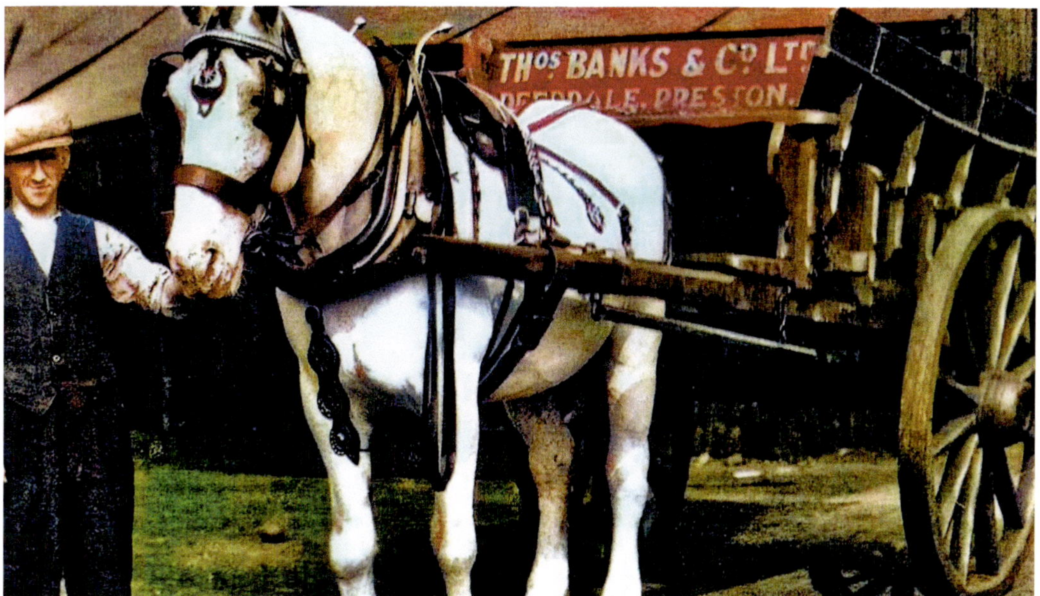

Thomas Banks & Co. Ltd, Fletcher Road, 1935

The Deepdale-based coal merchants, who operated from Fletcher Road until 2024, still offer a delivery service for coal and logs, along with a chimney sweep service. Back in 1935 they transported coal by horse-driven carts. John Smith of Crook Street, Ribbleton, proudly stands alongside the magnificent animal reputed to be the oldest working horse in town.

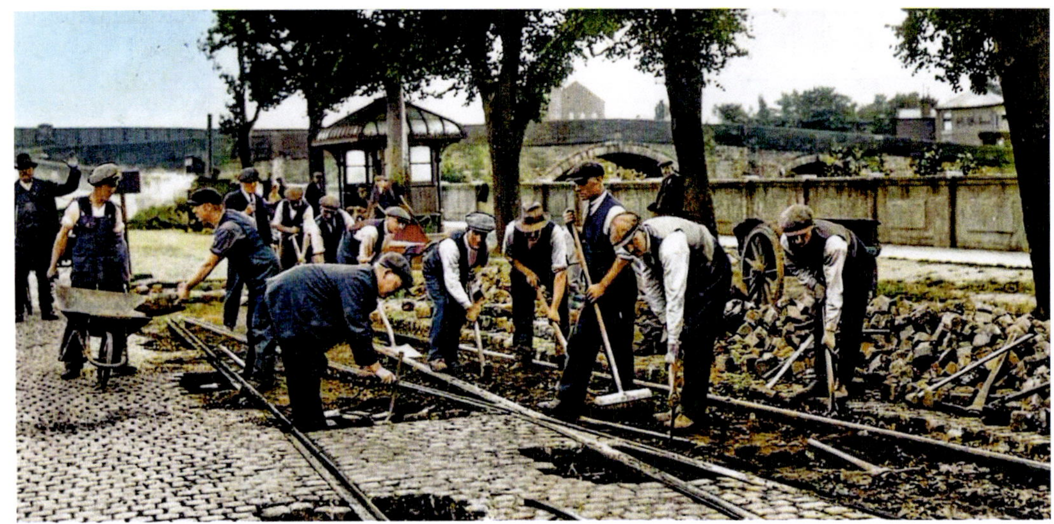

Broadgate Tram Terminus, 1936

The fact that electric trams had become redundant was confirmed when Preston Corporation workers began removing all signs of the pioneering service, although the ornate tram shelter would remain for bus passengers. The Penwortham Old Bridge can be seen in the background, beyond which, to the left, is the iron girder bridge of the old West Lancashire Railway. Built in 1882 for the Preston to Southport service, it carried passengers to the Fishergate Hill station until 1900. Only the stone piers of the bridge remain, carrying service pipes. The old Fishergate Hill station was demolished *c.* 1978.

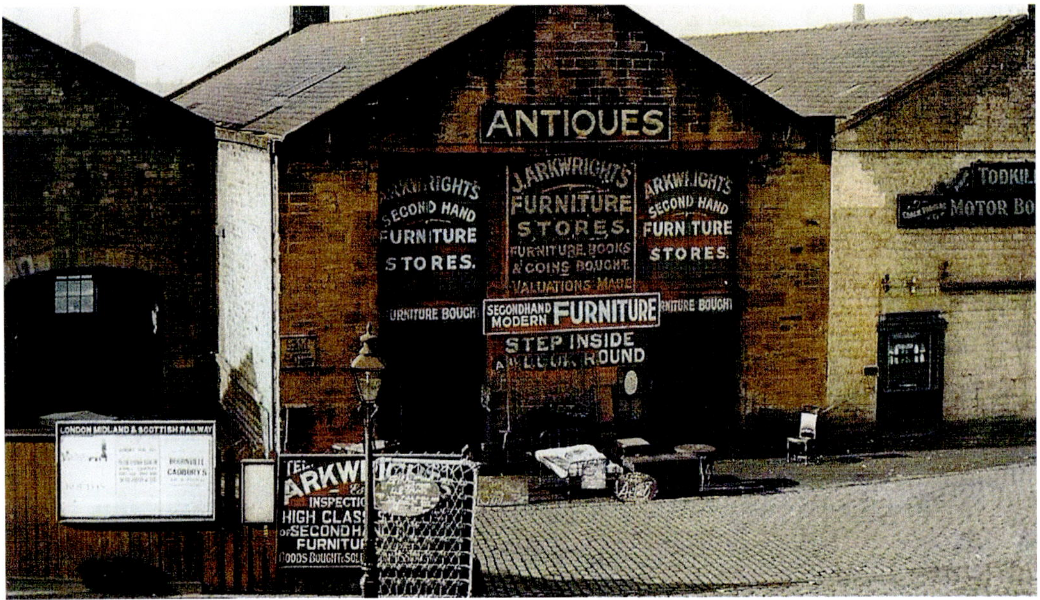

Old Canal Warehouses, Corporation Street, 1938

The centrally placed warehouse, home to John Arkwright's Furniture and Antiques Stores from 1876, and the adjacent property occupied by Todkill's & Son Ltd Motor Body Garage were due for demolition as the land was bought by Bradshaws for their car showrooms. The warehouse to the left survived until the mid-1980s, occupied by monumental stonemason Edward Sharples.

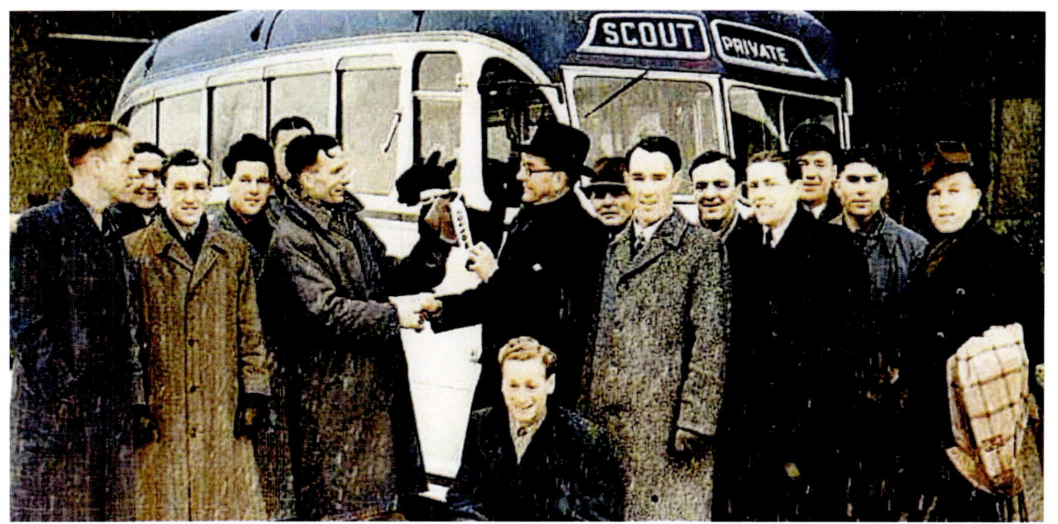

Preston North End Away Day Travel, January 1947

The team is all wrapped up in the icy conditions and are presented with a lucky black dog mascot as they prepare to board the Scout Motors coach destined for Burnden Park, Bolton. The New Year's Day trip during the freezing winter of 1946–47 was also taken by many PNE fans – a crowd of 42,000, including over 2,000 who had travelled by rail. Nat Lofthouse put Bolton Wanderers ahead five minutes before the interval, but PNE turned the tables with late goals from Bobby Beattie and Jimmy McIntosh to win 2-1. PNE finished the first post-war season in seventh place in the top flight.

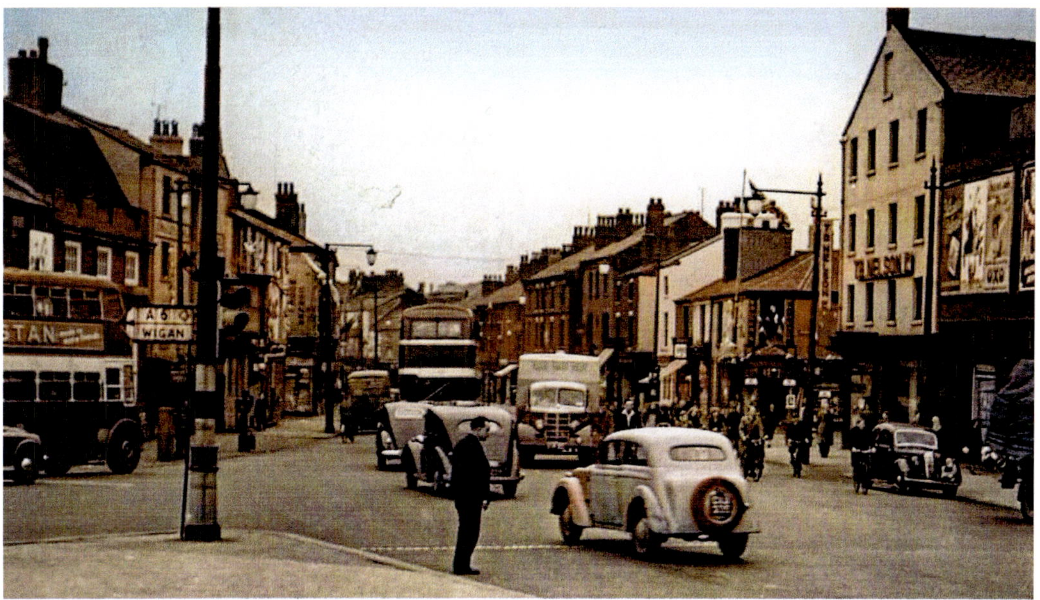

Church Street at the Stanley Street Junction, 1953

It looks like rush hour as buses, saloon cars and bicycles head in both directions. It was a time when there were calls for a roundabout to be installed and a one-way system introduced on Park Road (part of the present Ringway). There were no cycle lanes back then, but the many bike riders didn't seem too bothered about that.

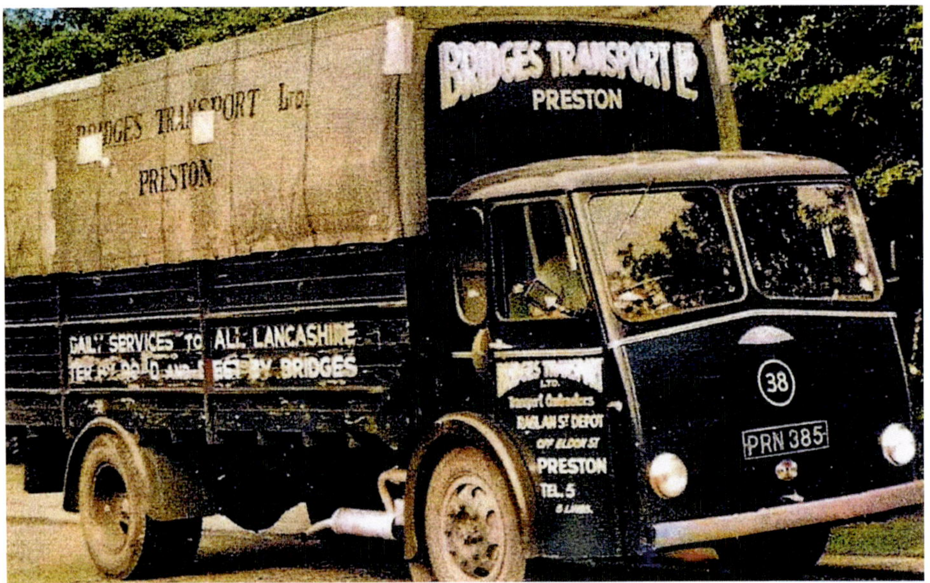

Bridges Transport Ltd Haulage Contractors, 1955

The fleet of Bridges vehicles were a common sight heading out of their Raglan Street depot. Harold Bridges, the son of a Warton gamekeeper, became known as Preston's 'Mr Transport' as he built up his vast motor haulage empire to over 100 vehicles and 400 employees. His slogan 'Send It By Road, It's Better by Road, And Best By Bridges' attracted plenty of custom during his forty-seven years in the haulage business. The company was taken over by Tayford's of Scotland in 1968, who kept the name and moved to Leyland. They became insolvent in 1988.

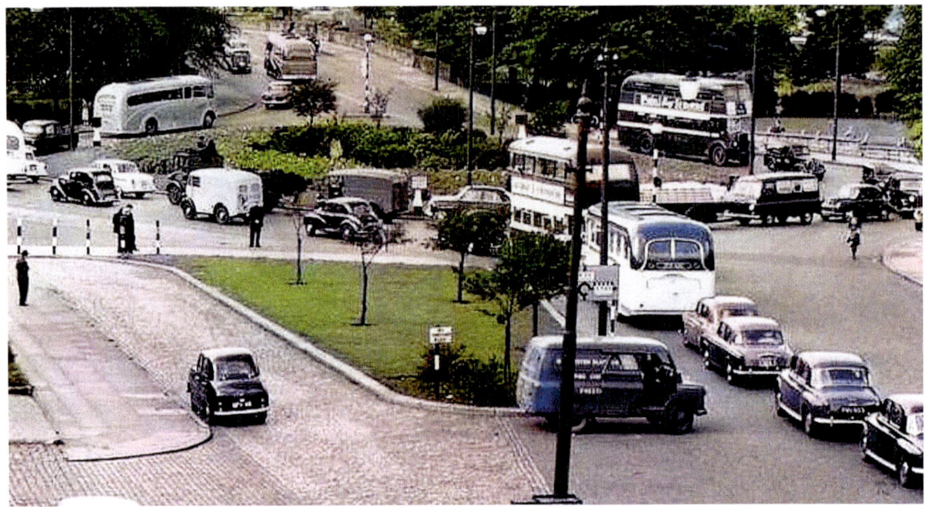

Fishergate Hill, Strand Road, August 1957

Resurfacing work on Liverpool Road over the bridge led to week-long commuter chaos, with traffic at a standstill. Penwortham Bridge (1915) with its three arches spanning the River Ribble provided a direct route to Penwortham and beyond. It remains a popular alternative, even though the spectacular 1980s Penwortham flyover is the choice of many, having been built to ease the congestion on the A59.

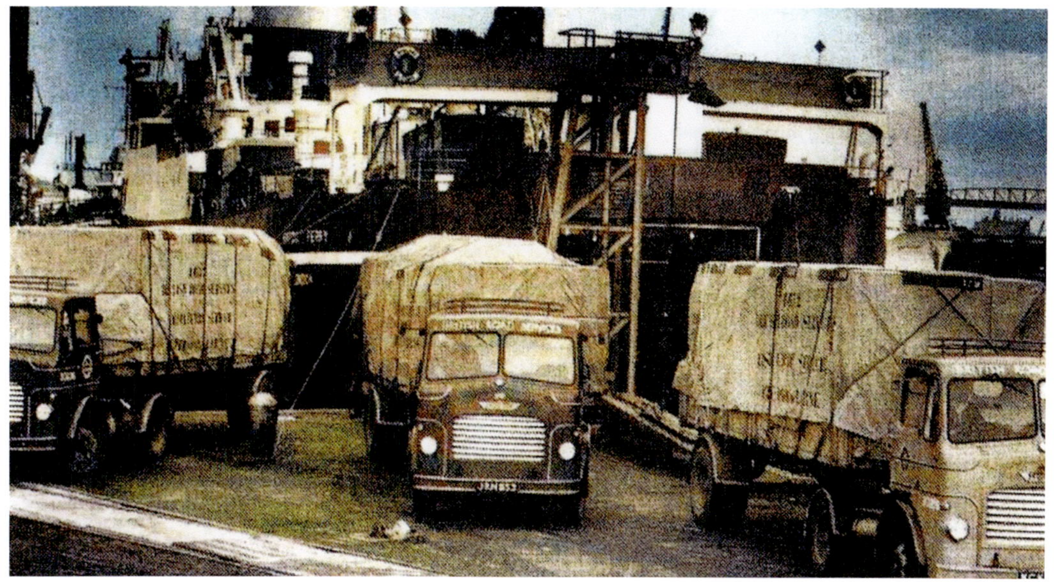

Bardic Ferry, Preston Docks, 1957

This newcomer to the vehicle ferry fleet made its first runs between Preston and Larne, Northern Ireland, in September 1957. The ferry had a crew of fifty, accommodation for fifty passengers and space for eighty vehicles. Three return trips a week made it a profitable service, running until 1974. British Road Services lorries can be seen disembarking.

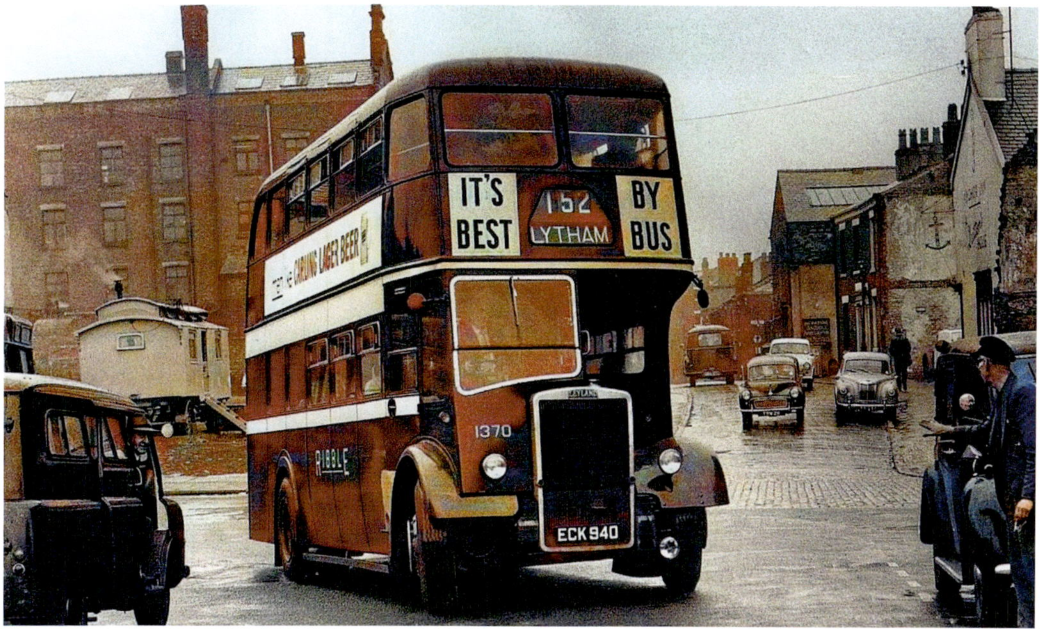

Ribble Bus on Lords Walk, July 1961

'It's Best By Bus' was the slogan displayed on the Leyland-manufactured bus. Not that taxi driver Stanley Cosgrove, to the right of the image, would necessarily agree, being the secretary of the local Taxi Owners Association. The Anchor Inn, at the corner of Nile Street, can be seen further along to the right.

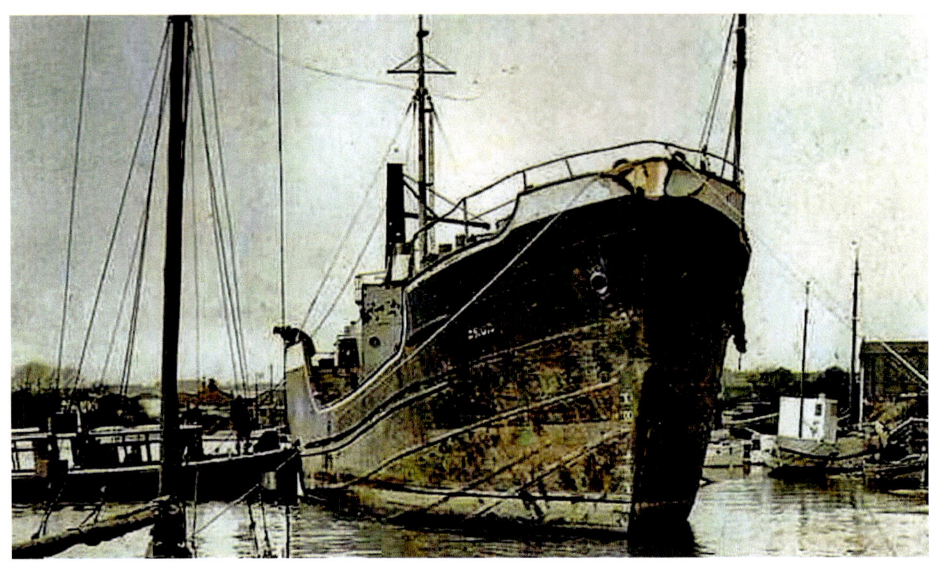

MV *Druid* Enters Preston Docks, August 1962

This stricken cargo ship from Glasgow had capsized in rough seas days earlier. Its captain, William John Ross, and two crew members had drowned in the tragic event. Gale-force winds rolled the vessel completely over before righting itself, tipping the six-man crew overboard. At the inquest a verdict of 'death by misadventure' was recorded, and no blame was attached to the skipper at a Ministry of Transport inquiry.

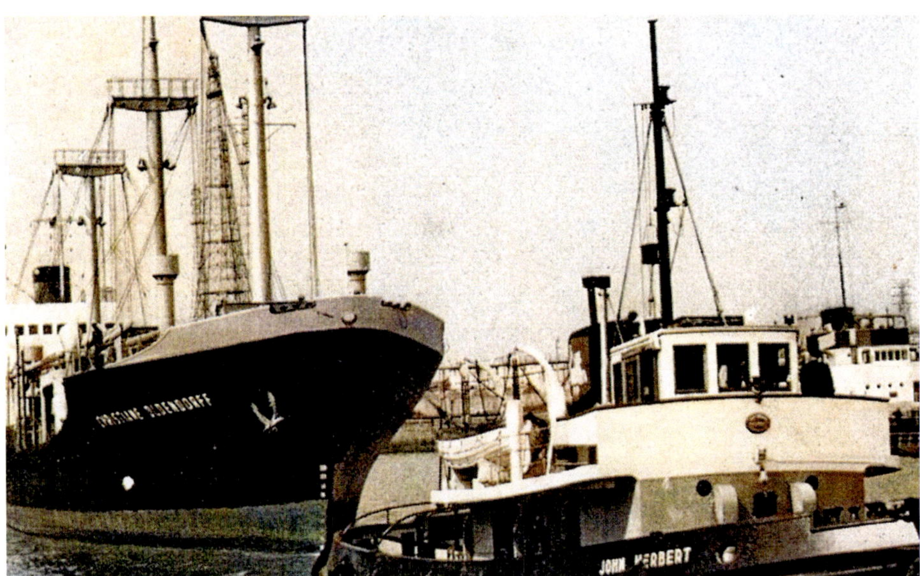

Tugboat *John Herbert* Guides a Vessel into the Preston Dock, 1962

This vessel was one of four twin-screw motor tugs purchased in the 1950s and named after local politicians – Edgar Hewitt, John Herbert, Frank Jamieson and Charles Hearn, all long-serving town councillors. They were all built by Henry Robb Ltd, Leith, costing between £50,000 and £80,000 each. Alderman John Herbert, who had been on the Town Council since 1919, was on hand to see his vessel floated in 1955.

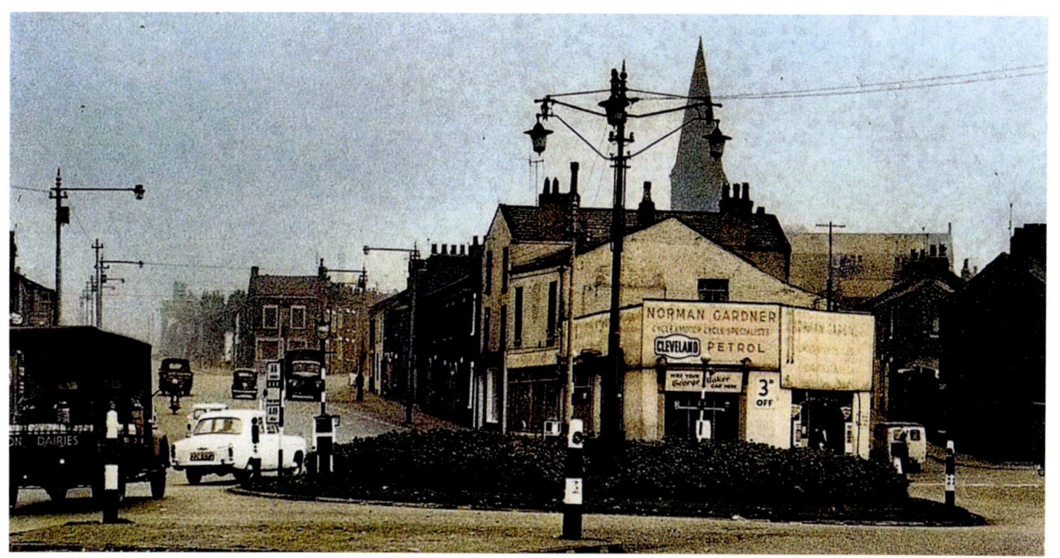

Roundabout, Garstang Road, North Road, Moor Lane, October 1962

Since the introduction of this roundabout, the scenery has certainly changed. In the distance, where North Road met Lancaster Road, the Church Hotel stood on the corner. The spire of St Thomas's Church has dominated the scene since 1838, but all the properties around it have been demolished. In 1968, work was underway on the estate of Quikbuild Homes on the North Road redevelopment, which changed the landscape that we see to this day.

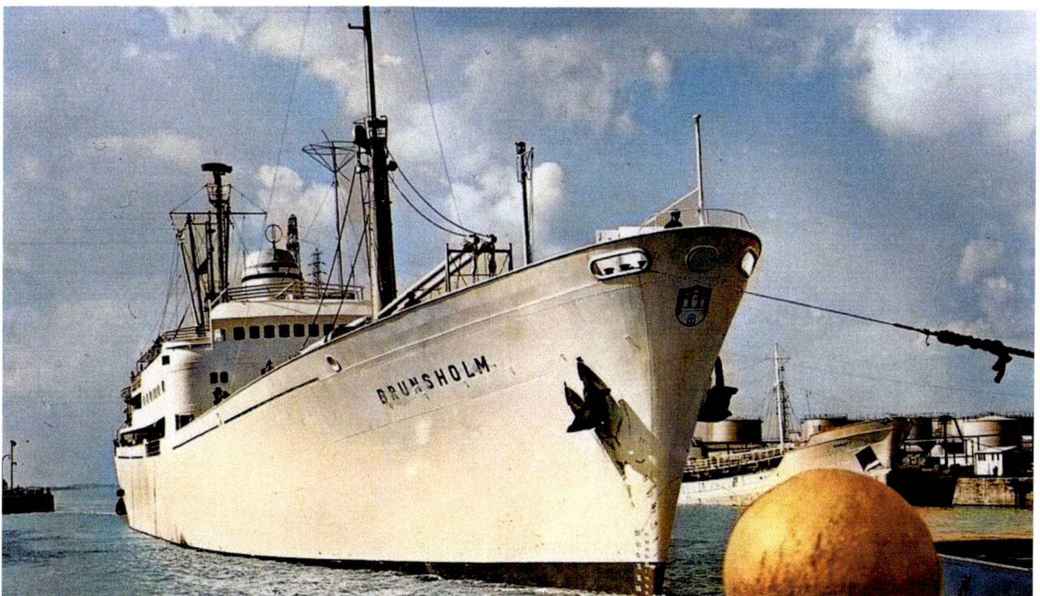

Preston Docks, August 1963

MS *Brunsholm* arrives on its maiden voyage in 1963 with a cargo of bananas from the West Indies. The banana trade from there, begun in 1919 by Matthew Wade, Preston's 'Banana King', had been taken over by Geest Industries in 1953. This regular trade with the West Indies came to an end in 1971 as Geest required larger boats and the Ribble Channel was too shallow for them.

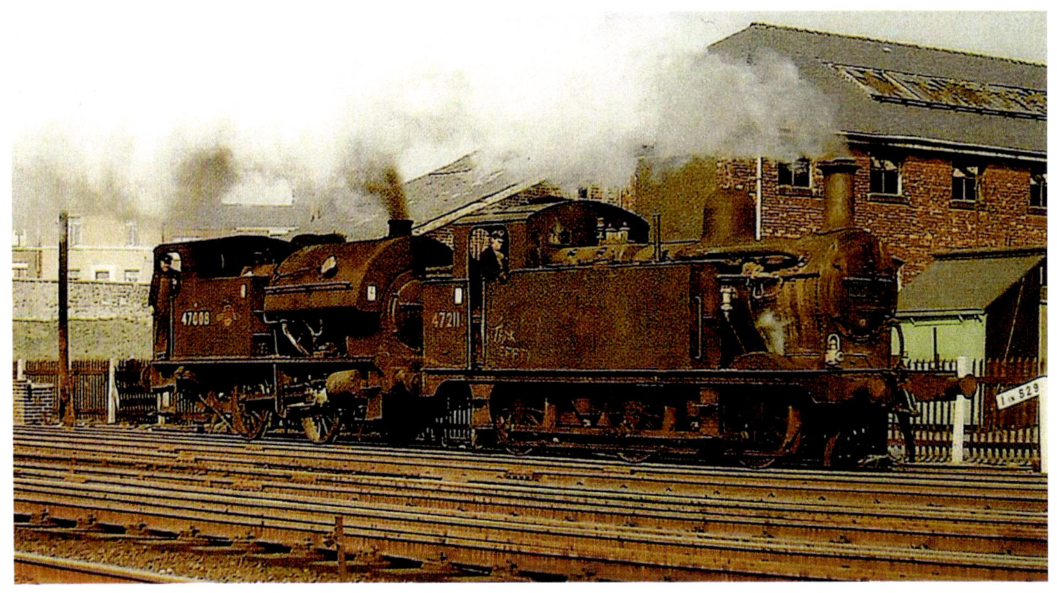

Heading for Lostock Hall Sheds, March 1964

After a day on the rails at Preston Docks, saddle tank No. 47008 and Jinty No. 47211 are seen heading for the locomotive shed at Lostock Hall. The Preston loco shed in Croft Street had been destroyed in June 1960 following a huge blaze. Months later, this pair of steam locomotives were withdrawn from service as steam power on the railways was in decline.

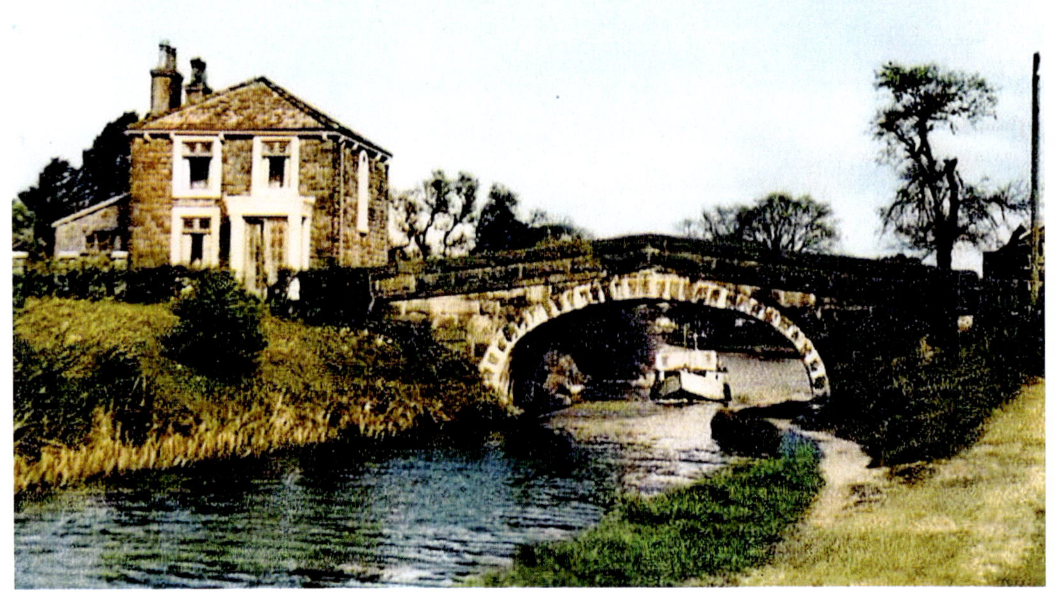

Lancaster Canal, Cottam, 1965

A leisure craft approaches Bridge No. 19. To the left is the former canal ranger's house on Cottam Lane, known as Bridge House these days, where by the 1960s you could buy an ice cream or a lollipop after your canal journey. No longer could you travel to the centre of Preston along the waterway, which by then terminated at the bottom of Tulketh Brow.

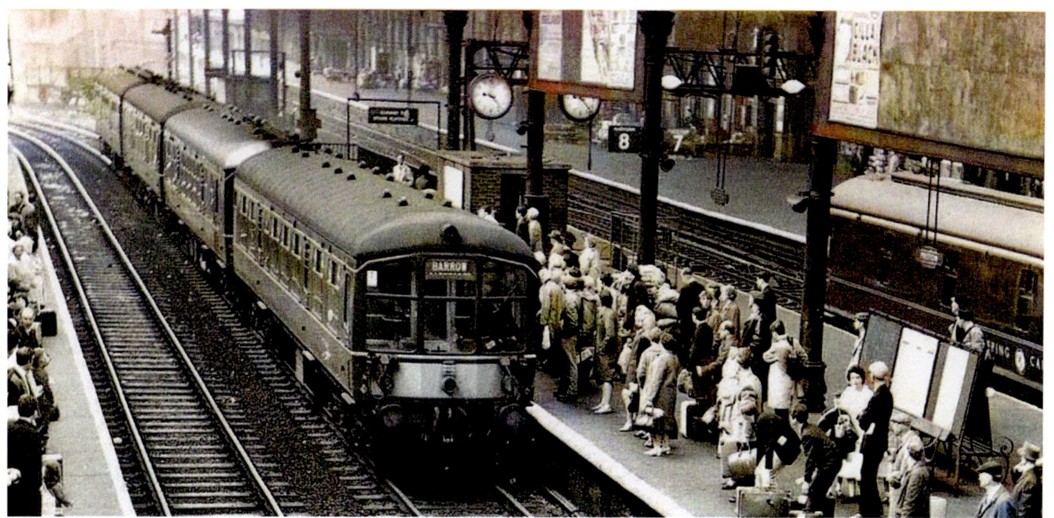

Preston Railway Station, July 1965

This image was taken during the Preston holiday fortnight, with crowded platforms as passengers wait to depart. On some trips the steam engines had given way to the first generation of diesel railcars. Back then, the fortnight break known as 'Wakes Weeks' meant daily trips to the seaside with a bucket and spade, with no shortage of excursion trains running.

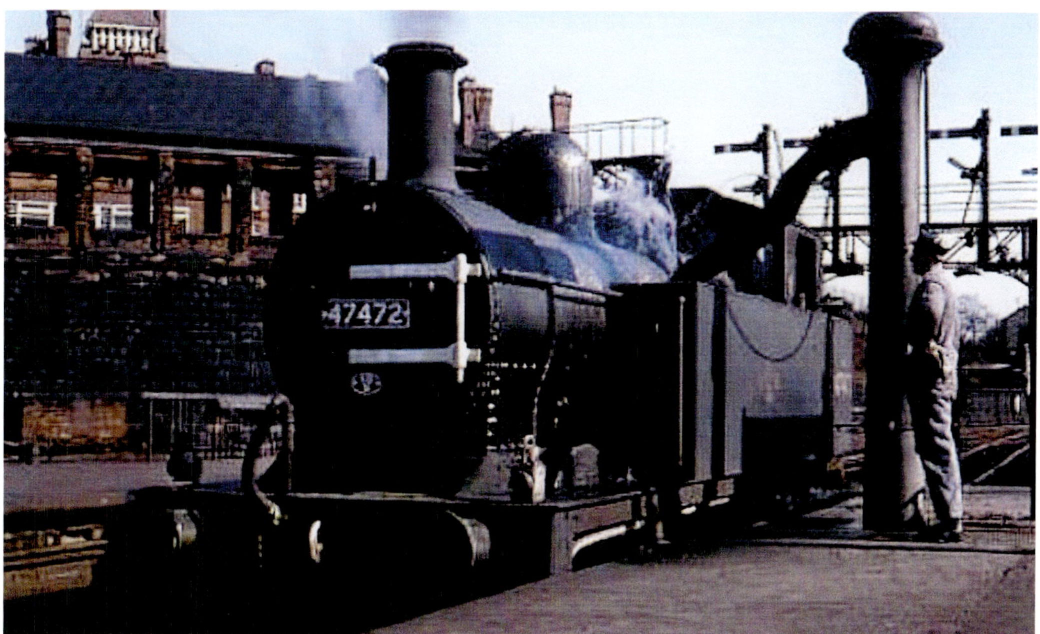

Pilot Engine No. 47472, September 1966

Like lots of my generation, I spent many an hour trainspotting from various vantage points close to my local station watching the steam engines pass by. They were often shrouded in smoke, their livery concealed by layers of soot and grime. One engine that was familiar to us all was engine No. 47472 of 1924 vintage. In the background is the old, covered walkway at the south end of Platform 6 which led to the Park Hotel, an ideal vantage point for viewing the locomotives.

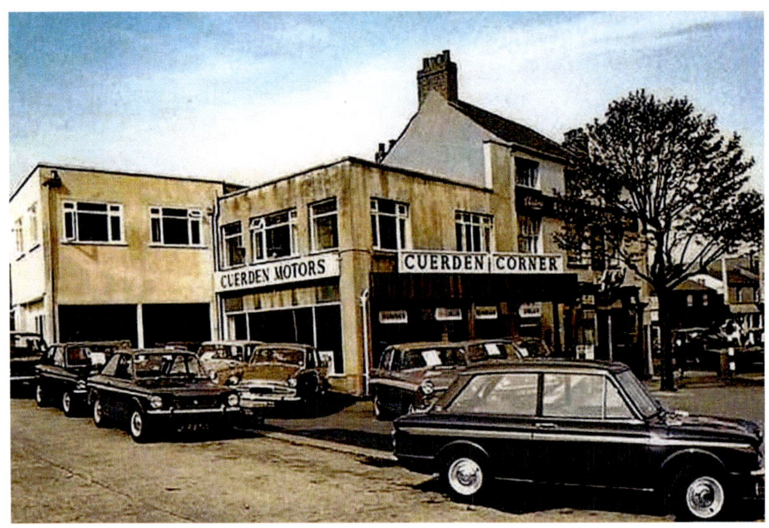

Cuerden Corner, Stanley Street, 1967

Cars with 'For Sale' stickers line the forecourt and Dale Street at the popular showroom. Cuerden Motors, part of the Rootes Group, also had showrooms on Manchester Road, Preston, and King Street, Blackburn, with a garage on Grimshaw Street. The premises are now home to the kitchen designer Stuart Frazer. The neighbouring Kings Arms public house was Joplins for a while, but after reverting to its original name, closed in 1999. Part of it became the Art Cafe for a short while, but it was vacated in 2022.

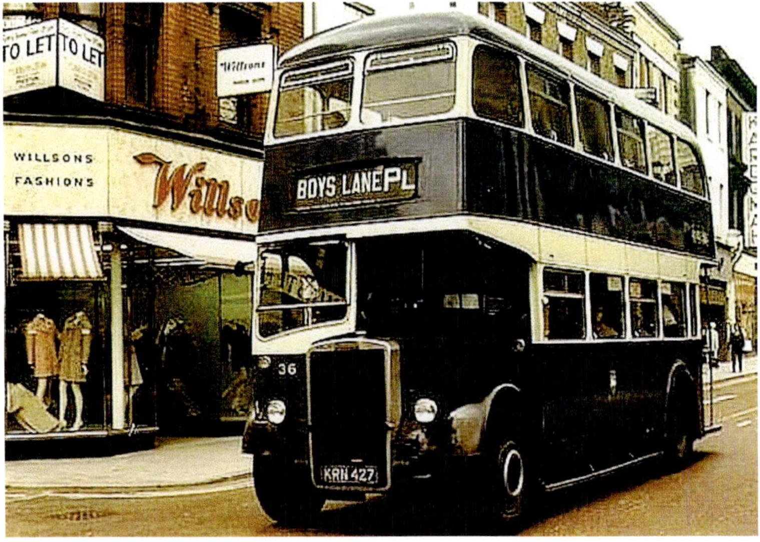

Fishergate, 1967

It is destination 'Boys Lane' for this double-decker bus. Those were the days of bus conductors and open access at the rear, where you could hop on and off at your peril. To the left of the image was the ladies fashion store Willsons, at No. 100 Fishergate, a survivor of the 1930s; today it is a Red Cross charity shop and previously a Virgin Media store. To the right is the sign for the Kardomah, a popular café and tearoom, and a refreshment stop for shoppers before its closure in 1966.

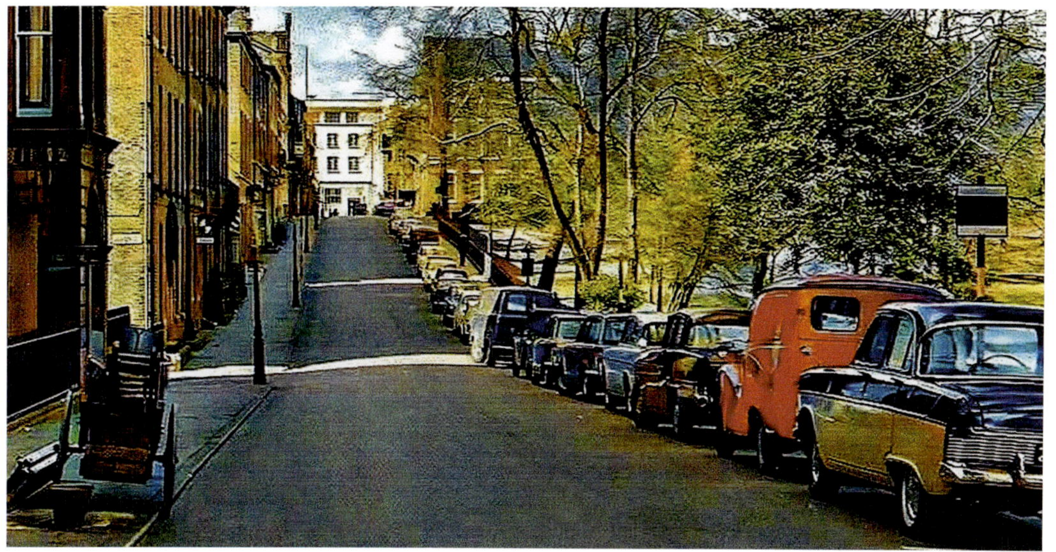

Winckley Square, West Side, November 1967

This autumn day began with a touch of frost on the grassy slopes, as a line of vehicles (all classics today) are parked neatly along one side of the thoroughfare. To the left there are no yellow lines to deter parking, nor parking meters; just a window cleaner's cart, ladder and bucket are on the pavement at that side. Parking restrictions are certainly part of Winckley Square today. In 2025, it was the most ticketed area in the county, with 1,063 penalty charges handed out.

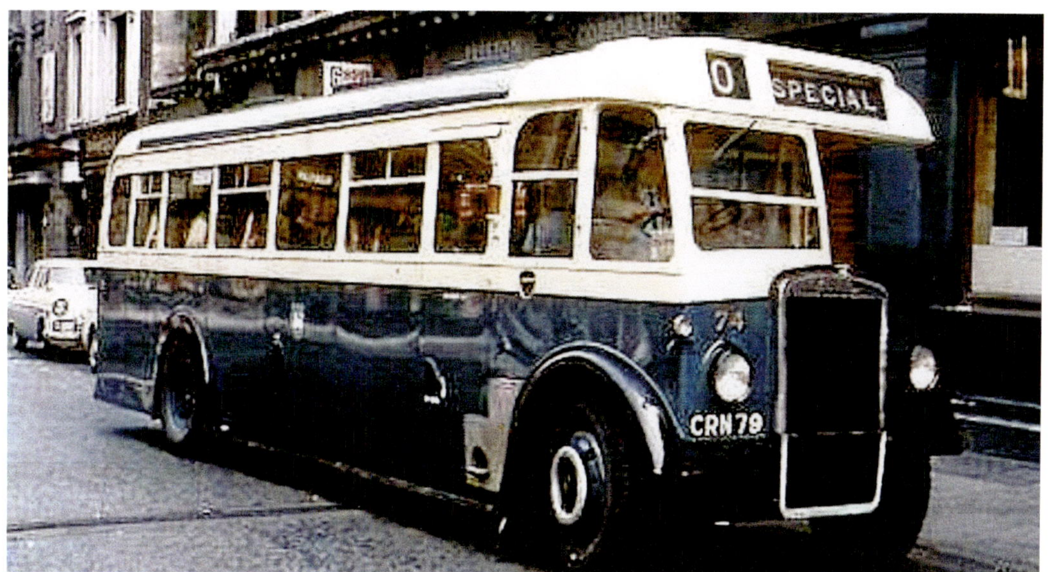

Supermarket Special, Lancaster Road, *c.* 1968

This special bus service ran throughout the day, taking customers to and from the Dundonald Street supermarket for free. The bus was built in 1949 and covered the route for four years from 1964 before double-deckers took over. The store, which started life in the converted Cliff cotton mill, was originally known as Fame and became Gem in 1964, before Associated Dairies expanded and took over making it an Asda. It ceased trading in 1986 when Asda opened their Fulwood store.

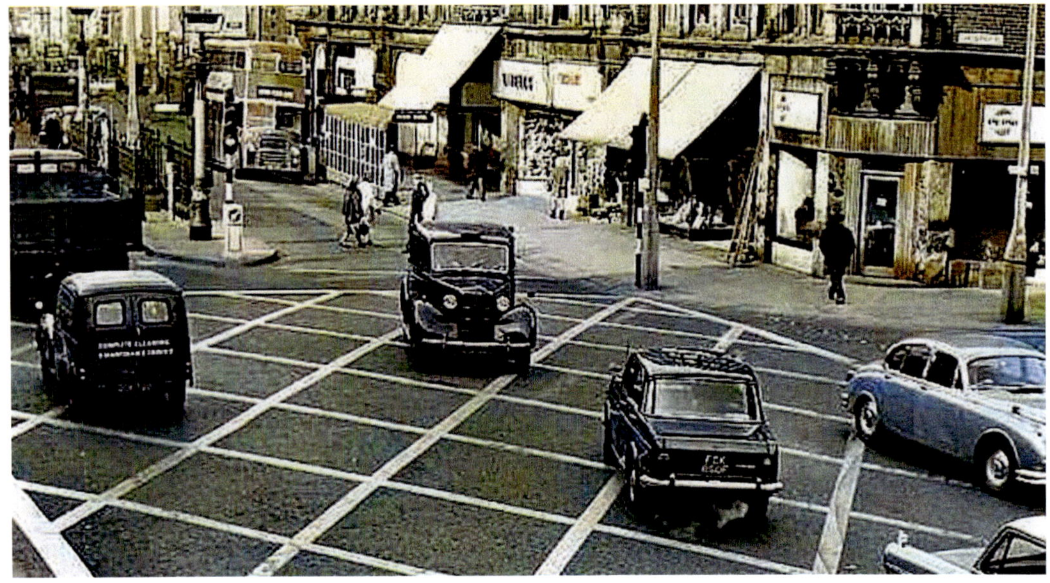

Church Street and Lancaster Road Box Junction, March 1969

The latest solution to traffic problems was introduced on this busy intersection, where traffic flowed either side of the underground toilet island. There were also traffic lights on the junction and the bus shelter for Moor Nook stood in front of the Miller Arcade. To the right, on the corner of Lancaster Road, the former Kings Arms was trading as the Long Bar, which since 2012 has been the Baluga bar.

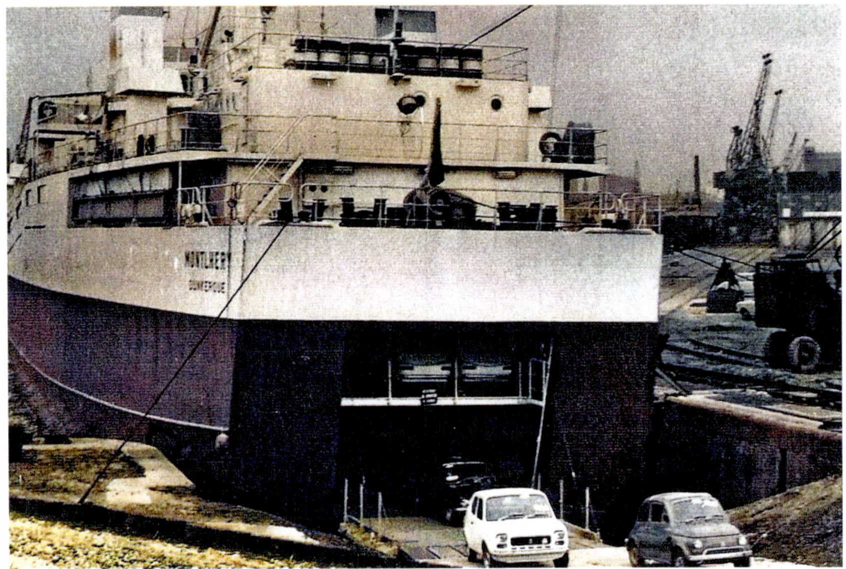

Preston Dock, 1972

A cargo of Fiat cars arrived from Vado, Italy, aboard the transporter MV *Montlhery* and can be seen unloading on a makeshift ramp at the south-west corner of the main dock basin. Its sister vessel, MV *Monza*, also covered the route, but the shipment service was eventually lost to Ellesmere Port. The year 1972 saw the lucrative exporting of coal and coke, particularly to Ireland, come to an end.

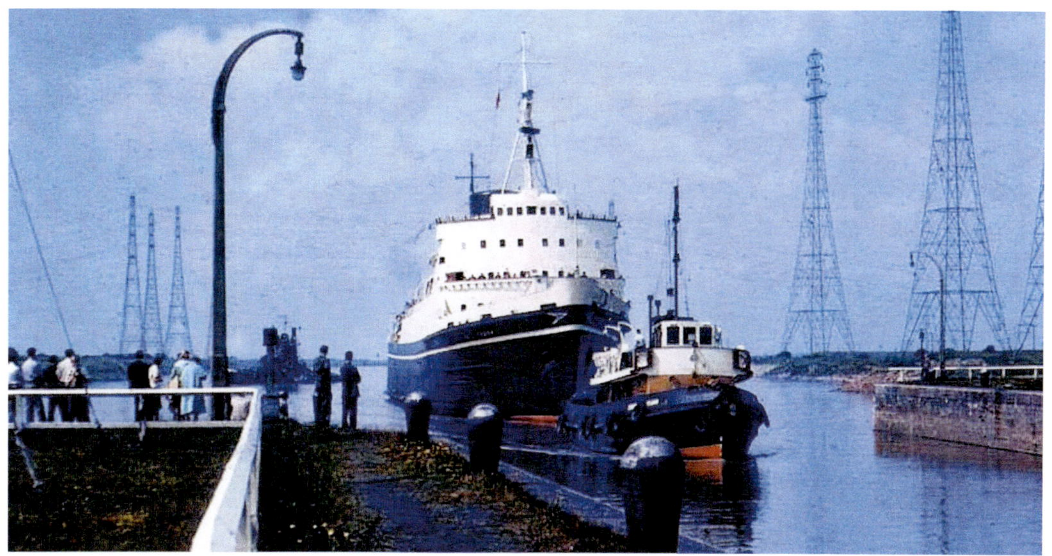

Ionic Ferry Entering Preston Dock, 1972

The _Ionic Ferry_ first sailed from Preston to Larne in October 1958, joining its sister ship, the _Bardic Ferry_, which had first been employed on the route from September 1957 with a full load of vehicles, containers and passengers. The vessel owners, the Transport Ferry Services, were sold to the European Ferries Group in 1972 and, as routes were reorganised, the _Ionic Ferry_ sailed from Preston for the last time in July 1973 and the _Bardic Ferry_ said goodbye to Preston in June 1974.

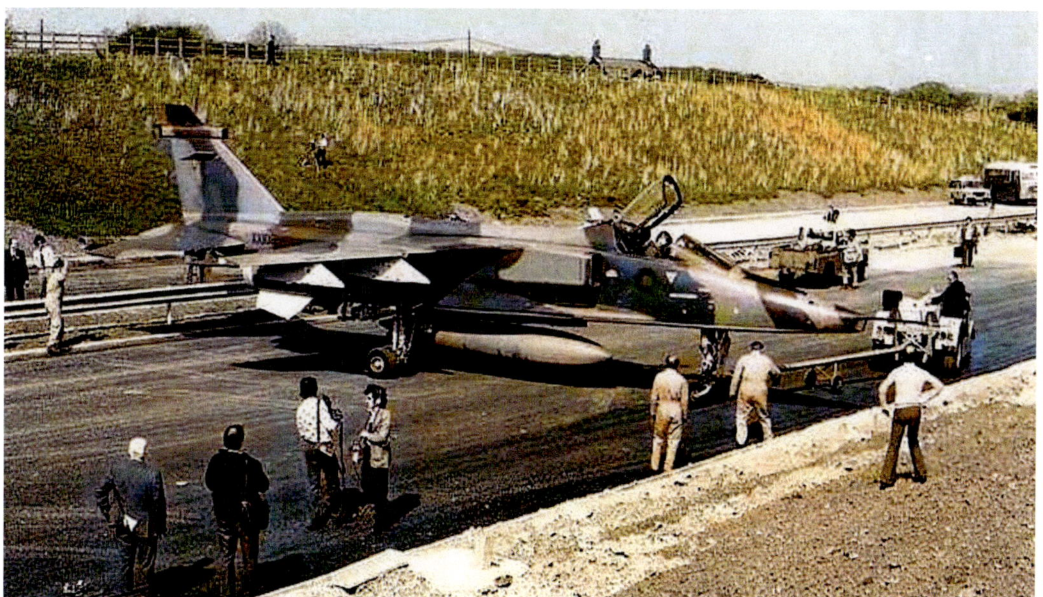

Jaguar on the M55 Motorway, April 1975

Prior to the opening of this motorway connecting Preston to Blackpool, it was used for a test run to see if fighter jets could land on motorways. The British Aircraft Corporation conducted successful trials from their nearby Warton factory. The twin-engine Jaguar, a supersonic aircraft, was developed jointly by the UK and France. The RAF retired their squadron of Jaguars in 2007.

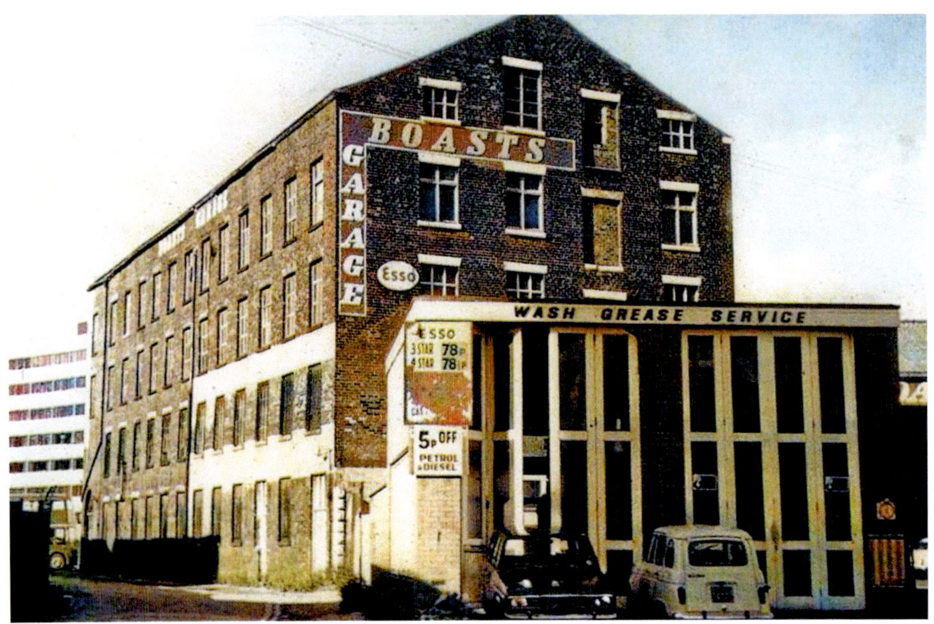

Boasts Empire Garage, Derby Street, 1977

These premises, viewed from the bus station, were once the John Booth's Phoenix Ironworks. In the 1950s, A. Boast & Co. became a leading local removal and storage company. The Esso sign, according to the adverts of the day, was the sign 'For Happy Motoring' and four-star petrol was 78p per gallon. A Sainsbury's store was built on the site in 1978, which became Tradex from 1992 and today is a B&M bargains outlet.

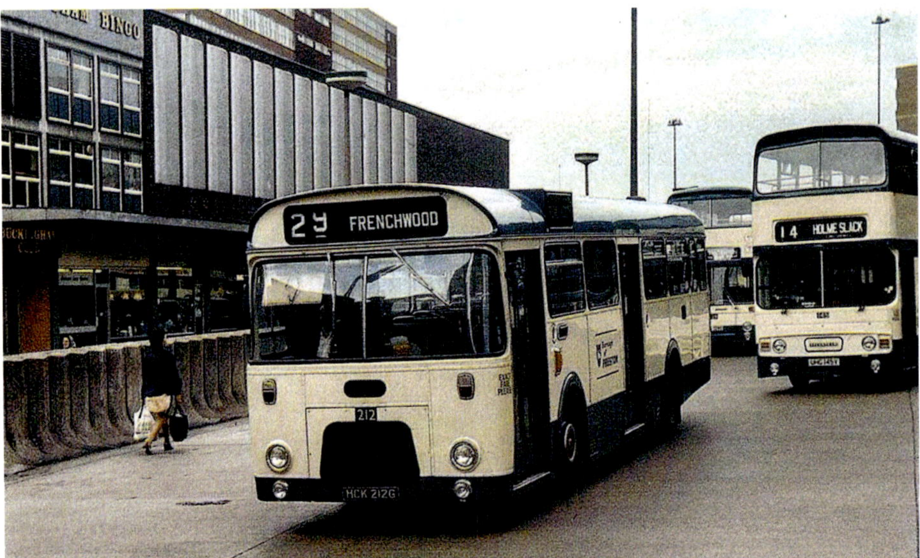

Preston Bus Station, Tithebarn Street, 1981

Opened in 1969, the brutalist-designed bus station had a subway access from St John's Shopping Centre, shown to the left. The buses seen departing displayed the recently introduced destination numbers which replaced the old P1, P2, FP and GL lettering.

Sport and Leisure

Living in an industrial town, the people of Preston have certainly always earned their leisure time. As the centuries progressed, local pursuits of pleasure took different and diverse paths. Back in 1656, Preston Corporation bought a bull purely for the purpose of bullbaiting in the Market Place; cockfighting was another popular pursuit from that period. In the years ahead, fox hounds would be seen scampering through the area as hunting became a popular pursuit of the nobility and their associates. Dog racing and horse racing gradually became common occurrences, and by 1726 horses were competing on Preston Moor. The gathering of folk for sporting events gradually became an opportunity for social mingling, including fashionable balls and concerts. The images that follow chronicle later developments, both socially and in sporting circles.

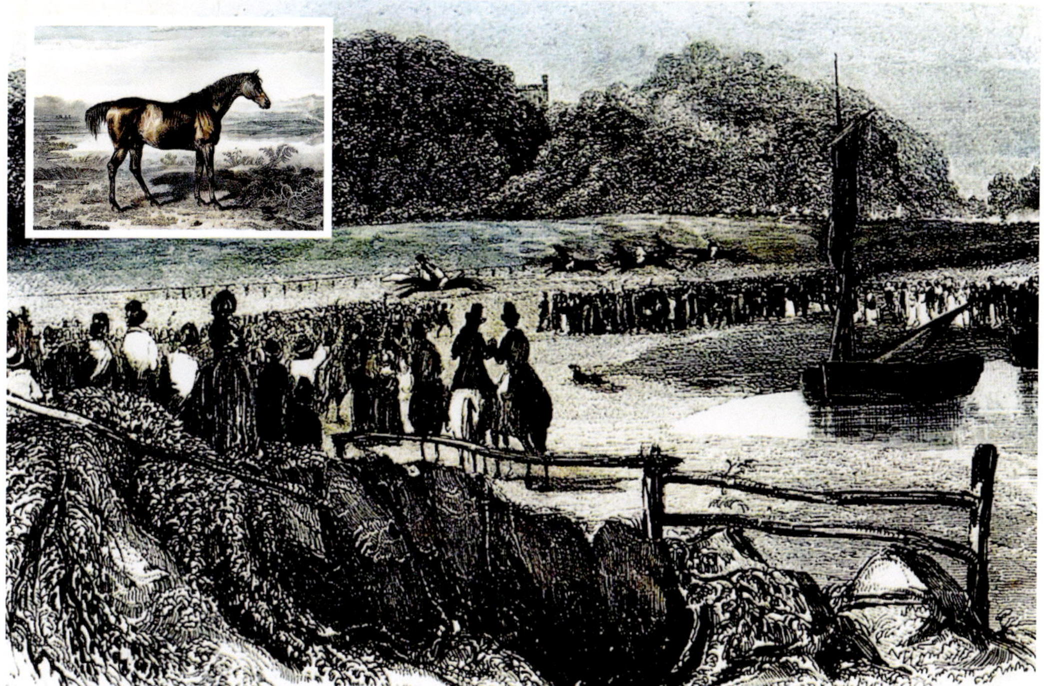

A Day at the Races, Penwortham Holme Guild, 1842

There were two days of horse racing held with significant prize money, despite the nobility choosing not to patronise the events. The fun for the spectators was plentiful, with horses bolting, throwing their riders and even turning tail. Further race meetings were held at Penwortham Holme from 1845 to 1848, when a confrontation between soldiers and the Preston constabulary led to the discontinuation. *Inset*: The record-breaking horse Doctor Syntax won seven Preston Gold Cups, the last one in 1821.

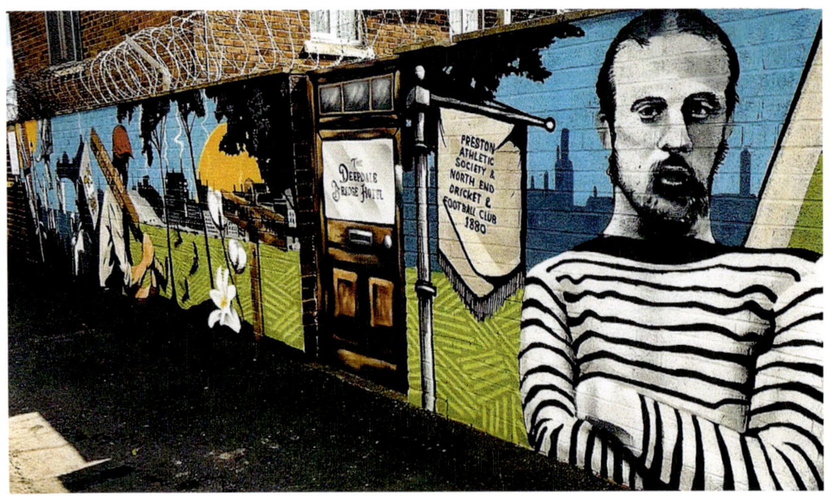

Alan Kelly Way, 1860s Onwards

Thanks to the 80-metre-long mural on the wall of the Kimberley Barracks, behind the Alan Kelly Stand, created by local artist Shawn Sharpe, a colourful history of Preston North End is now on display. The fact that a cricket bat and the Preston Guild of 1862 feature is a reminder of North End roots being traced back to a cricket match at the Guild. When those cricketers from the Ashton Marsh moved to Moor Park and later leased a field at Deepdale, they fittingly took the name Preston North End. The club played rugby from 1877 and turned to Association Football three years later.

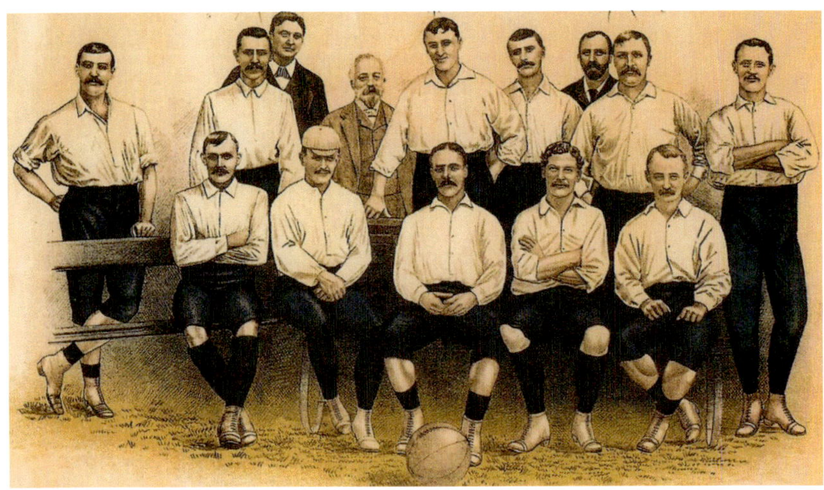

Invincibles, Preston North End, Season 1888/89

The football team would compete in the Lancashire FA Cup from 1880, winning it in 1887, and the FA Cup from 1883, reaching the final in 1888. Under the guidance of Major William Sudell, the team were founder members of the Football League, winning their opening fixture against Burnley at Deepdale by 6-2. By early January 1889, following a 4-1 win at Deepdale against Notts County, they were declared champions and would go on to remain undefeated, winning eighteen of their twenty-two fixtures. They went on to reach the FA Cup final at the Oval, Surrey, where they defeated Wolverhampton Wanderers 3-0, winning the trophy without conceding a goal in their five cup ties. Consequently, they were talked about as being invincible.

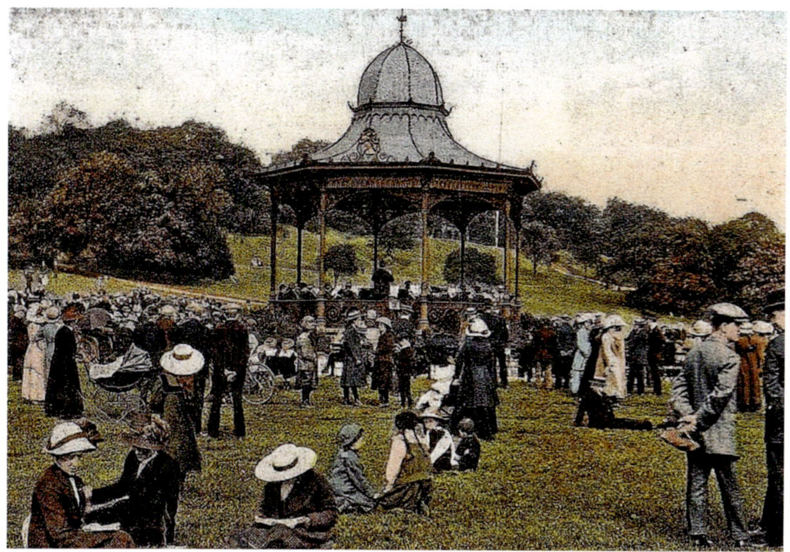

Avenham Park Bandstand, 1906

Preston's public parks were certainly an attraction for visitors to the town and those who enjoyed relaxation outdoors or sporting pursuits. The construction of the bandstand on Avenham Park cost £435 and enhanced the park's popularity. It was opened in early August 1903 in the centre of the valley, with a vast crowd enjoying music from the Northern Military Band. For the next fifty years it was a focal point, and concerts galore were held there until it was removed in 1953.

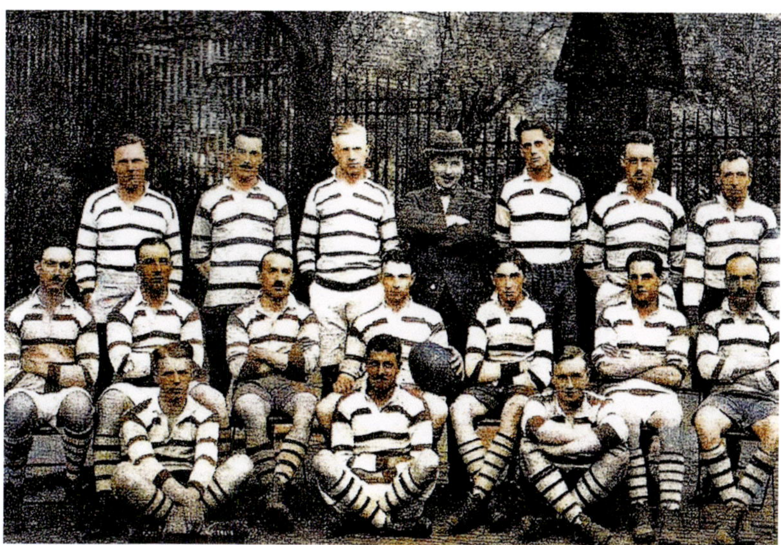

A New Beginning for Preston Grasshoppers, Season 1921/22

The rugby union club are pictured ahead of their opening match of the season in October 1921. The club had reformed in January following the First World War and they began with a 16-0 victory over Leyland Electrons. They acquired a field on the south side of the Ribble, near the tram bridge, for their home fixtures. Both teams changed into their match kit at the Bull & Royal Hotel on Church Street and walked the ¾ mile to the playing field. The club was formed in 1869 and has had notable successes along the way, these days competing in the National League North.

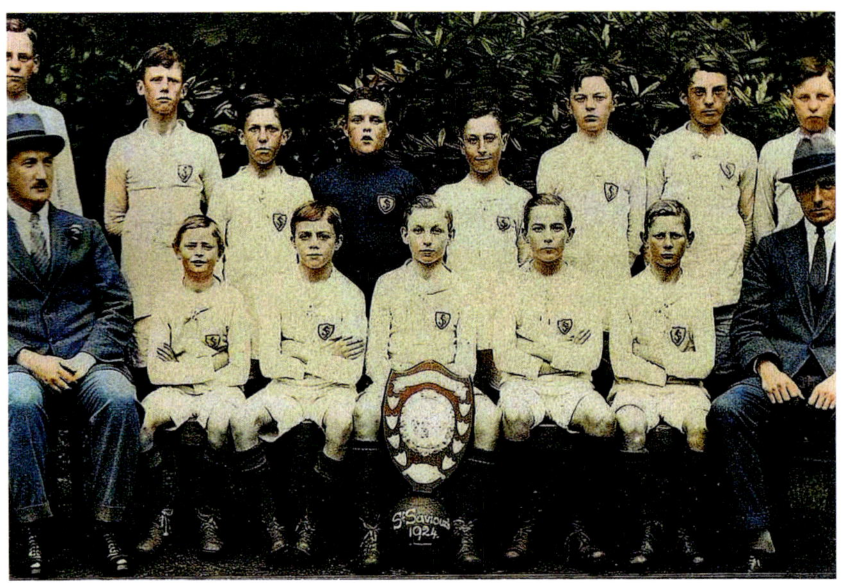

St Saviour's Sunday School Footballers, May 1924

The winners of the Preston Sunday School Football League proudly display the shield after their name is added. After a season of Saturday afternoon soccer on the local park pitches, they had only lost two out of thirty League matches, pipping St Paul's to the title by a single point.

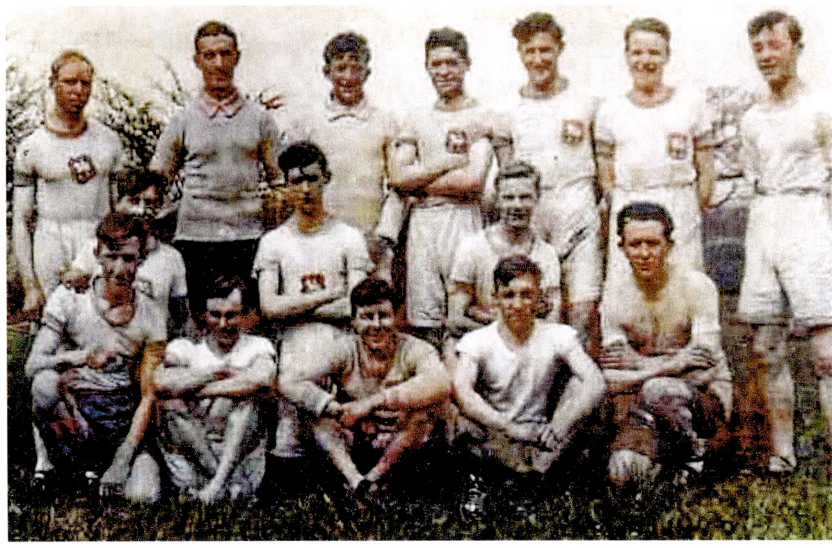

Preston Harriers, Haslam Park, May 1924

The club was formed in September 1881 after a gathering of enthusiasts at the White Horse Inn, Friargate, wanting to form a 'Hare & Hounds' club. Among their members in 1924 was John Higginson, who won the triple jump at the British AAA Championship that year and represented club and country at the Olympic Games in Paris, finishing in thirteenth position. Two years later he won the AAA title again and set a British triple jump record of 14.25 metres. Other notable Harriers in the past century have included Eric Turner, Andrew Holden, John Nuttall, Steve Tunstall and Helen Clitheroe.

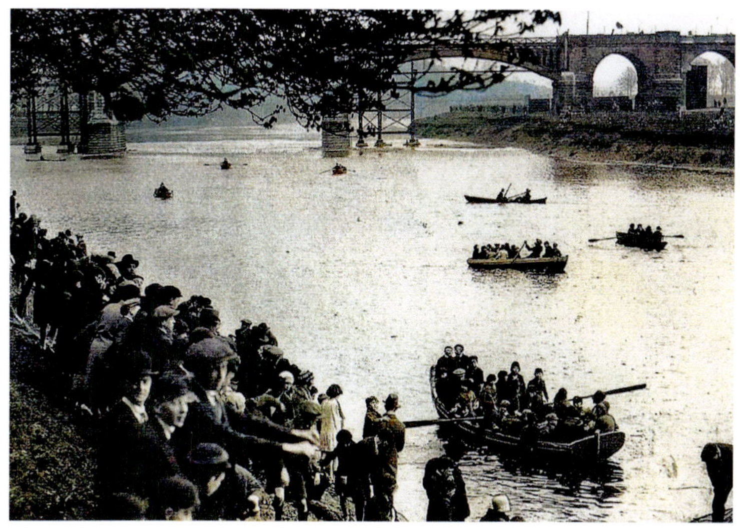

Messing About on the River, April 1929

On Easter Monday the usual egg rolling took place on the slopes of Avenham Park, with hard-boiled eggs decorated with all the colours of the rainbow and chocolate eggs wrapped in gold or silver foil cascading down the valley. For many of the adventure seekers, the hiring of a rowing boat was an irresistible temptation. It had been a tradition since John Crook and his sons had occupied the Pleasure Boat Inn along Riverside. After the building of the Continental Hotel in 1911 boats could still be hired from the adjacent boathouse.

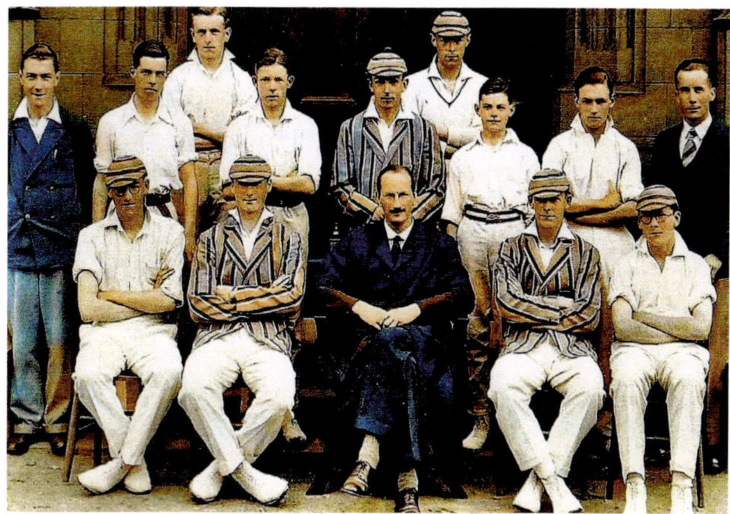

Preston Grammar School Cricket Team, 1929

Headmaster Norman Hodgson, appointed in 1926 on a salary of £750 per annum, is pictured centrally on the front row with his cricketers around him. It had been a good year on the cricket field for the PGS boys, who had beaten their local rivals, the Preston Catholic College, by three wickets at Walton. The PGS, with origins back to Stoneygate in 1666, moved to Cross Street in 1841, the premises being bought by Preston Corporation twenty years later for £1,500. They moved again in 1913 to Moor Park Avenue, where PGS merged in 1969 with the girls' Park School to form the Sixth Form College.

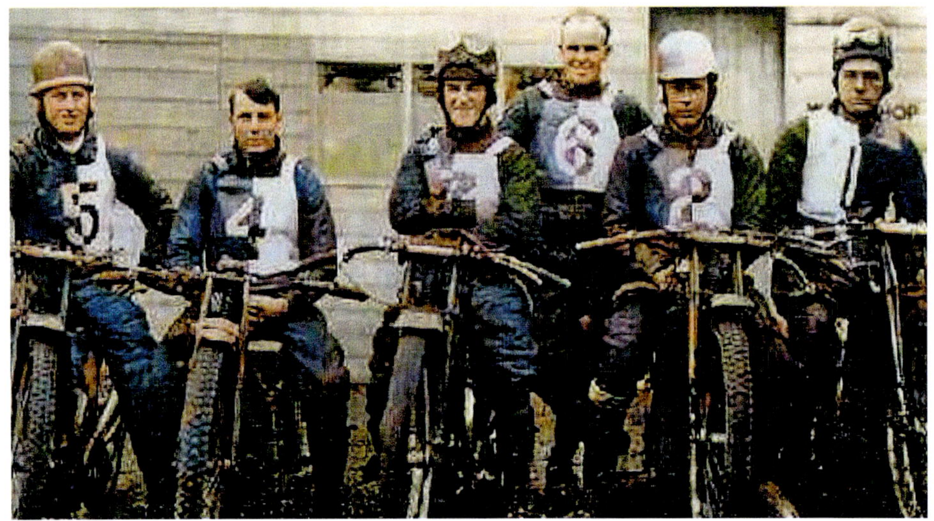

Preston Speedway Club, Farringdon Park, 1929

Members of the club that won the British Dirt Track KO Cup in October 1929 and finished second in the Northern Dirt Track League pose for the camera. For the Farringdon Park fixtures, crowds of over 10,000 were common, but the dangers of the sport were to lead to the deaths of John Proctor Stockdale of Lancaster, Jack Smith of Bolton and James Carnie from Broadgate on the Preston track in 1929 and 1930. Unfortunately, the club ran into financial difficulties and in July 1932 the liquidators moved in and the club disbanded.

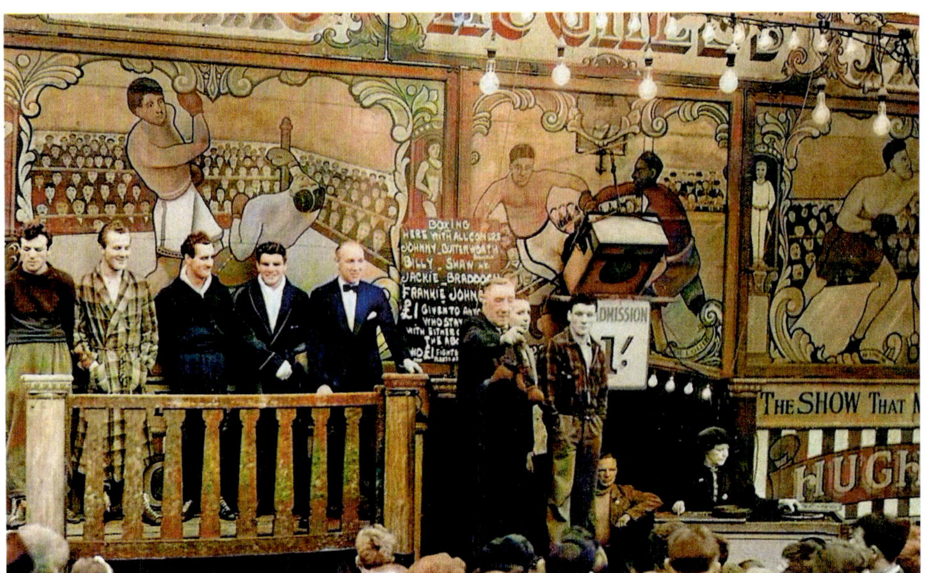

Bert Hughes Touring Boxing Booth, 1935

This touring sporting attraction was a regular visitor to the Whitsuntide Fair in Preston in the 1930s. It was an opportunity for local lads to challenge the professional boxers of the era. Jack 'Kid' McCabe, a Leyland lad who fought in several memorable bouts at the Majestic, Marathon and Royal Hippodrome in Preston, would face a dozen challengers a day in the boxing booths later in his career, mostly defeating them in a couple of rounds.

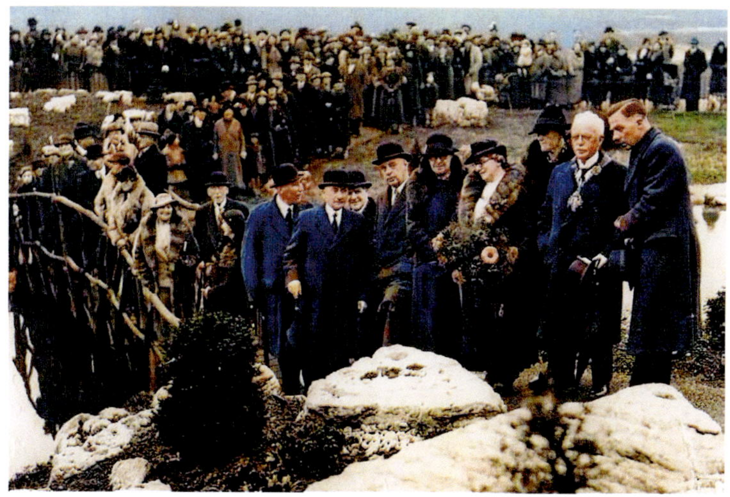

Japanese Gardens, Avenham Park, November 1936

Parks Superintendent Mr Algernon Birkinshaw and his assistant Mr Arnold Victor Pearson were heavily involved in the creation of these gardens on the site of the former duck pond. The gardens were officially opened by Mayor James Harrison. Creating the rock garden was a mammoth task costing £3,000 – over £170,000 today – most of the money being spent on labour at a time when unemployment levels were high. The selection of suitable rocks was a priority and, after scrutinising various locations, the pair decided that they should come from Slack Head, Milnthorpe and from the back of the Fairy Steps at Arnside. Despite a misty, murky morning, a great crowd gathered to experience the delights of the enchanting gardens.

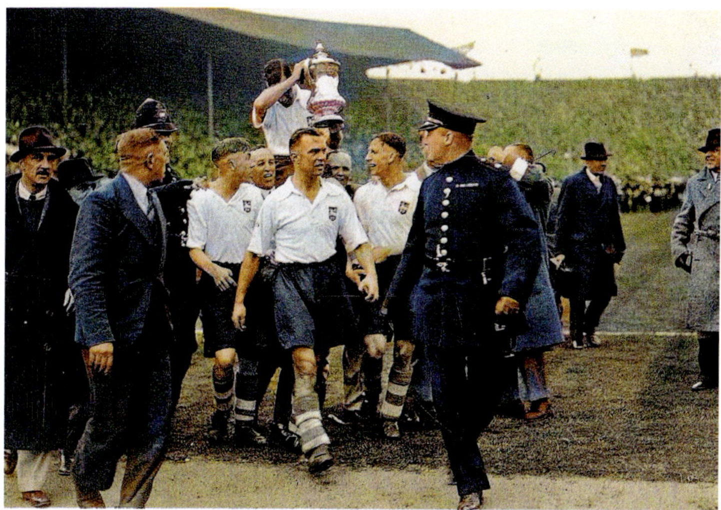

PNE FA Cup Winners, Wembley Stadium, April 1938

There was no hiding the delight on the faces of the Preston North End players as FA Cup-winning captain Tom Smith is carried shoulder high with the gleaming silver trophy aloft. North End's victory, courtesy of a George Mutch penalty at the end of extra time, had earned a 1-0 victory over Huddersfield Town. Twelve months earlier they had suffered defeat by 3-1 against Sunderland on the Wembley turf. Only Bill Shankly, Frank Gallimore, Andy Beattie and Hugh O' Donnell were in the PNE side that returned to triumph as an injured Jimmy Milne missed out.

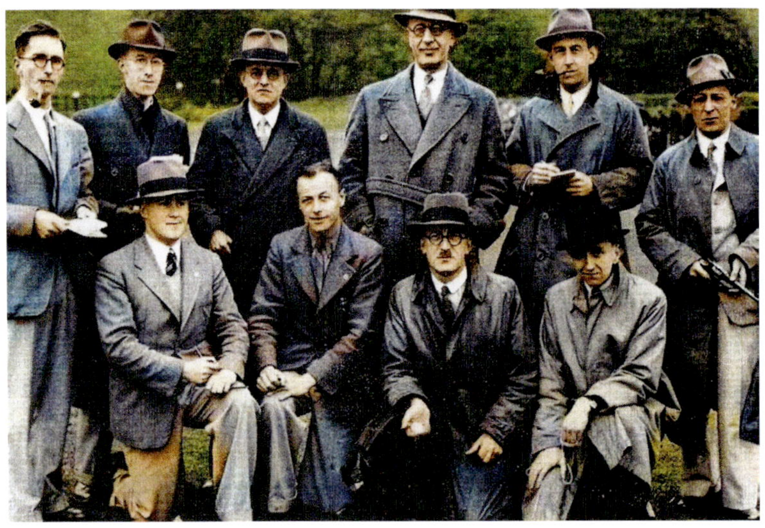

Preston Catholic College Sports Day, June 1938

The lay staff line up prior to officiating at the annual sports. Judging by their clothing of raincoats, overcoats and trilby hats, it wasn't a glorious summer's day. A couple of studious-looking gentlemen were enjoying a smoking pipe and, standing to the right, Mr Walter Allen was brandishing a starting pistol. For the overall winner of the games the Victor Ludorum Cup awaited. The headmaster of PCC from 1922 to 1940 was Father Francis Grafton. Generally, around 300 pupils attended the college based on Winckley Square each term.

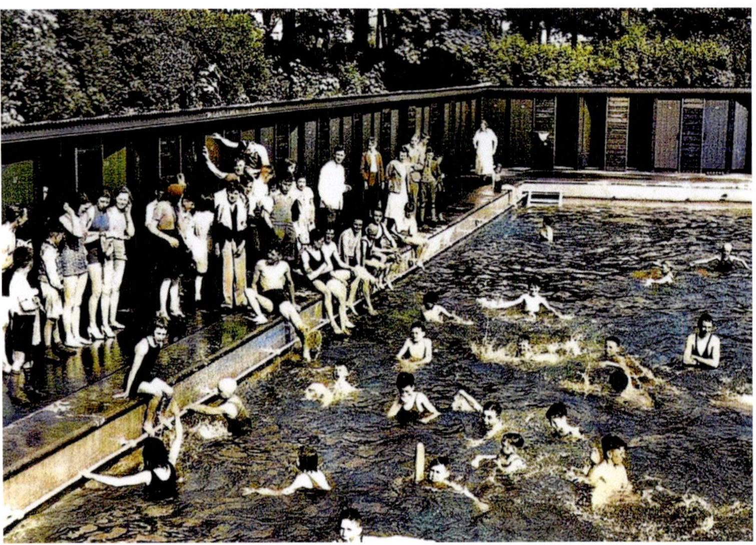

Haslam Park Open-Air Swimming Baths, 1939

Preston had three outdoor pools – on Moor Park (1905), Waverley Park (1924) and Haslam Park (1925) – in the twentieth century, all highly popular during the summer holidays. In April 1925, the Preston Corporation advertised for married Bath Attendants, who could earn up to £3 per week with bonuses and whose wife would be employed part-time when ladies or mixed bathing took place. The Moor Park pool closed in 1971 and the other two outdoor pools closed in 1987.

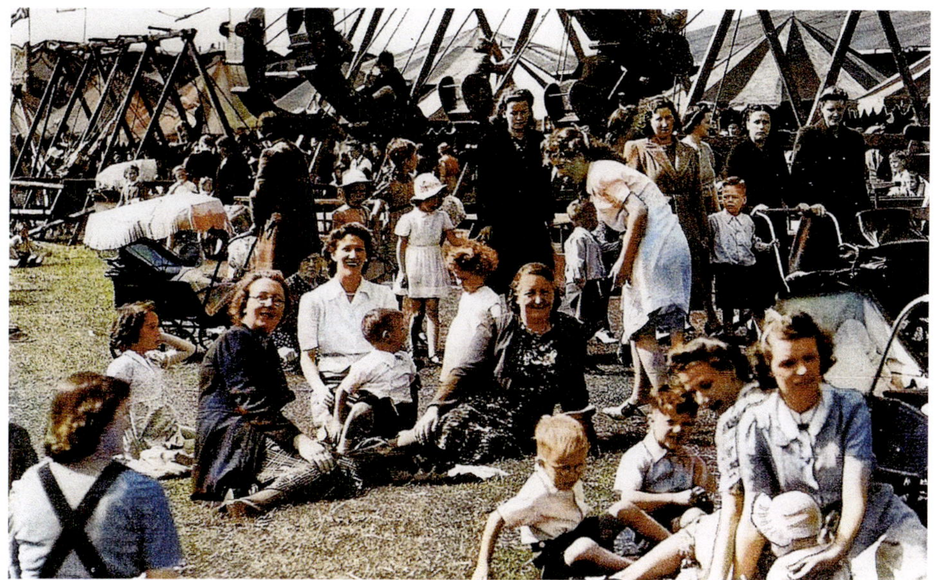

Moor Park, August 1944

With the world still at war the Preston Wakes Week holiday, held in mid-August back then, saw many content to stay at home, visiting attractions in the parks. This group of mothers were happy to relax as their children enjoyed the fun of the fairground on Moor Park. Sheep dog trials, a dog show and a fashion parade on Avenham Park all added to the holiday pleasures.

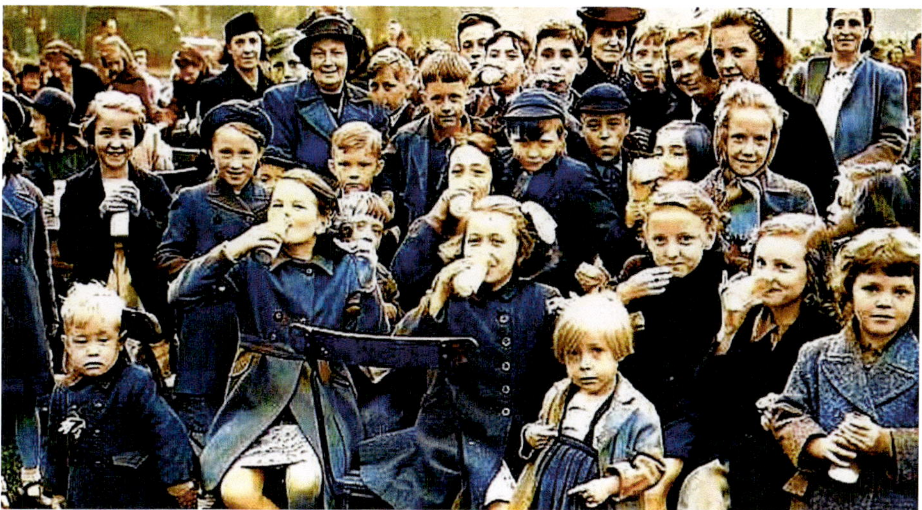

Avenham Park Victory Celebrations, June 1946

A bottle of milk was all that was needed for these children as they celebrated the end of the Second World War. Unfortunately, within an hour of gathering on the park and a greeting from Mayor Alderman Herbert Rhodes, a prolonged downpour halted the entertainment, forcing all to run for shelter. When the rain stopped even those children who had taken a drenching helped to devour the 14,000 sandwiches and cakes provided, along with 500 gallons of milk, in ⅓ pint bottles as the brass bands entertained them. The day of celebration ended with a searchlight tattoo featuring both the Loyal and East Lancashire regiments.

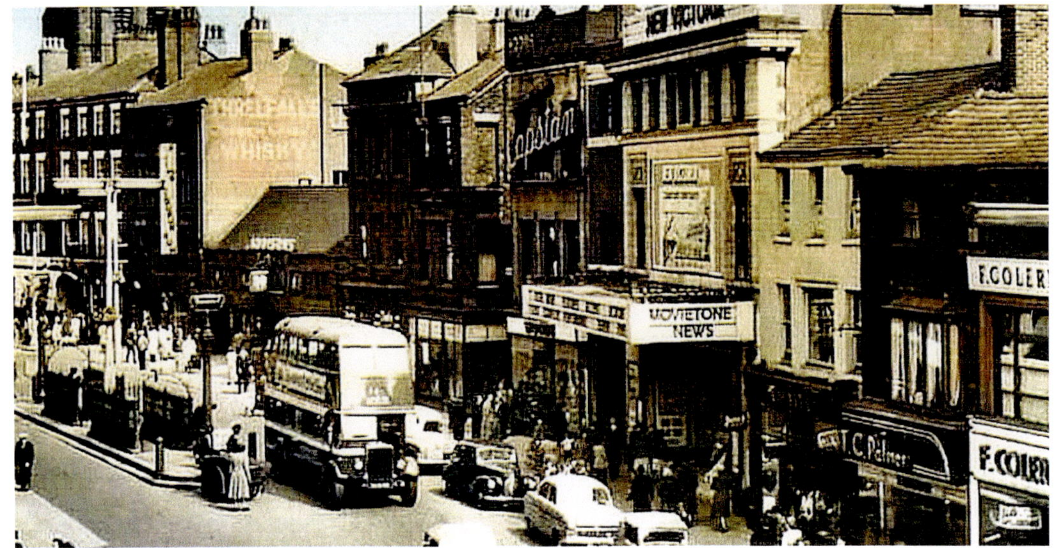

New Victoria, Church Street, 1950

Opened in 1928, the first colour movie in town was shown here in 1935. It was renamed the Gaumont in 1952, and from 1963, as part of the Top Rank organisation, it became the Odeon cinema until closure in 1992. To the left of the cinema is Woods tobacconist shop, where you could get your packet of cigarettes for the cinema – ashtrays were provided on the back of seats. It was only in 2007 that smoking was banned in cinemas.

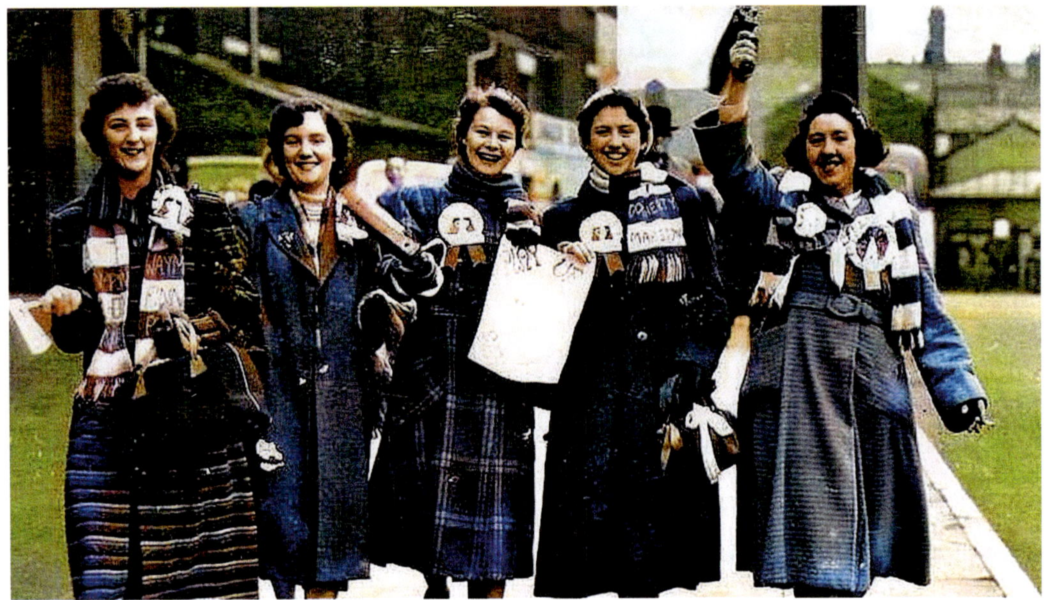

Come on North End, March 1954

It was FA Cup semi-final day and these five young ladies are gathered at the Tithebarn Street bus station to travel to Maine Road, Manchester, to cheer on PNE against Sheffield Wednesday. Goals from Charlie Wayman and Jimmy Baxter earned a 2-0 victory, making the trip by Mavis Thompson, Anne Collinson, Eileen Sharples, Dorothy Robinson and Edith Barker more than worthwhile.

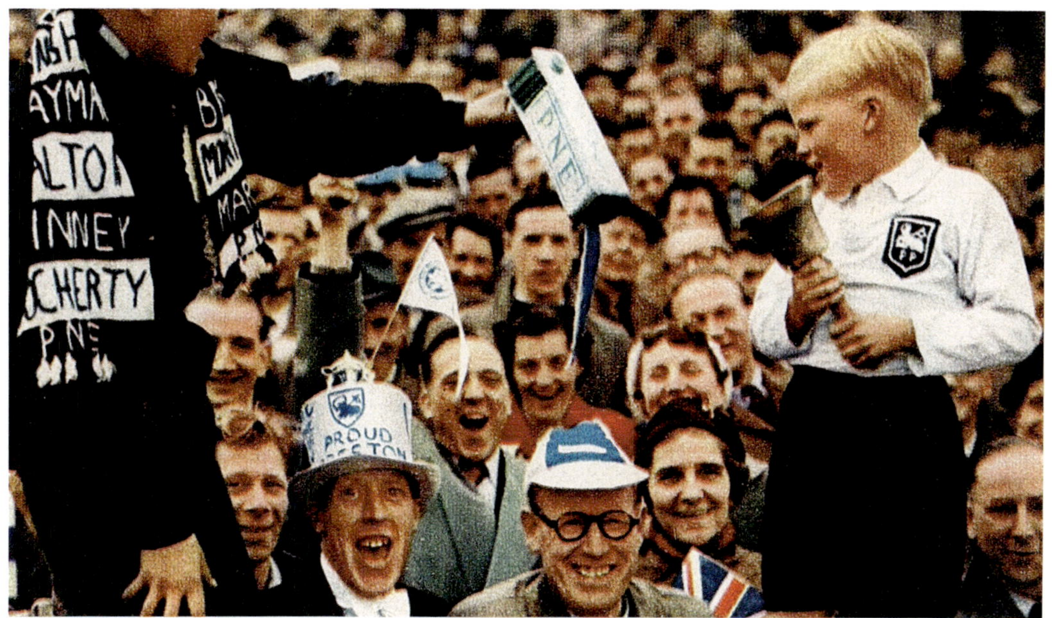

Above: PNE Supporters at Wembley with Club Mascot Bobby Rowe; *Below*: Tom Finney Leads Out Preston North End at Wembley

The FA Cup final of 1954 against West Bromwich Albion was a great occasion, although the outcome was a disappointment. Despite North End going behind to a Ronnie Allen goal after 22 minutes, they equalised a minute later through Angus Morrison and took the lead early in the second half as Charlie Wayman netted despite offside claims. Unfortunately, an equaliser from an Allen penalty was followed by a late winner from Frank Griffin, which secured the cup for WBA.

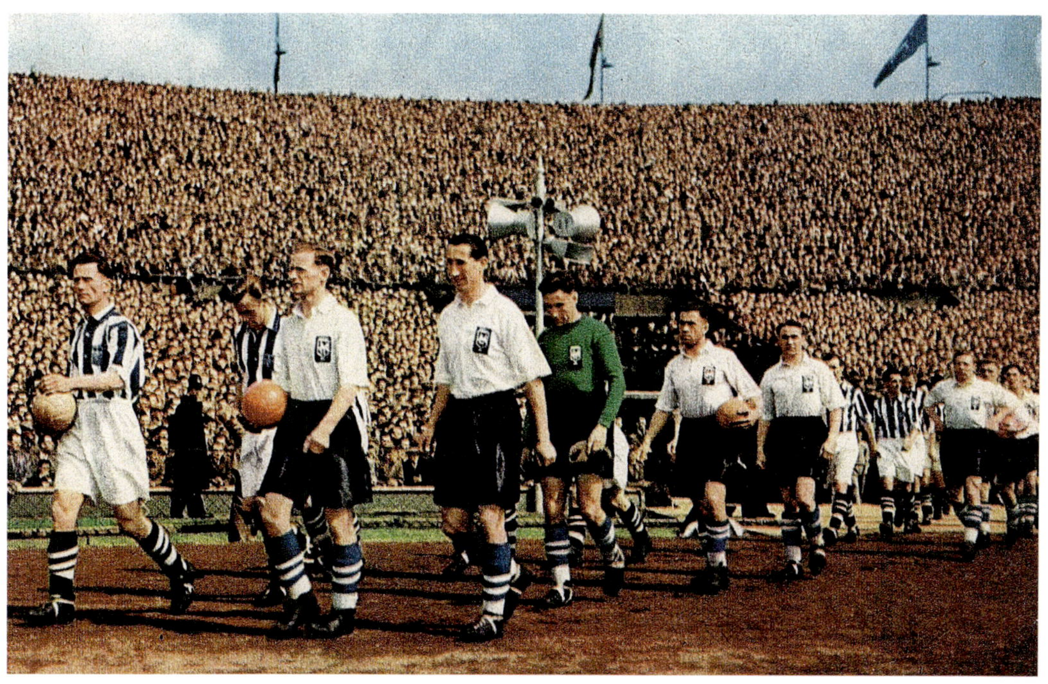

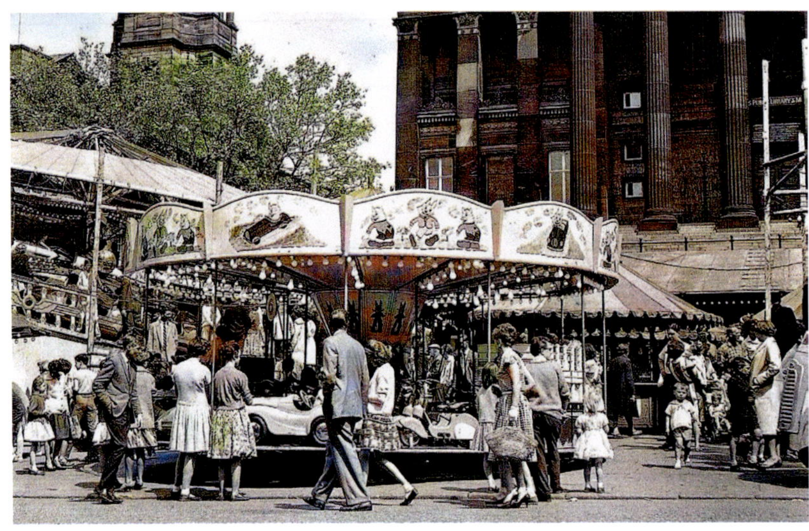

Whitsuntide Fair, Market Square, June 1960

The fairground was a highlight of the Whitsuntide holiday (Spring Bank Holiday from 1971). The Market Square and Covered Market were packed with flying aeroplanes and boats, prancing horses, the waltzer, dodgem cars, swing boats, Green's amazing caterpillar ride, Barry's wall of death with its daredevil motorcyclists, Mitchell's speedway and Shaw's monorail. All of this alongside novelty stalls, sideshows and a chance to stick three darts in a playing card as you attempted to win a goldfish swimming in a plastic bag of water.

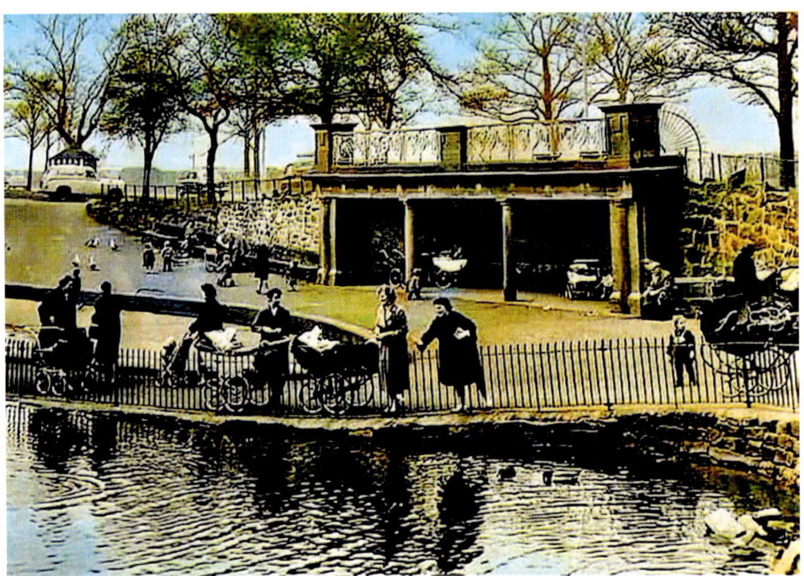

Serpentine Lake, Moor Park, June 1961

A *Lancashire Evening Post* photographer (their van is parked to the top left) had come to capture the pleasant scene. Mums and their toddlers were attracted to the lake on this sunny day, where there were ducks to feed and an oval paddling pool for kiddies to splash about in. The Serpentine Lake had been developed in 1866. A bridge, previously over the lake on Avenham Park, had been lengthened and placed over it at the southern end.

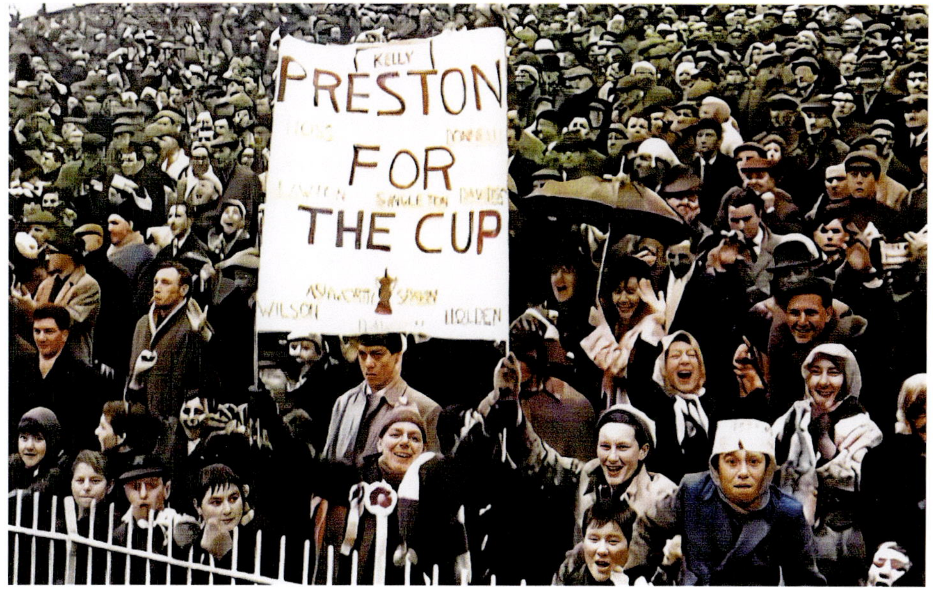

Preston North End Supporters at Villa Park, 1964

This enthusiastic crowd had a clear message that Preston were 'Up For The Cup' once again in 1964 for the semi-final at Villa Park against Swansea Town. Despite the rain and a muddy pitch, North End triumphed 2-1 thanks to Tony Singleton's long-range strike. Awaiting them in the FA Cup final were West Ham United. Second-tier PNE led twice in the Wembley encounter through Doug Holden and Alex Dawson, but after Geoff Hurst equalised a last-minute winner from Ronnie Boyce gave West Ham victory by 3-2. It had been a season to remember for PNE, with a Wembley outing and just missing promotion to the top tier as they finished third behind Leeds Utd and Sunderland in the days before play offs were introduced.

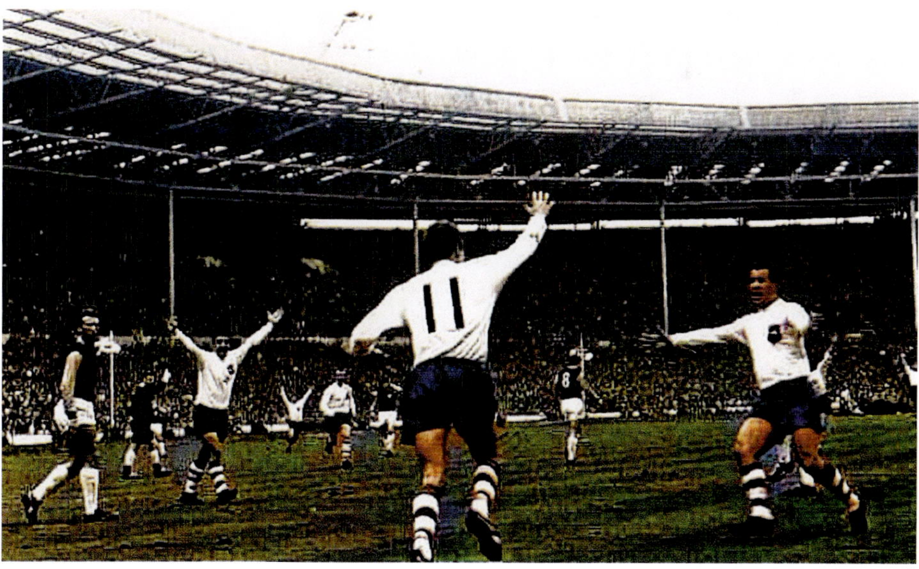

FA Cup Final PNE vs West Ham Utd, Wembley 1964

A triumphant Doug Holden (No. 11) turns away after giving Preston the lead in the tenth minute.

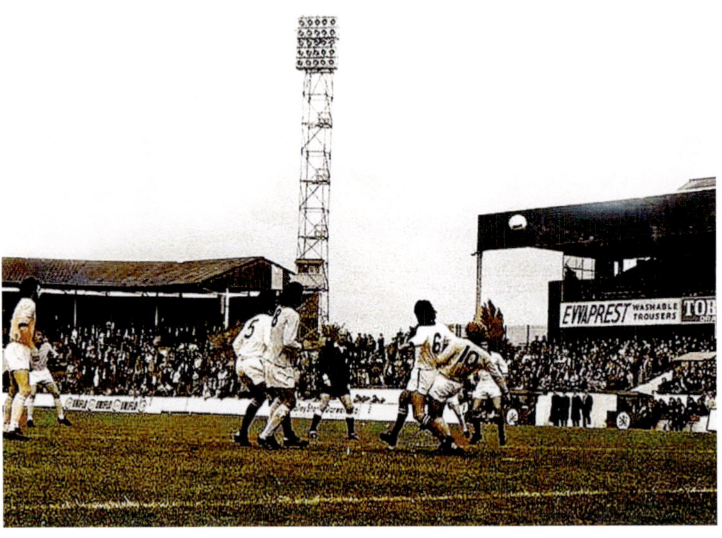

PNE vs Walsall, August 1974

Having dropped to the Third Division under manager Bobby Charlton, he made a return to the field as the team ditched their traditional blue shorts and turned out in an all-white kit. Charlton, Tony Morley and Mike Elwiss were on the score sheet in a 3-2 victory. North End finished in ninth position as away-day crowds flocked to see Charlton play. He resigned early in the 1975/76 season despite a promising start after a fall out over the transfer of centre-half John Bird to Newcastle.

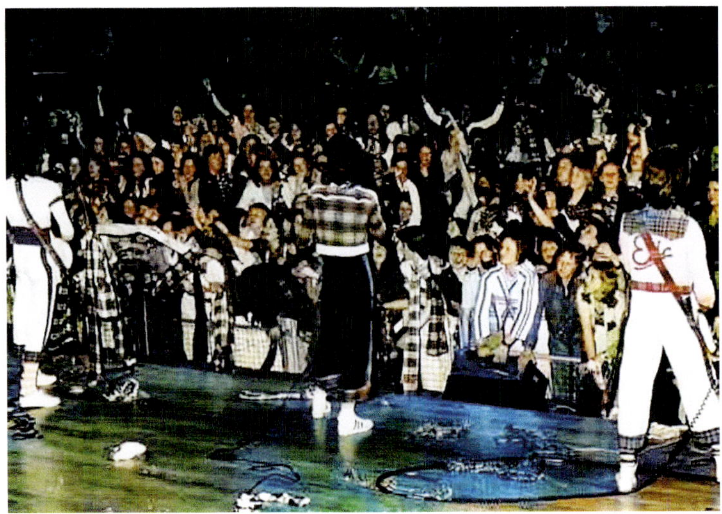

Bay City Rollers, Guild Hall, May 1975

The appearance of Alan & Derek Longmuir, Stuart 'Woody' Wood, Eric Faulkner and Les McKeown on the stage led to mass hysteria among the sellout crowd. The audience, mainly consisting of teenage girls, were screaming, shouting and singing along to their favourite tunes, including their recent chart topping single 'Bye Bye Baby'. The tartan-clad musicians were interrupted by a power failure, but they returned to more rapturous applause. Despite the crush when girls rushed towards the stage to be confronted by fifty stewards, only a few minor injuries occurred.

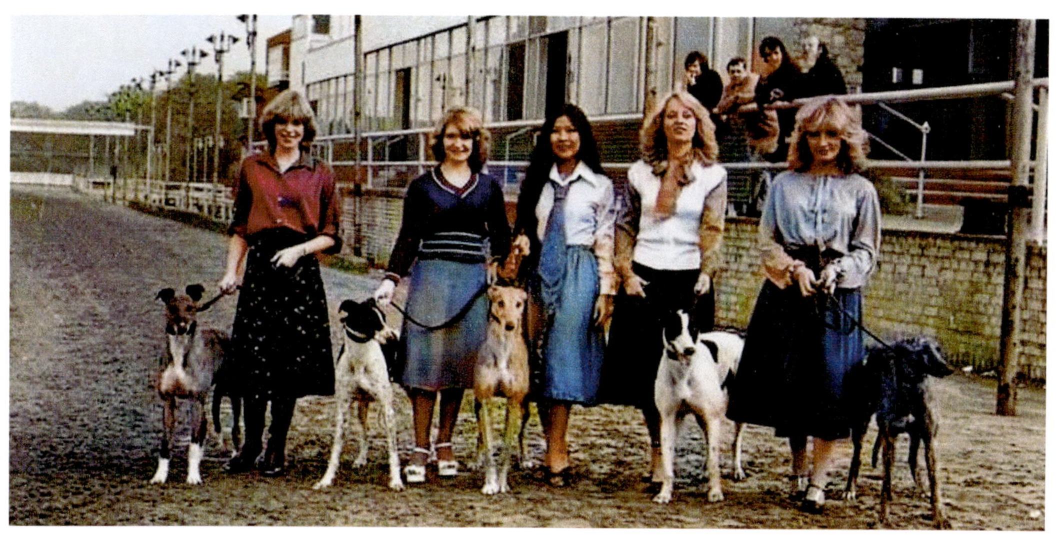

Preston Greyhound Stadium, October 1978

A line-up of local ladies along with their chosen four-legged friends prior to a fundraising event. The Acregate Lane track opened in May 1932 as one of the finest tracks in the north of England. Meetings were held three times a week, often with a ten-race calendar. The stadium was used as a base for American troops during the Second World War. It also survived devastating fires in 1948 and in 1972. Unfortunately, in early December 1988, it was forced to close due to financial difficulties, and in July 1989 the bulldozers moved in as plans for a housing estate were drawn up.

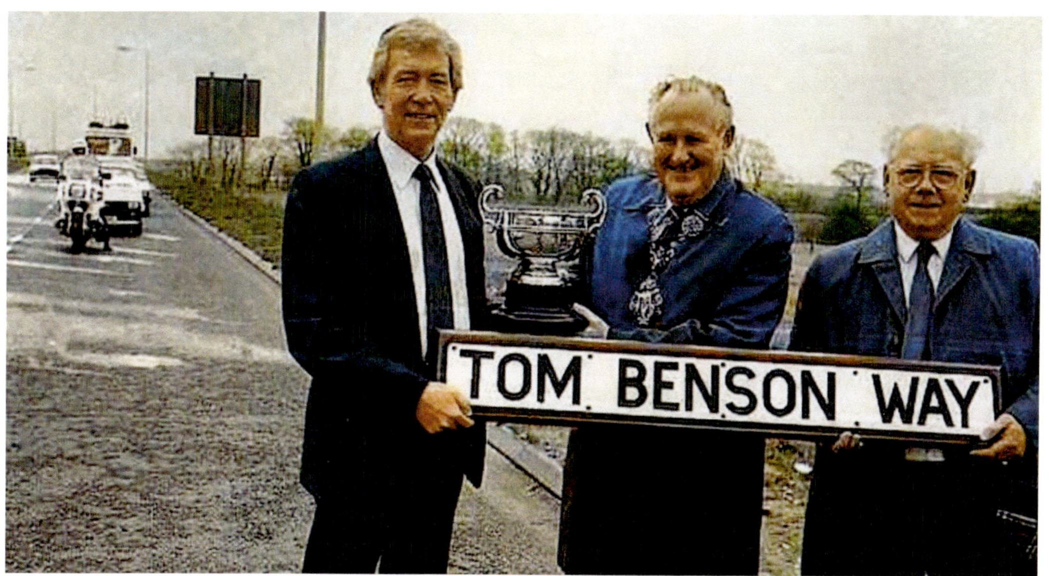

Tom Benson Way, 1987

The Preston-born, nonstop-walking world record champion had the Ingol Distributor Road named after him. Opening in December 1985, it cost over £4 million. Mayor Richard Atkinson and his Labour colleague Joseph Ward (future mayor) presented a delighted Tom Benson with a road sign as a cavalcade of cars are brought to a halt. Tom Benson claimed six world titles, including a record-breaking 414.8-mile trek around Moor Park in 1984. He died in Exmouth in June 2013, aged eighty.

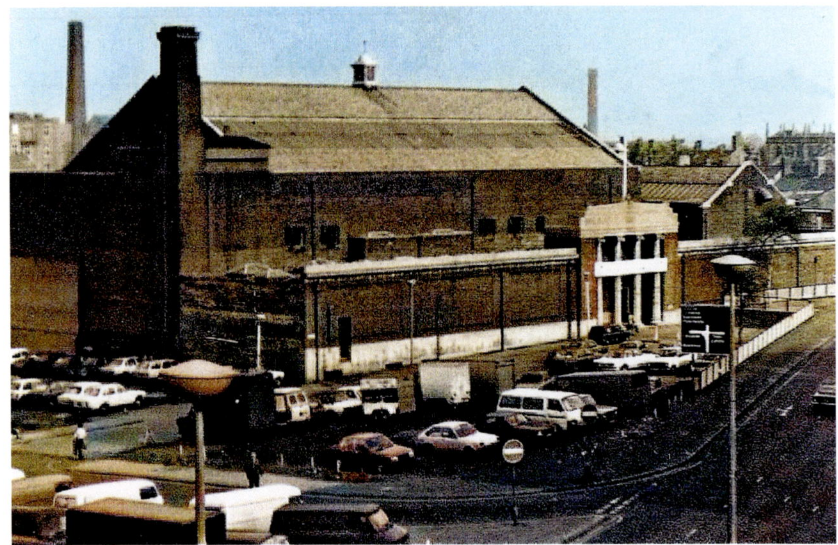

Saul Street Baths, Ringway, 1990

These baths opened in 1936, replacing the original public swimming baths erected in 1851. They also doubled up as the Queens Hall for concerts, dancing and sporting action by boarding over the large pool. In a deal worth over £800,000, the Saul Street baths site was sold in October 1989 to the Home Office to build a new Preston Crown Court, which opened in 1995.

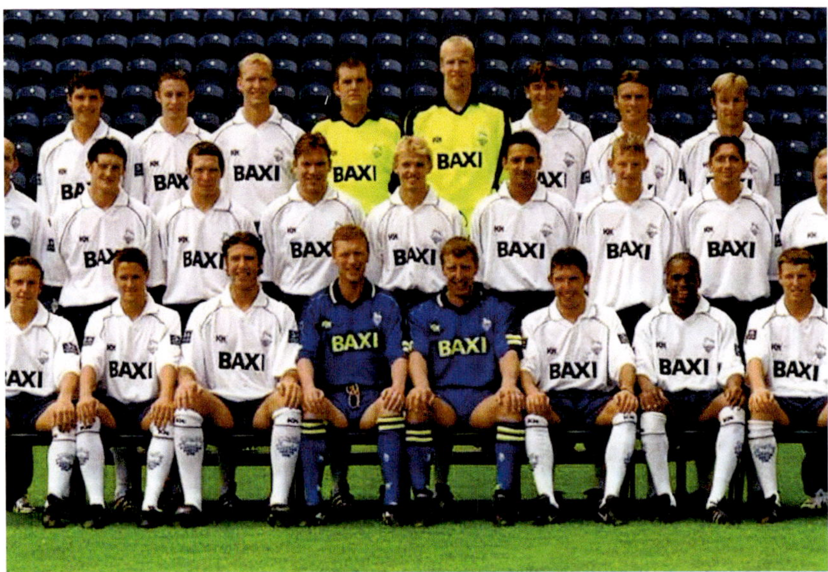

Baxi Boys of Preston North End, 1998

Ready for another season under manager David Moyes. Since the takeover of PNE by Baxi in October 1994, and guided by chairman Bryan Gray, the club's fortunes were on the up, as the Baxi shirts replaced the Coloroll-sponsored shirts. Having clinched the Third Division title in 1996 under manager Gary Peters, they went on to clinch the third-tier Division Two title in season 1999/2000 under David Moyes. A year later they reached the 2001 Play Off final at the Millennium Stadium, where a 3-0 defeat to Bolton Wanderers ended their Premier League bid.

Working and Industrious Lives

Generations of Preston folk have toiled to earn a living and provide food and shelter for their dependants. There is a certain fascination about how we earn our daily bread, with a great diversity in the occupations we are engaged in. Over the years the work available has changed considerably. Locals are rarely employed in the textile industry today. We still have buses, but no conductors. Milk men, coal men and chimney sweeps are rare indeed and wheelwrights, millwrights and clog makers have mostly laid down their tools. Sauntering through the city streets today, you may see a window cleaner up his ladder, a traffic warden handing out a ticket, street vendors offering a quick switch to their phone provider or energy supplier, or even a couple of police officers on patrol. Our working lives have stored up memories that we cherish, and the images that follow may stir some recollections of that colourful industrious existence.

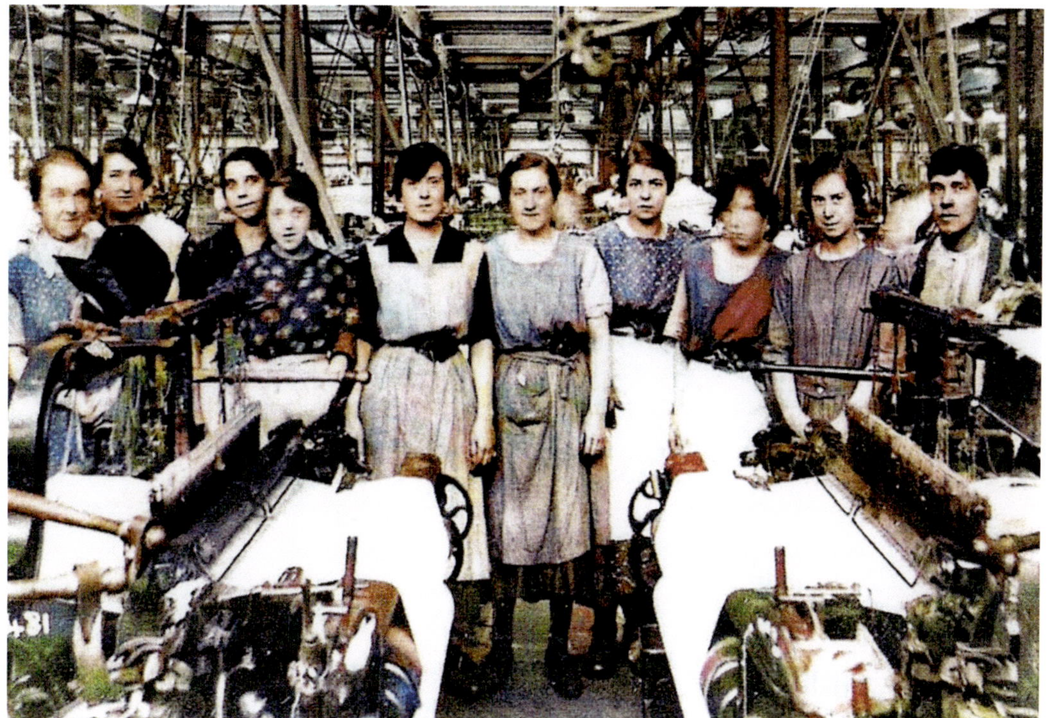

Horrockses Centenary Mill, New Hall Lane, November 1918

At the conclusion of the First World War the mill workers of Horrocks, Crewdson & Co., posed for a photograph as they went about their daily shift. During the war, employees of the firm had contributed to the War Relief Fund; by the end of the conflict over £16,000 had been delivered to charities.

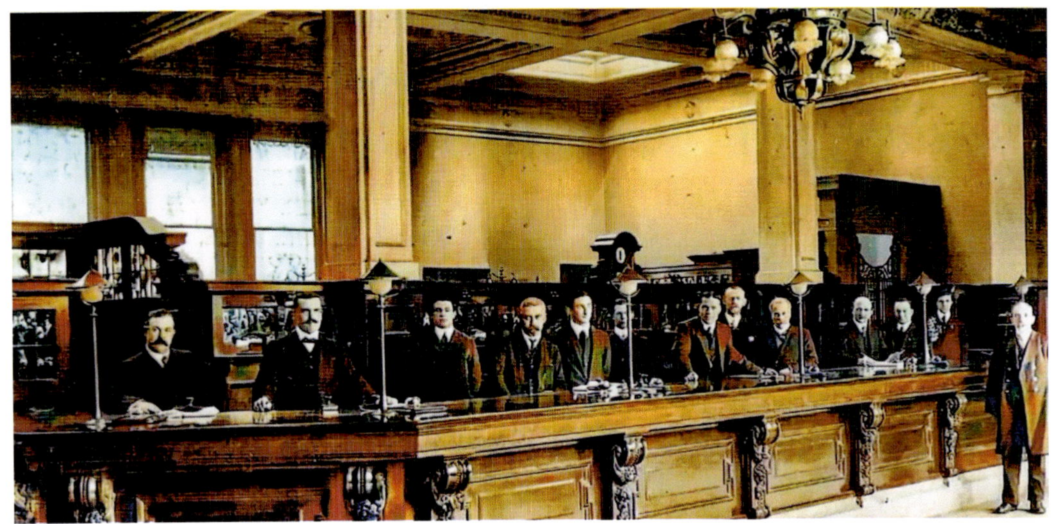

Preston Savings Bank, Church Street, 1920

This branch of the bank was opened in late July 1907 when tribute was given to Alderman William Bryham Roper, actuary of the bank, who had given fifty years' service to the institution, starting as a clerk in their Lune Street branch. It was remarked that only the prudence and thrift of the Preston people had made the building possible. In post-war days it was a TSB bank, but after closure lay neglected until JD Wetherspoons moved in and created the Twelve Tellers public house, which opened in January 2015. If you count the tellers behind the counter, you will see the pub is aptly named.

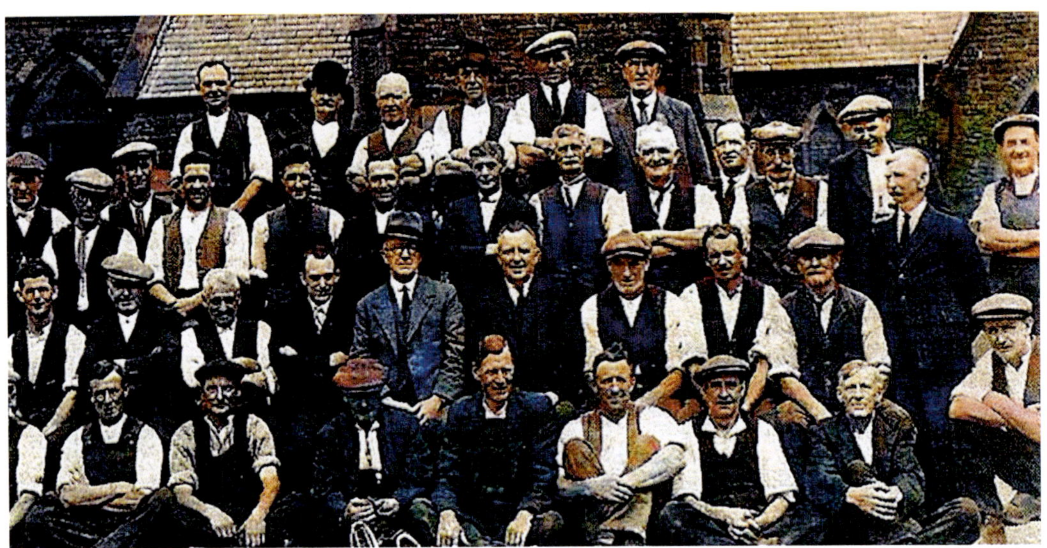

Preston Cemetery Workers, 1924

In 1914, gravediggers threatened to strike before being given a pay rise to 25s for a five-and-a-half-day week. A decade later, the forty-strong workforce pictured here were praised for the close-cropped lawns and well-tended paths that greeted visitors. Although the men didn't wear an official uniform, they were generally happy to wear a waistcoat, a union shirt (mainly collarless) and many wore a flat cap. Between 1855 and 1925, when the cemetery was extended, there were 162,000 interments recorded. Sixty years later, with a much bigger area to tend, the cemetery staff only numbered fourteen.

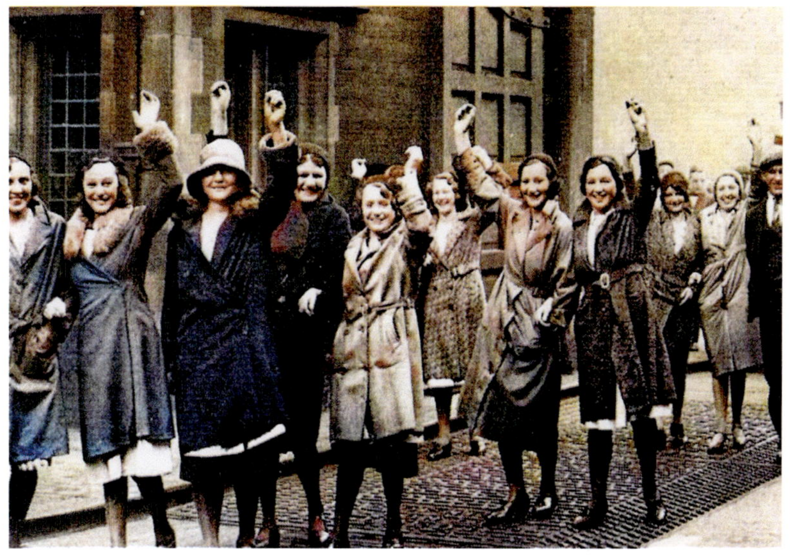

Horrockses Yard Works, Stanley Street, 1928

The mill lasses have ditched the clogs and shawls as they stand on the weighbridge at the factory entrance by the side of the Horrockses office block (1912), smiling and waving their hands for the camera. It was the roaring 1920s and they dressed accordingly. The business, by then known as Horrocks, Crewdson & Co. Ltd, had a worldwide reputation for producing quality cotton goods. The mill was demolished in 1964/65 and the office on the left became a Barclays bank, demolished in 2004.

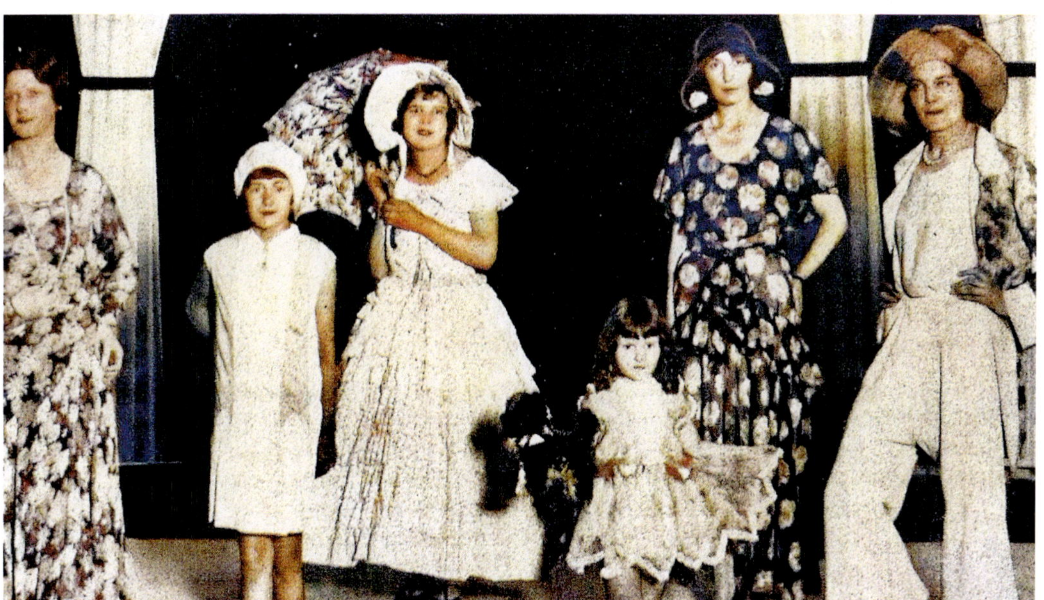

Preston Cotton Festival, Public Hall, July 1930

Such was Preston's position in the cotton industry that it was decided to hold a Cotton Festival there to showcase the products produced in local mills. Tours of the mills were arranged to see the latest automatic looms. In the Public Hall the latest frocks and fashions were on display, with models, mannequins and local lasses dressed in colourful cottons manufactured in Preston.

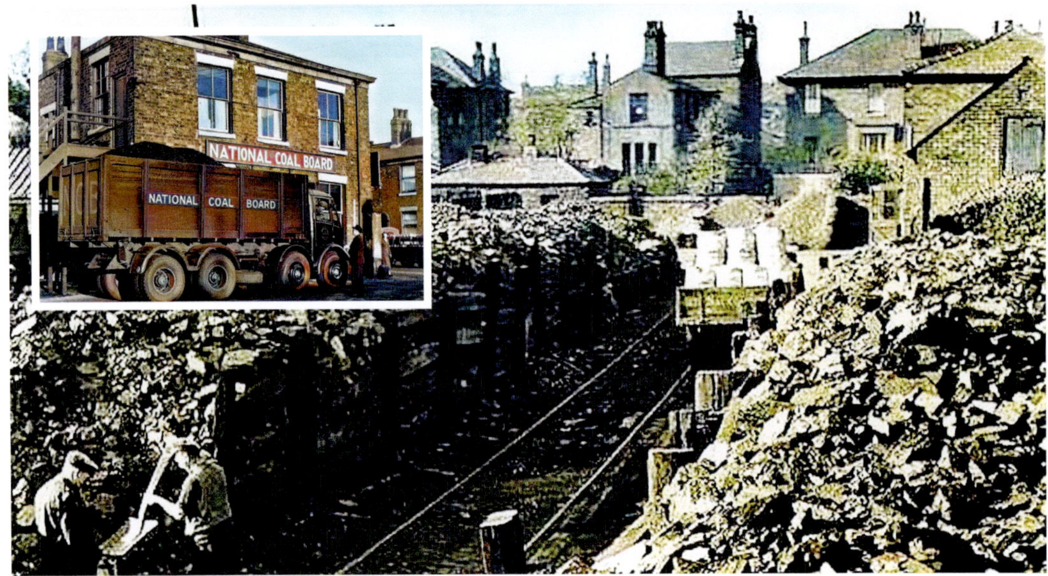

Coal Yard, Fletcher Road, 1947

The Labour government's introduction of the National Coal Board in July 1946 to run the nationalised coalmining industry made little difference to the working lives of these employees, who are busily bagging up coal for delivery. Forty years later, in 1987 the NCB was dissolved and became the British Coal Corporation, with the assets being privatised. *Inset*: National Coal Board lorry.

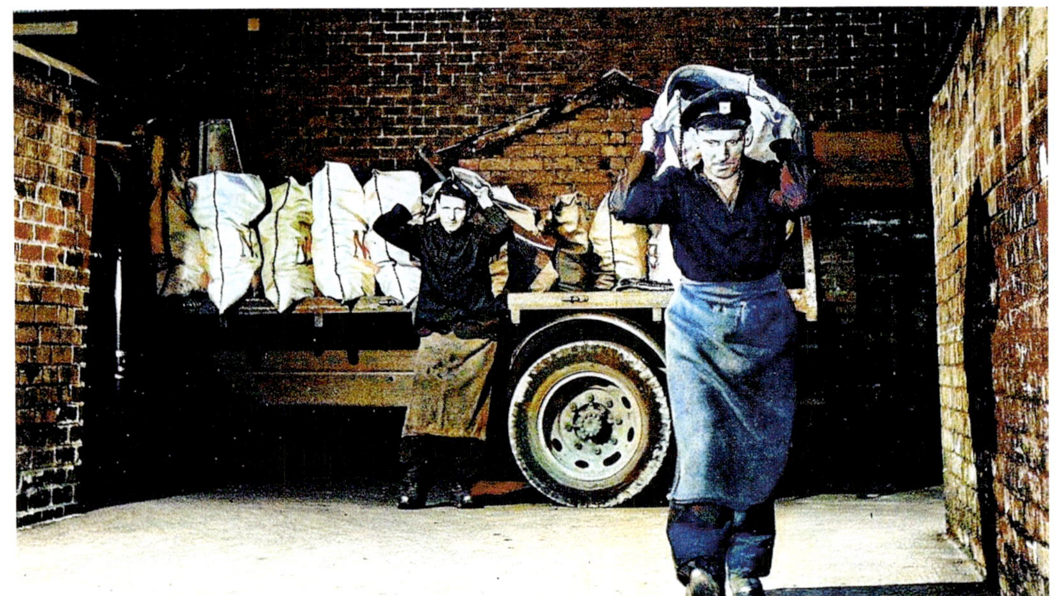

Coal Deliveries, 1947

The National Coal Board began operating with difficulty. It was the days of food and coal rationing, along with shortages due to miners' strikes. The coal men arriving on your street with sacks of the precious black stuff were a welcome sight. A youngster would often be asked by their mum to count the sacks delivered to your cellar or outhouse, lest you be short changed.

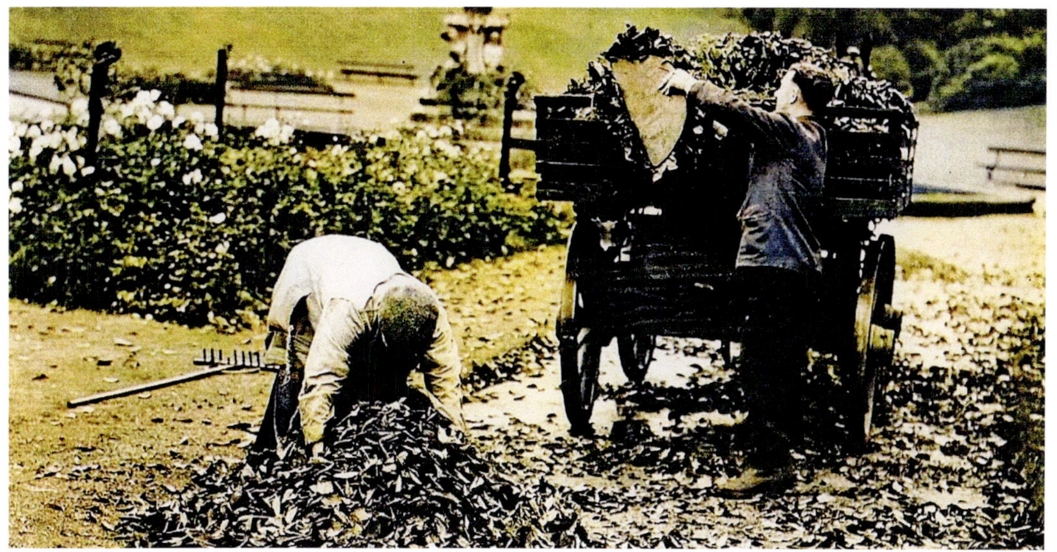

Miller Park, October 1949

Employees from the Preston Corporation Parks Department gather the autumn leaves with a horse and cart. Former military man Thomas Henry Jebb, who began as a gardener in 1931 with the Parks Department, was in charge of the horses on Avenham and Miller parks in his later years. A feature on Avenham Park from 1943, an annual horse show was held in August, when crowds exceeding 20,000 often attended.

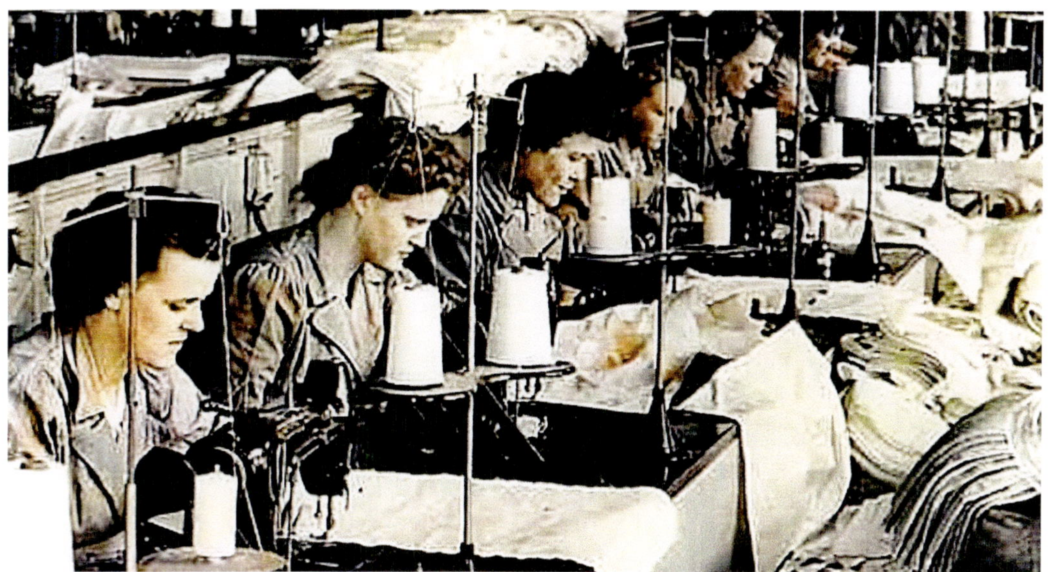

Horrocks, Crewdson Ltd Staff, December 1955

News that shares in the company had gained 2*s* reflected the boom in the textile trade that was taking place. The ladies in the sewing room were clearly busy, with sheets, pillowcases and towels in demand. During the 1950s the business was well established. Queen Elizabeth II had chosen one of their frocks – described as being patterned in a Victorian wallpaper design with tiny pink roses – from the 4 guinea range and had it made especially for her to wear on a tour of Jamaica, which helped to boost sales.

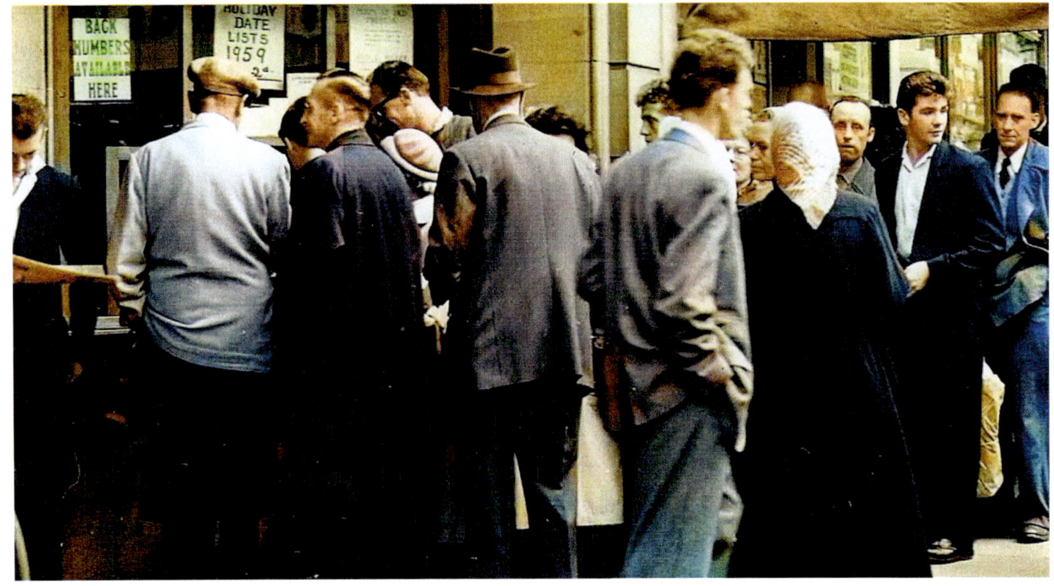

Lancashire Evening Post Kiosk, Fishergate, August 1959

The kiosk was always a popular place, but especially so on Thursday 6 August after the ending of a seven-week national printers' strike in which the working week was reduced to 42 hours from 44. It was the first time that *Post* production had been halted (except for the general strike of May 1926) since the paper was first published in October 1886. Folk were clearly eager to obtain a copy of edition No. 22,550, costing 2½*d*, with a promise that the news they missed would be included in forthcoming issues.

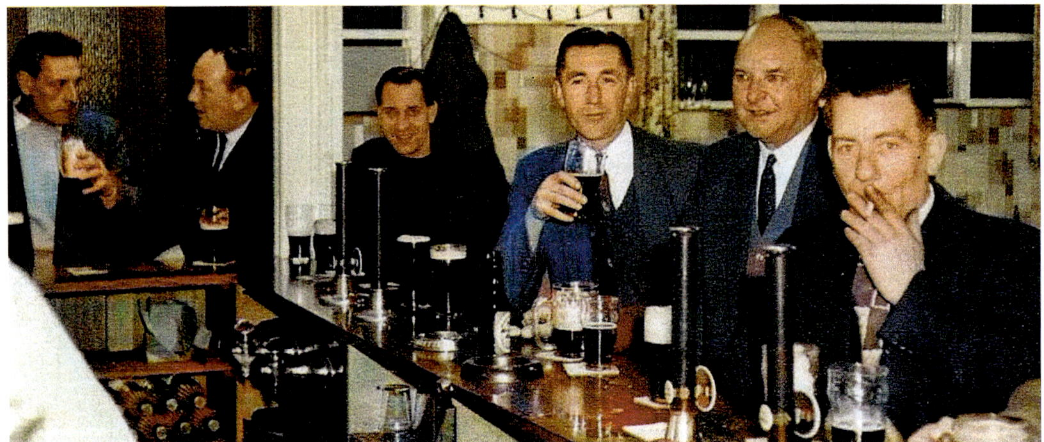

Larches Labour Club, 1962

Working men's clubs were very much part of the social scene in the post-war period. Larches was opened in 1959 and run by a club steward who was kept busy pulling pints for residents of the new Larches estate. Labour clubs with concerts, cabaret and dances were certainly popular then, entertaining many besides trade unionists for decades ahead. In July 1995, the *Preston Guild* magazine listed the following Labour clubs within Preston alone: Acregate, Deepdale, Fishwick, Greenlands, Ingol, Meadow Street and Parkfield, along with numerous other Catholic and social clubs. In 2010, Larches LC was ravaged by fire, and when vandalism followed it was demolished.

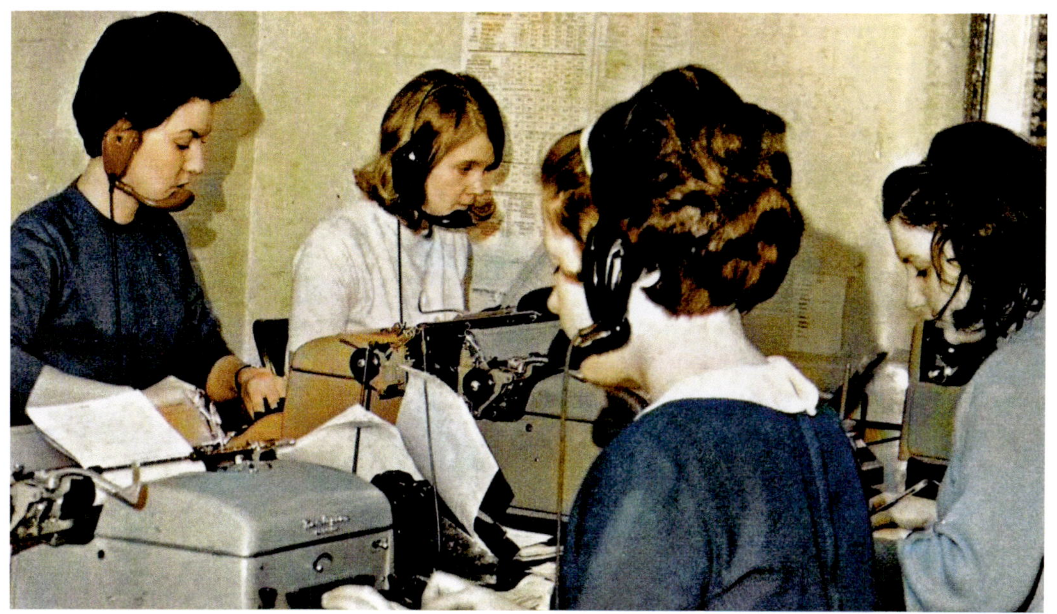

Lancashire Evening Post Offices, Fishergate, January 1967

The girls in the Tel-Ad department were busily tapping the keyboards. These were the days when the Dictaphone became commonly used by operators. Invoices and advertisements had to be dealt with, and journalists and reporters rang in with breaking news – all part of the daily newspaper's production.

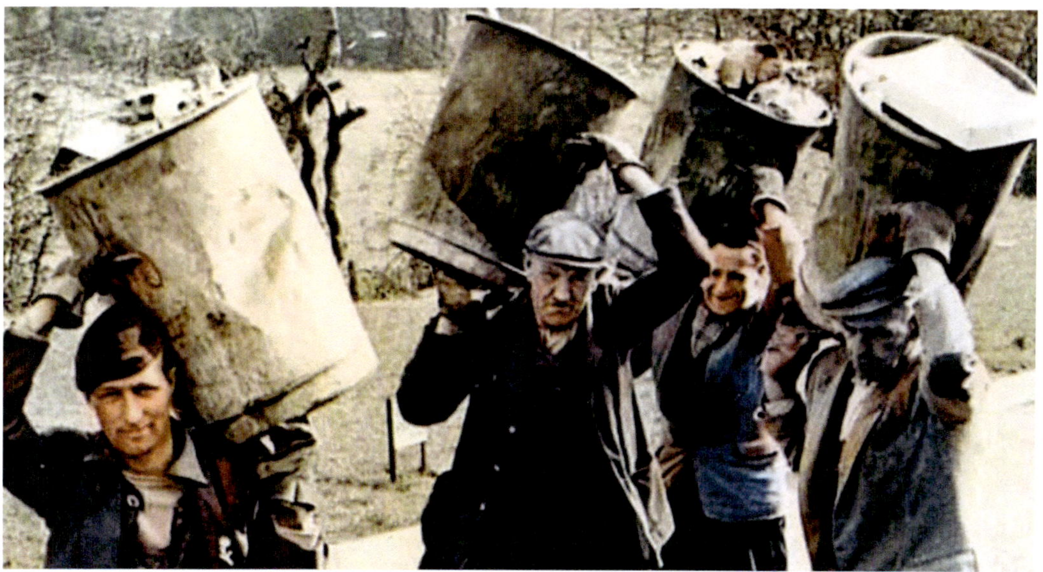

Dustbin Men on Duty, 1967

In the days before wheelie bins and recycling, the bin men carrying metal bins on their shoulders was a familiar sight. 'No hot ashes' was the order of the day and although they appeared 'suited and booted', the provision of high-vis workwear was far in the future. It was another twenty years before the first wheelie bins were introduced in Preston, and the current recycling bins were only phased in after the millennium.

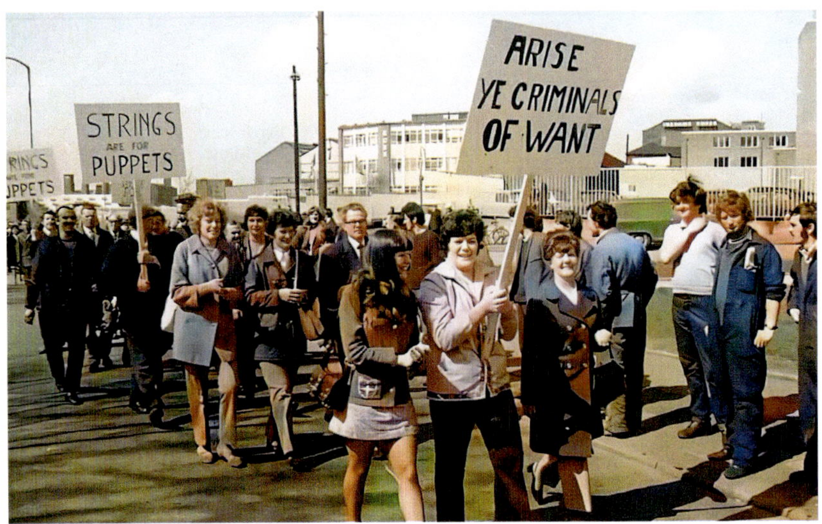

Workers from British Aircraft Corporation, March 1972

Striking workers from Strand Road pass the Goss Printing Press premises on Fylde Road. A number of Goss employees turned out to line the pavement in support as the strikers marched to the Market Square for a protest rally during a long-running wages dispute. Over 3,000 employees at the Warton, Samlesbury and Preston sites had, since February, been embroiled in a series of lightning strikes. According to local shopkeepers the dispute was damaging the local economy, with shopkeepers claiming trade was down by 25 per cent.

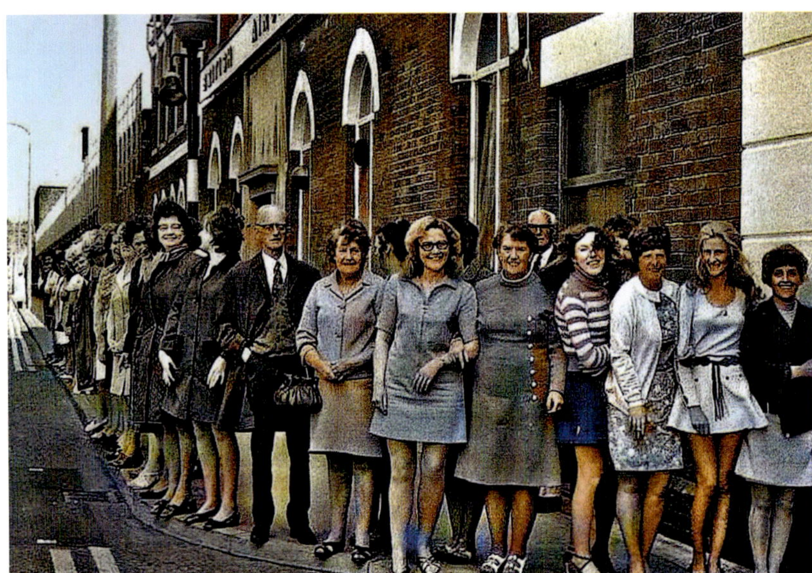

British Aircraft Corporation, Strand Road, June 1972

Staff line the pavement outside the aircraft-manufacturing plant awaiting the arrival of the Duke of Edinburgh. Prince Philip toured the military-manufacturing division of the plane makers at both Preston and Warton. He observed work being carried out on the Anglo-French Jaguar and the Anglo-German-Italian multi-role combat aircraft. The visit was a welcome distraction after the long-running strike action by the employees.

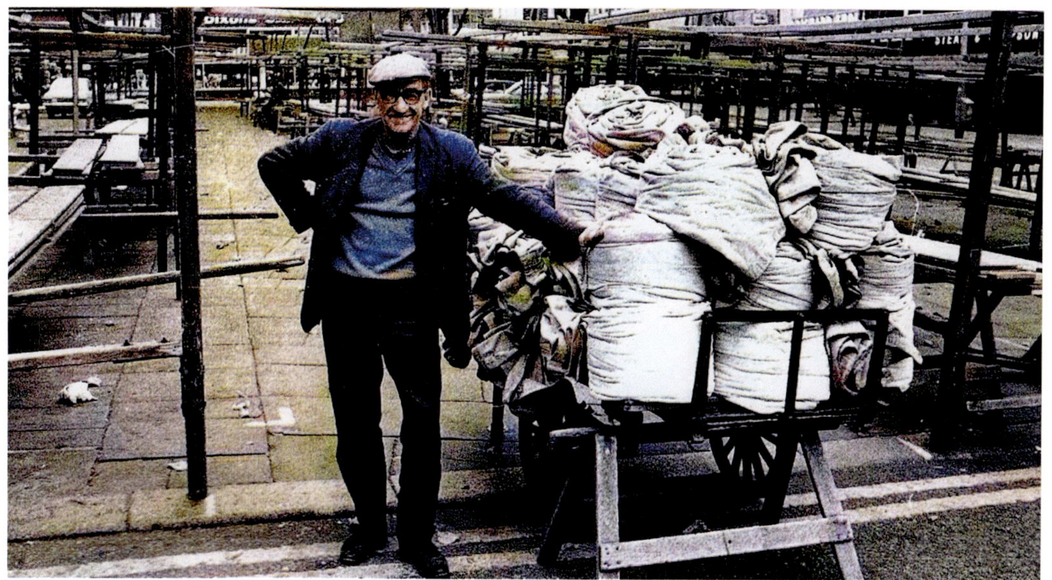

Flag Market Farewell, October 1972

For odd-job man Leslie Cairns, it was the end of an era as he packed up the canvas covers of the market stalls for the last time. The opening of a new Market Hall alongside the Covered Market left self-employed Mr Cairns redundant after a couple of decades. He was proud of never missing a day's work, come hail, high winds or heatwaves.

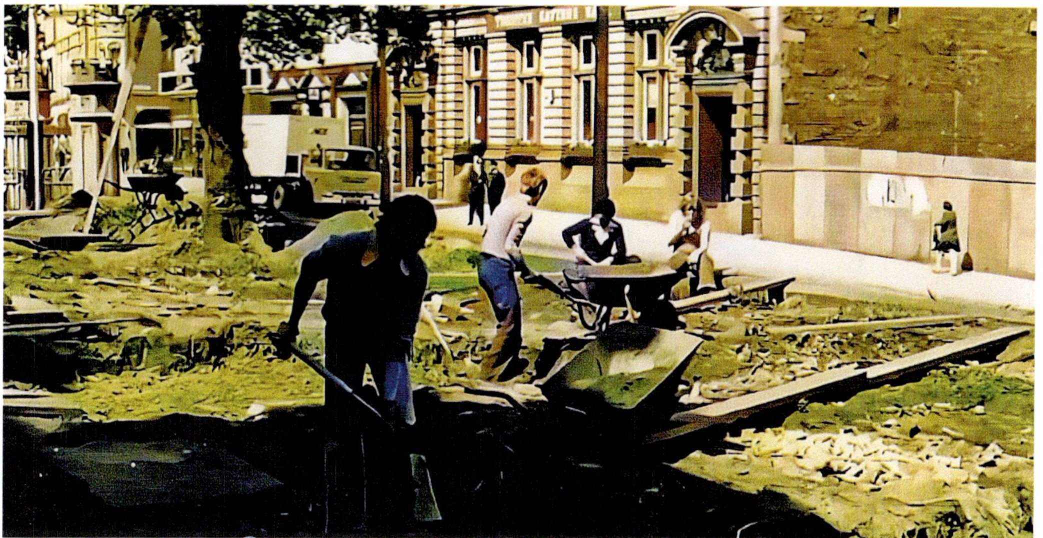

Preston Parish Church Graveyard, Church Street, 1977

As part of the government Job Creation Scheme, at a time when unemployment figures were high, these youthful workers were assigned the task of redeveloping and cutting back the graveyard at the front of the church. It meant breaking up the ancient tombstones, but there was no intention of disturbing the corpses, which were buried much deeper. The last burials had taken place in 1855 prior to the opening of Preston Cemetery in July 1855. The church became St John's Minster in 2003 and is now known as Preston Minster.

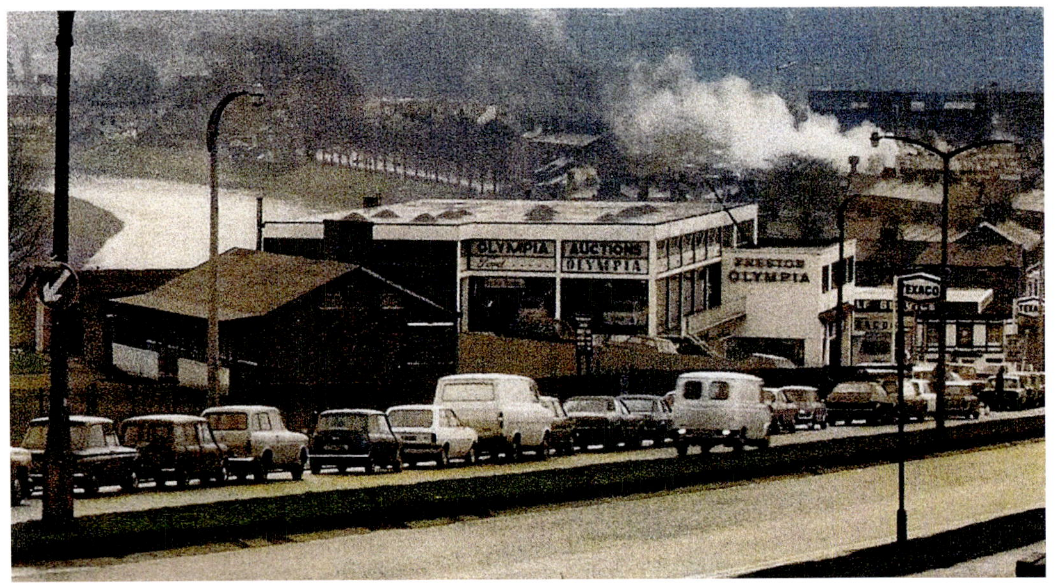

London Road, January 1979

Throughout the year oil tanker drivers were in dispute, with strikes leading to a shortage of petrol. Consequently, queues such as this one for the Texaco garage next to the Preston Olympia Auction car salerooms were commonplace as motorists quickly arrived when they learnt of a petrol station that had a supply.

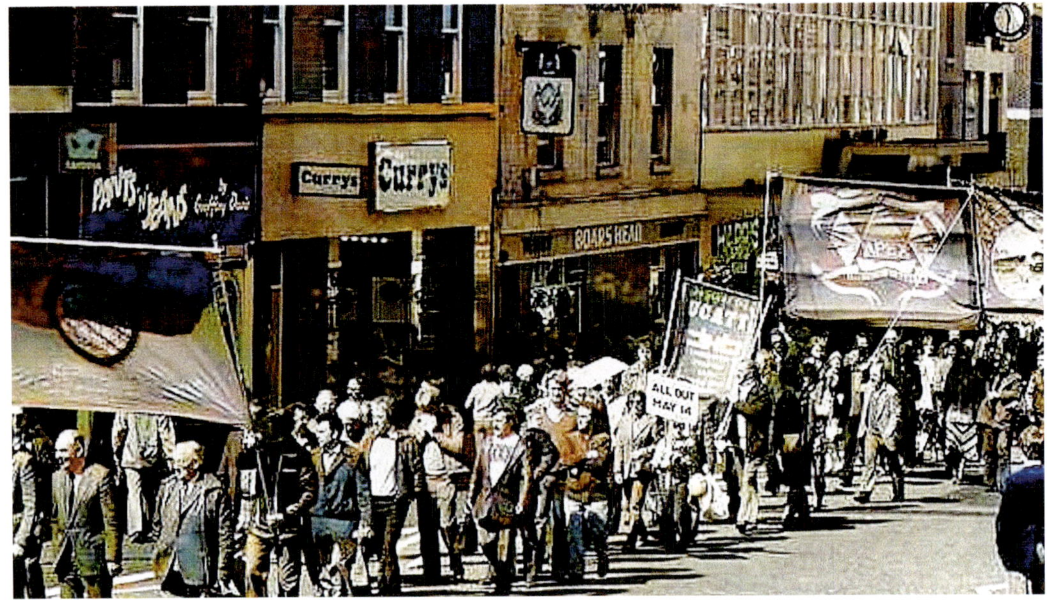

May Day Bank Holiday Protest March, Friargate, 1980

This holiday was introduced in 1978 by Labour Employment Secretary Michael Foot, and it soon became a day that trade unionists used for a rally or a protest march. On this occasion the marchers were displaying banners calling for a day of action a fortnight later against Margaret Thatcher's Tory government.

Parades, Pageantry and Processions

Having a Preston Guild every twenty years has ensured that the city continues to have the enthusiasm for parades and processions. They are mostly held to celebrate joyous occasions, with a colourful palette on parade. Although we no longer have the church processions of old at Whitsuntide, there are still many parish and parochial parades and processions. We have also been blessed by a Caribbean Carnival for the last fifty years. The annual carnival, also the Preston Guild, brings communities, cultures and faiths together, and a sea of people from diverse backgrounds line the procession routes. Folk from China, Asia, Africa and countries worldwide are clearly happy to parade together through Preston's streets. The images that follow are just a glimpse of processions of old, but they show they were just as colourful as modern parades, with the exception of the Caribbean Carnival, which is a true kaleidoscope of colour beyond comparison.

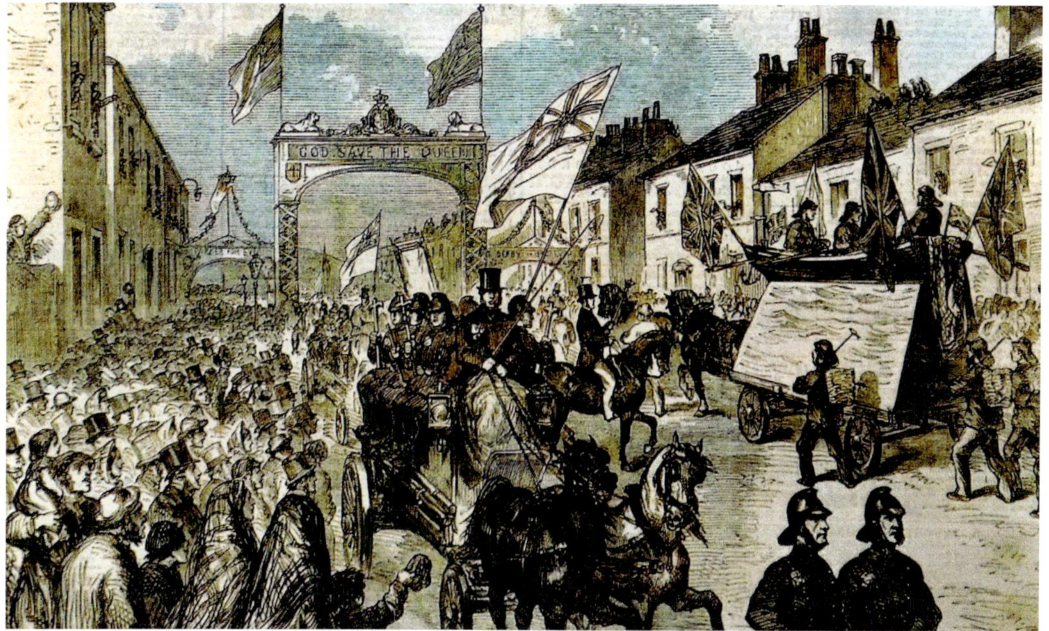

Preston Guild, September 1862

This was the scene recorded by the *Illustrated London News* as the Trades Procession made its way along London Road. Despite the cotton famine crisis, when poverty reigned, the enthusiasm for the Guild was undiminished. The Preston Fire Bridge volunteers can be seen in centre of the image, the horse-drawn fire engine having passed beneath one of the triumphal arches with its 'God Save the Queen' message. To the right are the fishermen in a boat aloft a horse-drawn cart.

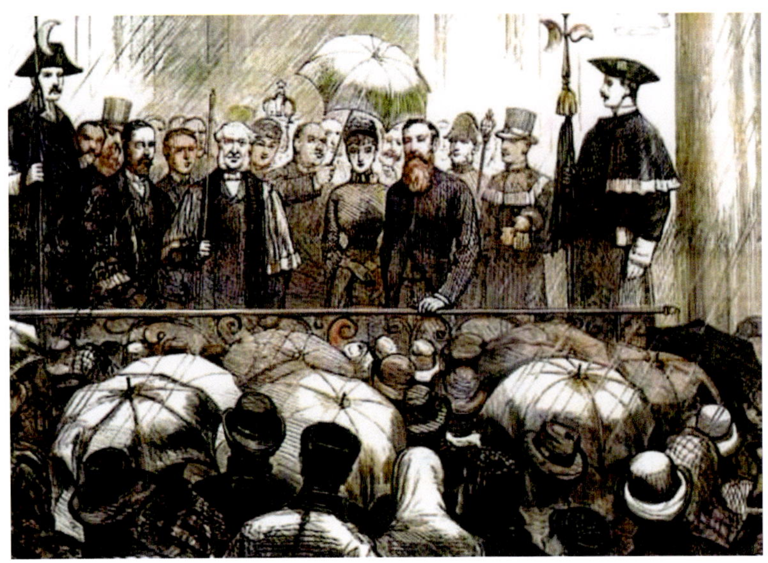

Preston Guild, September 1882

Guild Mayor Edmund Birley, cotton manufacturer, greets the crowd of onlookers in the Market Place from the steps of the Guild Hall to proclaim the Guild had arrived. He was in distinguished company, with the Duke of Cambridge among the dignitaries in attendance for a ceremony to lay the foundation stone of the Harris Library & Museum. Unfortunately, the multitude of umbrellas on view was a sign of things to come; the entire week had heavy downpours during the well-attended Church and Trade processions, with record crowds greeting the participants.

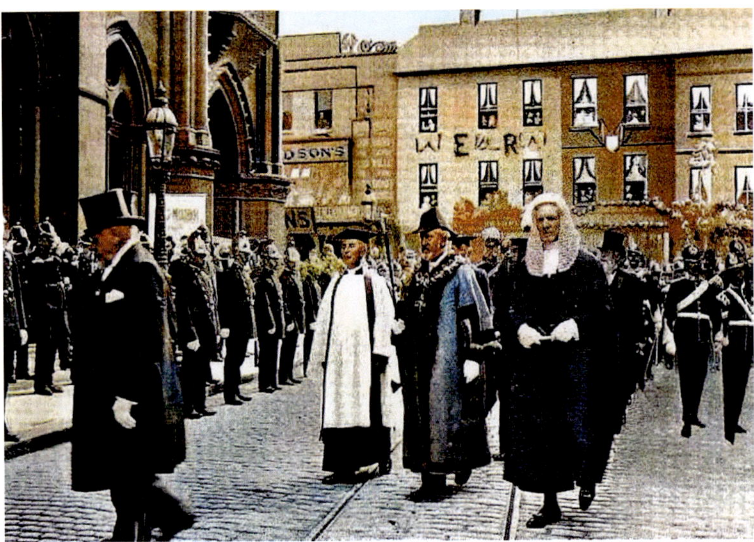

Preston Guild, September 1902

The Guild Mayor, the 16th Earl of Derby, escorted by the clergy and civic dignitaries, heads into the Guild Hall to proclaim the opening of events. A former Lord Mayor of Liverpool, with a distinguished Parliamentary career behind him, he fulfilled the role with great dignity. With the Guild celebrations held a few weeks after Edward VII's coronation, it was a lavish affair and it continued the Stanley family links with the Guild for over 350 years.

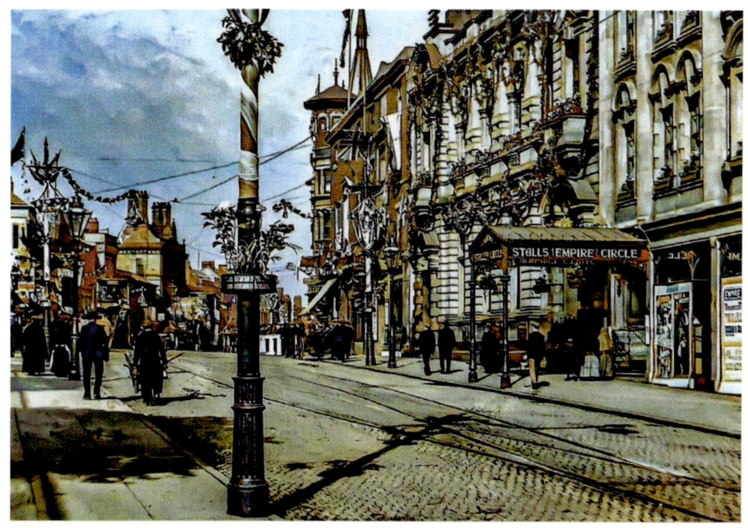

Coronation Day, Church Street, June 1911

The crowning of King George V and Queen Mary at Westminster Abbey was a grand event that Mayor of Preston Nathaniel Miller attended. It was followed by processions, parties and festivities on the London streets. Preston certainly decorated the main streets for the occasion, but according to a *Preston Herald* reporter the celebrations in town were lacking. The newly opened Empire Theatre, seen to the right, played their part in the celebrations with a Coronation Gala Week, with top vaudeville acts on stage.

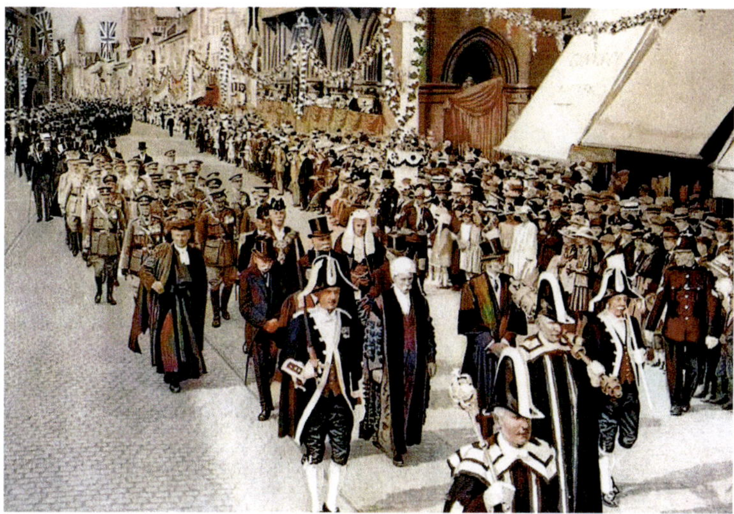

Preston Guild, 1922

On the first Sunday of September 1922, the longest mayoral procession on record left the Town Hall by way of Cheapside, taking a tour of the town via Lune Street and ending up at the parish church. Mayor Henry Astley-Bell, wearing his chain of office, can be seen flanked by dignitaries. Accrington born, he was a power in the cotton industry of Preston for over thirty years, connected to the Brookhouse, Progress and Raglan mills. A deeply respected alderman on the Town Council, he was made an Honorary Freeman of Preston in October 1935 and died, aged sixty-seven, in December 1937.

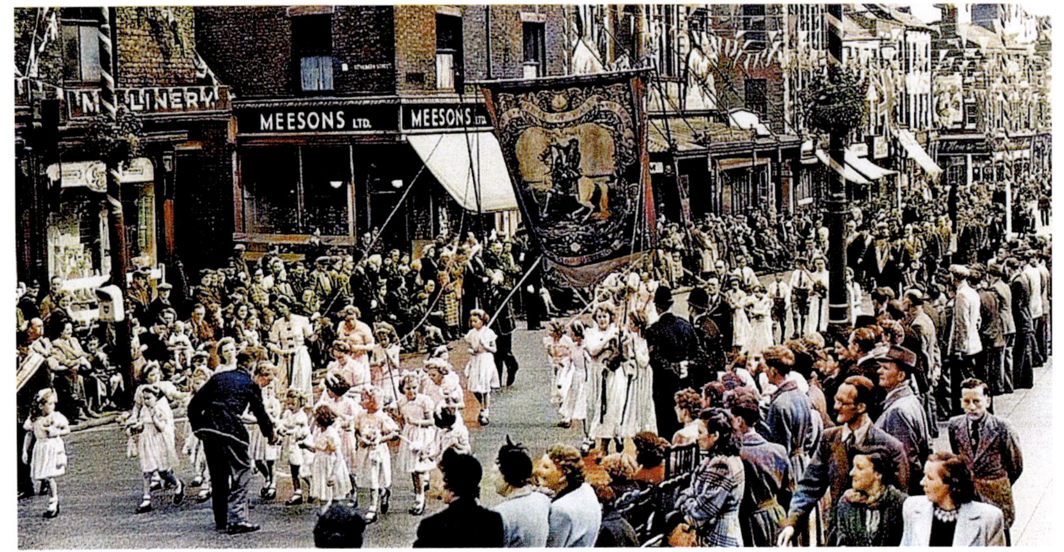

Preston Guild, September 1952

Crowds lined the pavement on both sides of Church Street as the Guild procession of churches passed by, painting a colourful picture. Those were the days when Tithebarn Street began on Church Street, with Goobys fashion on one corner and Meeson's sweets and tobacco outlet on the other. It was revealed later by the Town Council that the Guild had cost £70,000, with income from the events raising £29,000, leaving the ratepayers to fund the deficit. All agreed it was money well spent.

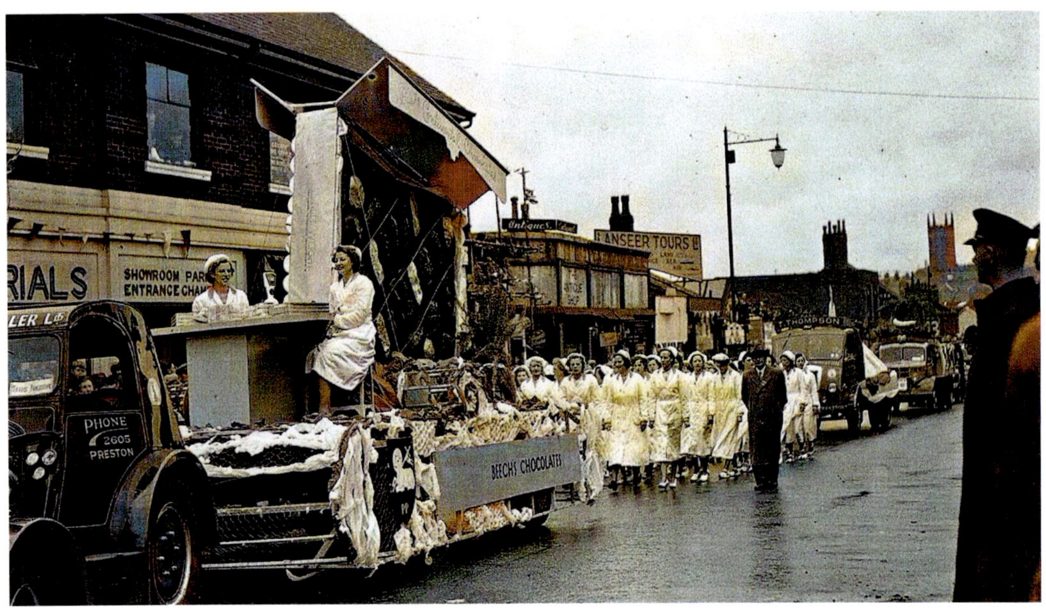

Beech's Chocolate Factory Float, Corporation Street, 1952

The Preston Guild Trades Procession, held on the Wednesday of Guild Week, was an opportunity for Preston's chocolate factory workers, predominately female, to remind us of the delicious delights they had been producing since 1920 when Edward Whiteley Collinson came to town and established his Fletcher Road factory. Despite the wet, drizzly day, nothing could dampen the enthusiasm on display.

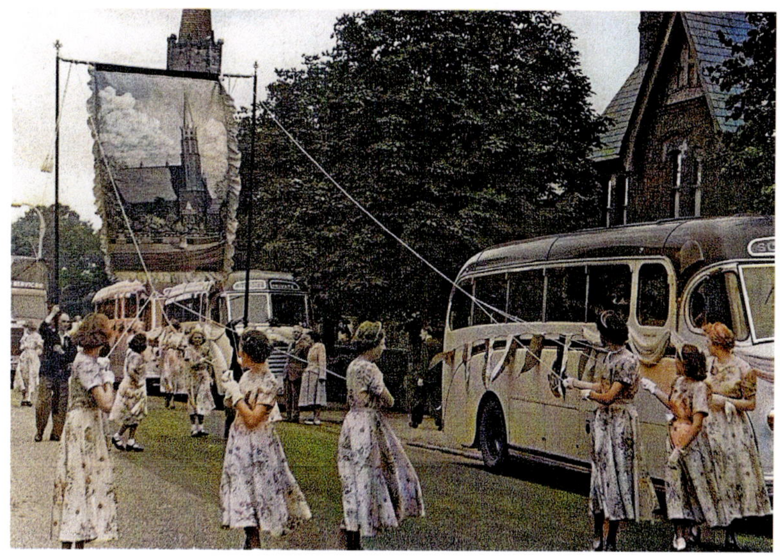

Fulwood Methodists, Garstang Road, Preston Guild, 1952

About to join the Free Churches Procession on the Tuesday of Guild Week, the young ladies of the church look immaculate in their floral dresses. Holding onto the guide ropes, they assist the two sturdy pallbearers carrying the banner displaying an image of their church building, which opened in 1912. Coaches are on hand to ferry older parishioners along the procession route, with over 11,000 participants in the parade.

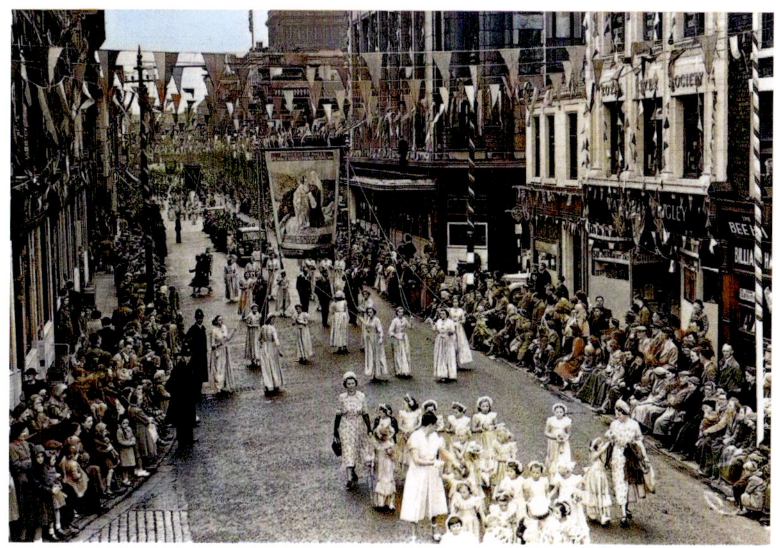

Preston Guild, Lancaster Road, 1952

On the Thursday of Guild Week, the Friendly Societies Procession took place, with over 3,000 participants. It was an opportunity for the women of the town who were Freemasons to make folk aware that freemasonry was not an exclusive male domain. Their banner proclaims the 'Princess of Wales - Female Orange Lodge', created in 1952 and still in existence today. Also in the procession that day for the first time were the OAP Association and the Hospital Welfare Society.

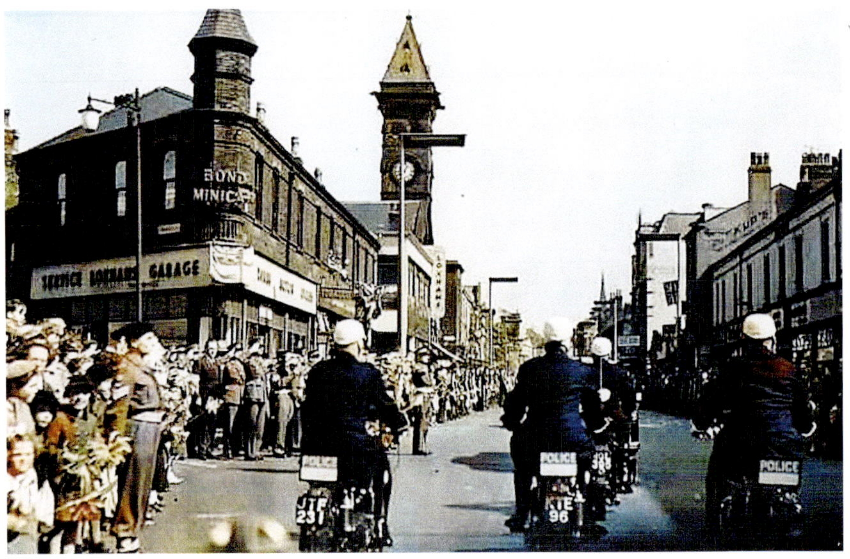

Royal Tour of Preston, April 1955

A motorbike police escort led the way from the railway station to Fishergate ahead of the car with Queen Elizabeth II and the Duke of Edinburgh on board. The royal couple, on a tour of the town, were greeted by saluting servicemen and Union Jack-waving crowds four or five deep lining the pavements. Cheering crowds continued to greet the royals on a journey that continued onto Lune Street, Moor Lane, Deepdale Road, Church Street and to the Town Hall, where a massed crowd on the Flag Market raised three cheers for Her Majesty prior to lunch at County Hall.

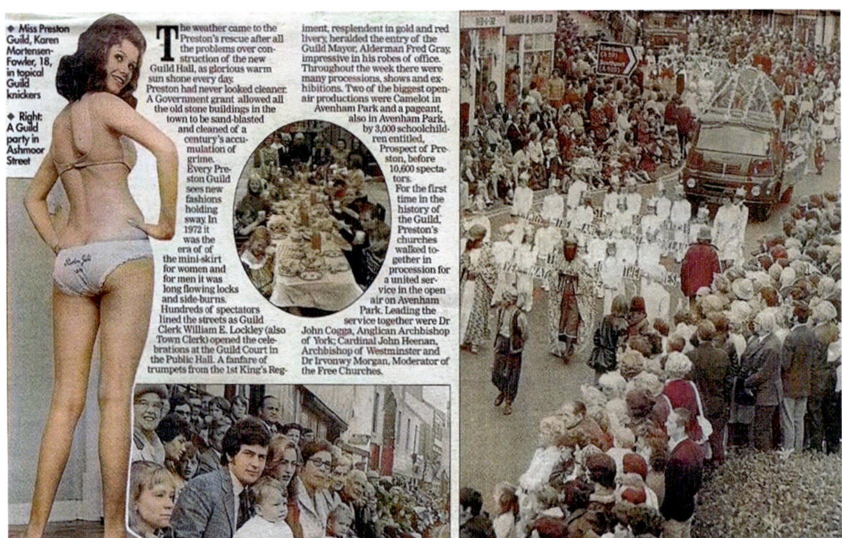

The weather came to the Preston's rescue after all the problems over construction of the new Guild Hall, as glorious warm sun shone every day. Preston had never looked cleaner. A Government grant allowed all the old stone buildings in the town to be sand-blasted and cleaned of a century's accumulation of grime. Every Preston Guild sees new fashions holding sway. In 1972 it was the era of of the mini-skirt for women and for men it was long flowing locks and side-burns. Hundreds of spectators lined the streets as Guild Clerk William E. Lockley (also Town Clerk) opened the celebrations at the Guild Court in the Public Hall. A fanfare of trumpets from the 1st King's Regiment, resplendent in gold and red livery, heralded the entry of the Guild Mayor, Alderman Fred Gray, impressive in his robes of office. Throughout the week there were many processions, shows and exhibitions. Two of the biggest open-air productions were Camelot in Avenham Park and a pageant, also in Avenham Park, by 3,000 schoolchildren entitled, Prospect of Preston, before 10,600 spectators.

For the first time in the history of the Guild,' Preston's churches walked together in procession for a united service in the open air on Avenham Park. Leading the service together were Dr John Cogga, Anglican Archbishop of York; Cardinal John Heenan, Archbishop of Westminster and Dr Irvonwy Morgan, Moderator of the Free Churches.

Preston Guild Celebrations, September 1972

It was a week of glorious weather, with sun-drenched spectators lining the routes as the processions took place, making this a Guild to remember. Pageants on Avenham Park and united church services all added to the feeling of togetherness and community spirit as the Guild Mayor Alderman Fred Grey carried out the historical role. It was even warm enough for Miss Preston Guild to show off her knickers.

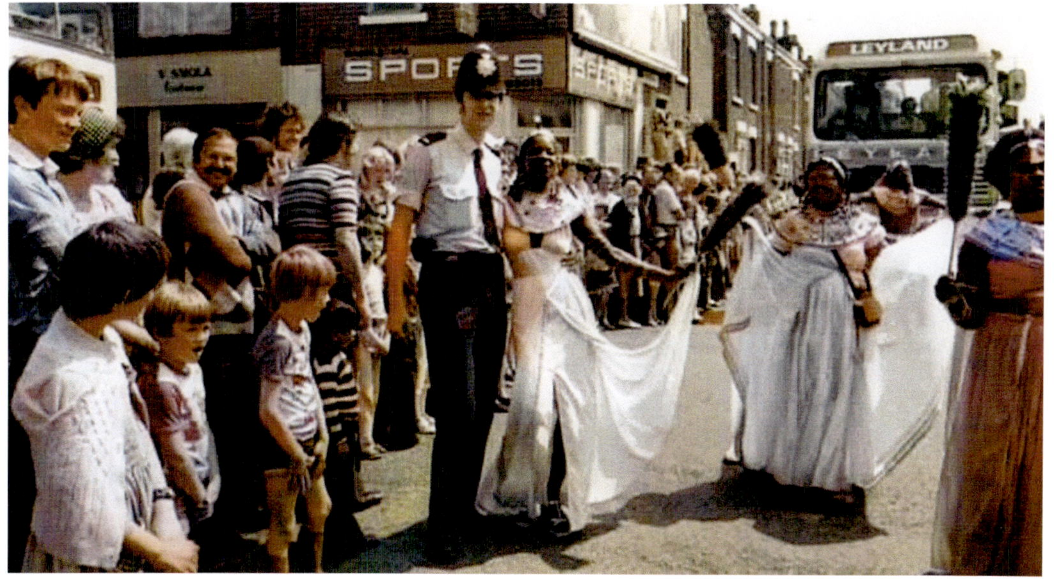

Caribbean Carnival Procession, 1978

The first procession took place in 1974 and four years later it had become well established. Traffic is halted as the colourful procession makes its way across Ribbleton Lane. Even the local bobby was enjoying the sun-soaked occasion as the local community embraced the carnival atmosphere. The community spirit is clear for all to see.

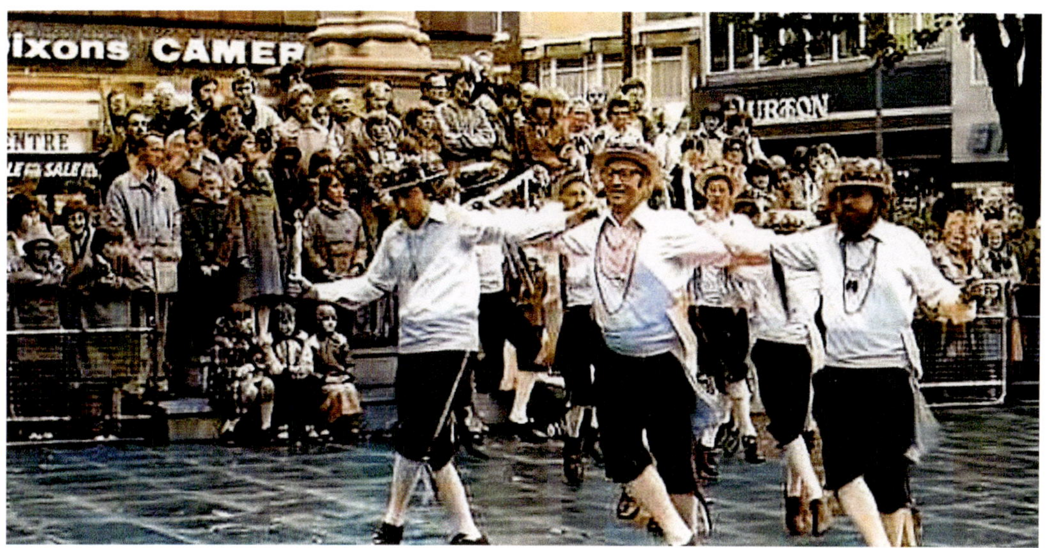

Morris Dancers, Market Place, May 1979

In 1179, King Henry II granted Preston a royal charter to officially make it a market town. To mark the octo-centenary of the original charter, Queen Elizabeth II paid a visit and unveiled the Obelisk (1782), which had been restored and returned after being at Hollowforth Hall since 1853. Among those keen to celebrate the occasion were the Preston Royal Morris Dancers, who performed in the Market Place. Reformed in 1978, the troupe can trace their roots back to the 1890s when appearances on May Day and Rose Queen festivals were commonplace.

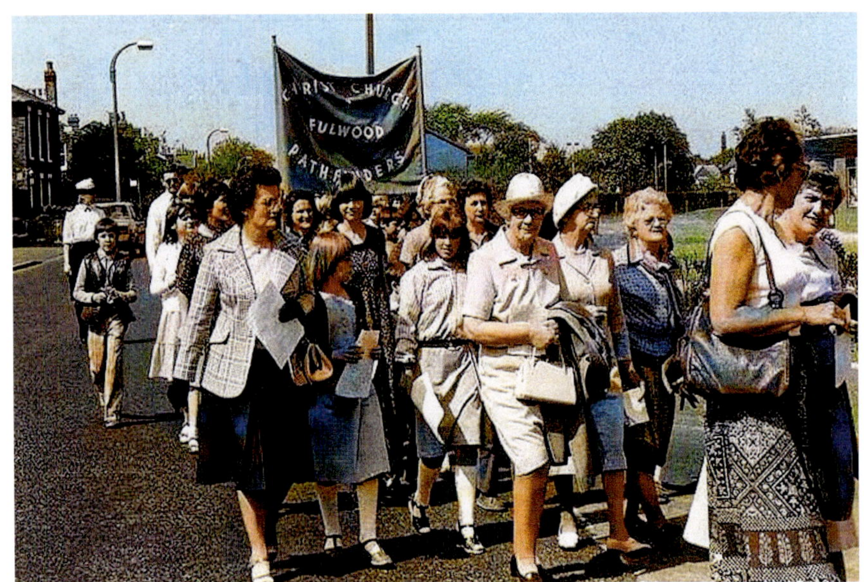

May Day Procession, Christ Church, Fulwood, 1980

The Anglican congregation from the Victoria Road, Fulwood, church strode out for the annual tour of their parish, with the banner proclaiming they are pathfinders on a journey through life. Their church, built in stone in a Gothic style, was opened in 1865 and cost £5,000 to build at a time when the township of Fulwood had a population of barely 2,500.

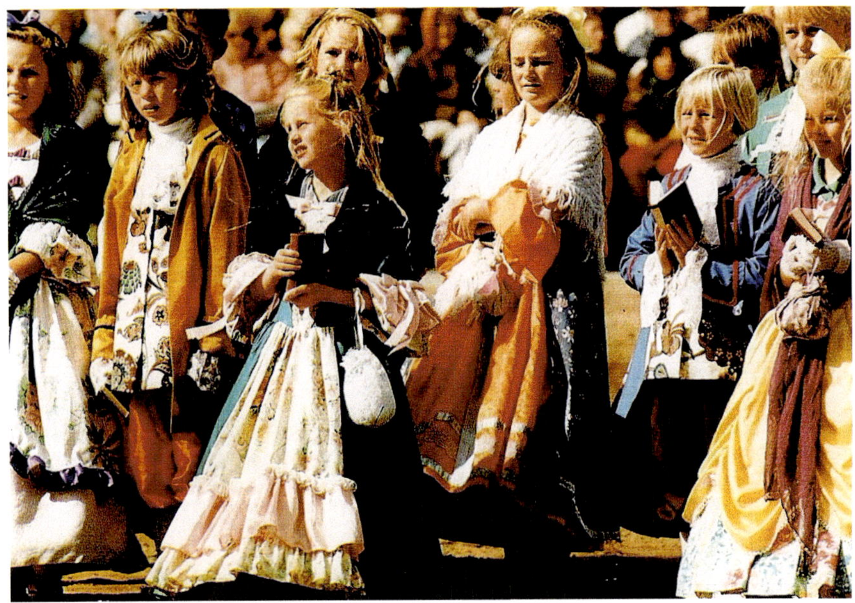

Schools Pageant, Preston Guild, 1992

The *Lancashire Post* brought us colourful images of the whole celebrations. Here schoolchildren take part in the 'Story of a Proud Town' wearing colourful authentic costumes from the past. Song, music and dancing were all part of the performance, as scenes from Preston's historical past were played out.

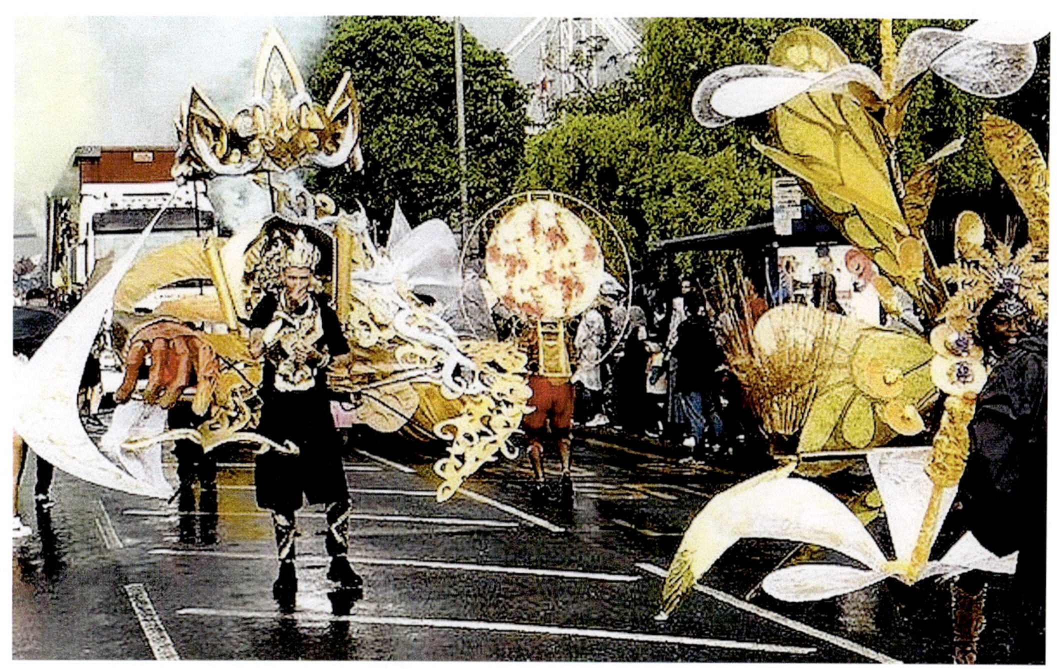

Above: **Caribbean Carnival, Deepdale Road, 2024;** *Below*: **Caribbean Carnival, Meadow Street, 2024**

The carnival began in the pouring rain on Spring Bank Holiday Monday amidst a sea of umbrellas. Souvenir sellers were on hand with flags, flairs and whistles as mementoes of the event. Happily, things soon brightened up as the spectacular costumes began to appear. Elaborate headdresses and costumes were commonplace, demonstrating the artistry and skill that go into making the carnival outfits. Shells, pearls, beads, gems, glitter and even peacock feathers were added to the enchanting designs. By the time the procession reached Meadow Street the showers had relented, and a sea of colour met the eyes as the music played and the dancing girls gyrated to the beat of the drums. In January 2025, an exhibition titled 'Sunshine, Soca and Spice' celebrated fifty years of the Preston Caribbean Carnival.

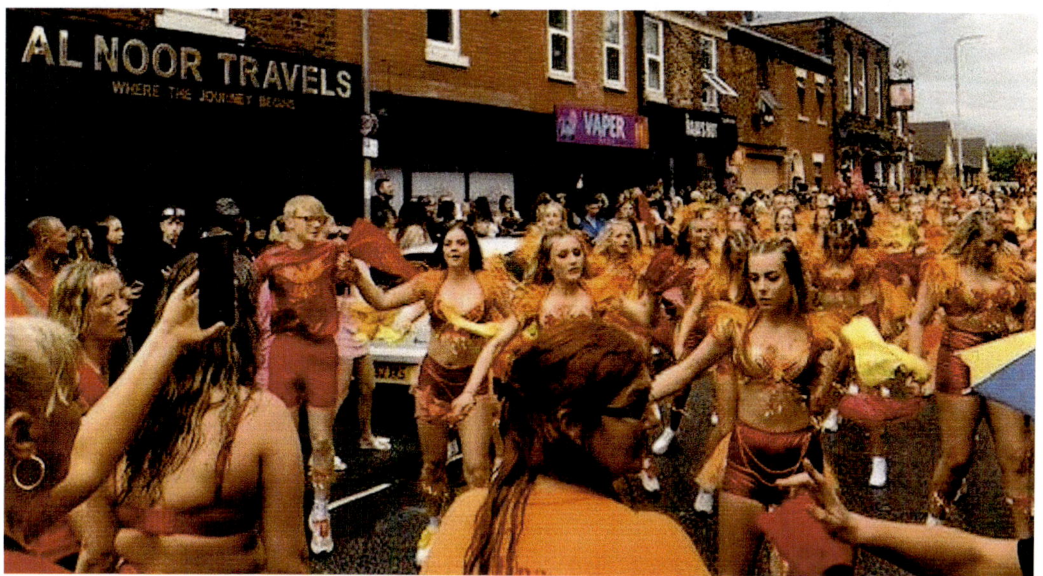

Acknowledgements

I must acknowledge the help given to me by the staff of the Harris Community Library in Preston over the years, who have willingly assisted as I delved into their archives, making historical information readily available to me. My appreciation also goes to the newspaper reporters of the past who, in chronicling the events of their day, left a valuable legacy. *The Lancashire Post, Preston Guardian, Preston Chronicle, Preston Pilot* and *Preston Herald* have all provided information from their publications. I appreciate the work of the photographers and illustrators of old, along with the postcard producers who left a rich legacy of images as they recorded our past.

Besides my own collection of images and illustrations, I would like to thank the Harris Museum, the Lancashire Library and the *Lancashire Post* (part of the National World group) for granting me permission to use images from their archives, or those that are nowadays stored in the Preston Digital Archive.

Also, my thanks go to Richard H. Parker, creator of the PDA, for use of their images, and to Mike Hill, editor of the *Lancashire Post*, who is ever helpful in my research and so enthusiastic with regards to local history.

My thanks also to Pat Crook for cheerfully checking my manuscript and putting her literary skills at my disposal.

About the Author

Keith Johnson is Preston born and bred. His previous works include the bestselling Chilling True Tales series of books featuring Preston, Lancashire and London, and the popular *People of Old Preston, Preston Remembered, Preston Through Time, Preston in the 1960s, Secret Preston, Preston in 50 Buildings, Preston History Tour, Preston at Work, A–Z of Preston, Now That's What I Call Preston, Preston's Military Heritage, Preston Murders and Misdemeanours, Celebrating Preston, Preston Reflections, Preston: A Potted History* and *Lost Preston*. For over twenty-five years he has contributed numerous feature articles on local history to the *Lancashire Post*, and since 2011 has written a weekly 'Court Archive' for the *LP Retro* magazine.

Keith was educated at St Augustine's Boys' School in Preston prior to attending the Harris College, now the University of Lancashire, where he gained his qualifications for a career in engineering, spending forty years working for the printing-press manufacturer Goss.